SiMPSONS™
COMICS
KNOCKOUT

MATT GROENING

TITAN BOOKS

SIMPSONS COMICS KNOCKOUT

Simpsons Comics #116, 117, 118, 119, 120

Published in the UK by Titan Books, a division of Titan Publishing Group Ltd.,
144 Southwark St., London SE1 0UP, under licence from Bongo Entertainment, Inc.

FIRST EDITION: JANUARY 2017

ISBN 978-1-78-565576-0

2 4 6 8 10 9 7 5 3 1

Publisher: Matt Groening
Creative Director: Nathan Kane
Managing Editor: Terry Delegeane
Director of Operations: Robert Zaugh
Production Manager: Christopher Ungar
Art Director: Jason Ho
Assistant Art Director: Mike Rote
Assistant Editor: Karen Bates
Production: Art Villanueva
Administration: Ruth Waytz
Legal Guardian: Susan A. Grode

Printed by TC Transcontinental, Beauceville, QC, Canada. 11/28/16

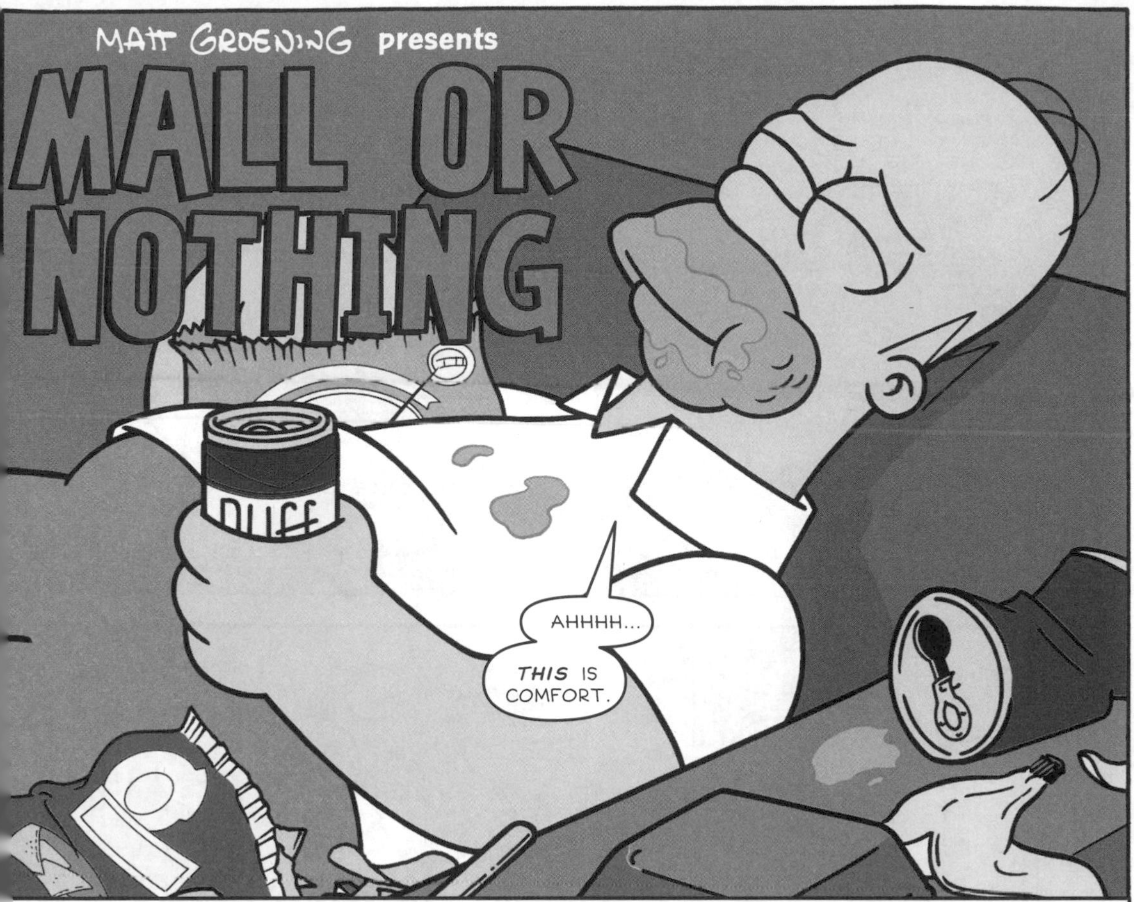
MATT GROENING presents
MALL OR NOTHING
DUFF
AHHHH...
THIS IS COMFORT.

CHUCK DIXON & ELMA BLACKBURN *STORY* | JOHN COSTANZA *PENCILS* | PHYLLIS NOVIN *INKS* | ART VILLANUEVA *COLORS* | KAREN BATES *LETTERS* | BILL MORRISON *EDITOR*

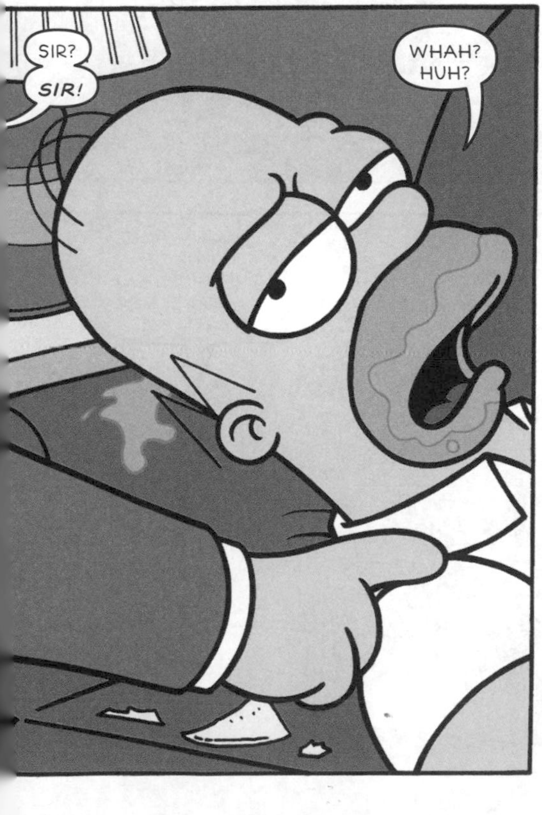
SIR?
SIR!
WHAH? HUH?

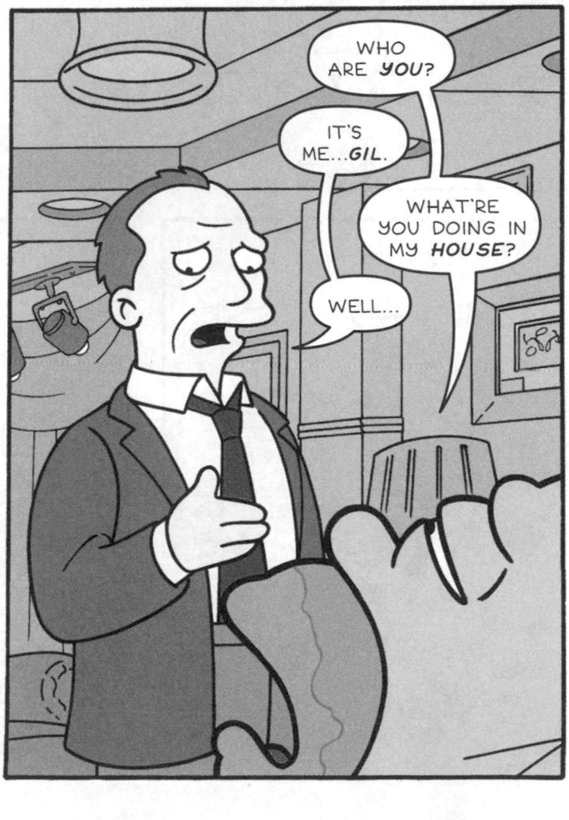
WHO ARE *YOU*?
IT'S ME...*GIL*.
WHAT'RE YOU DOING IN MY *HOUSE*?
WELL...

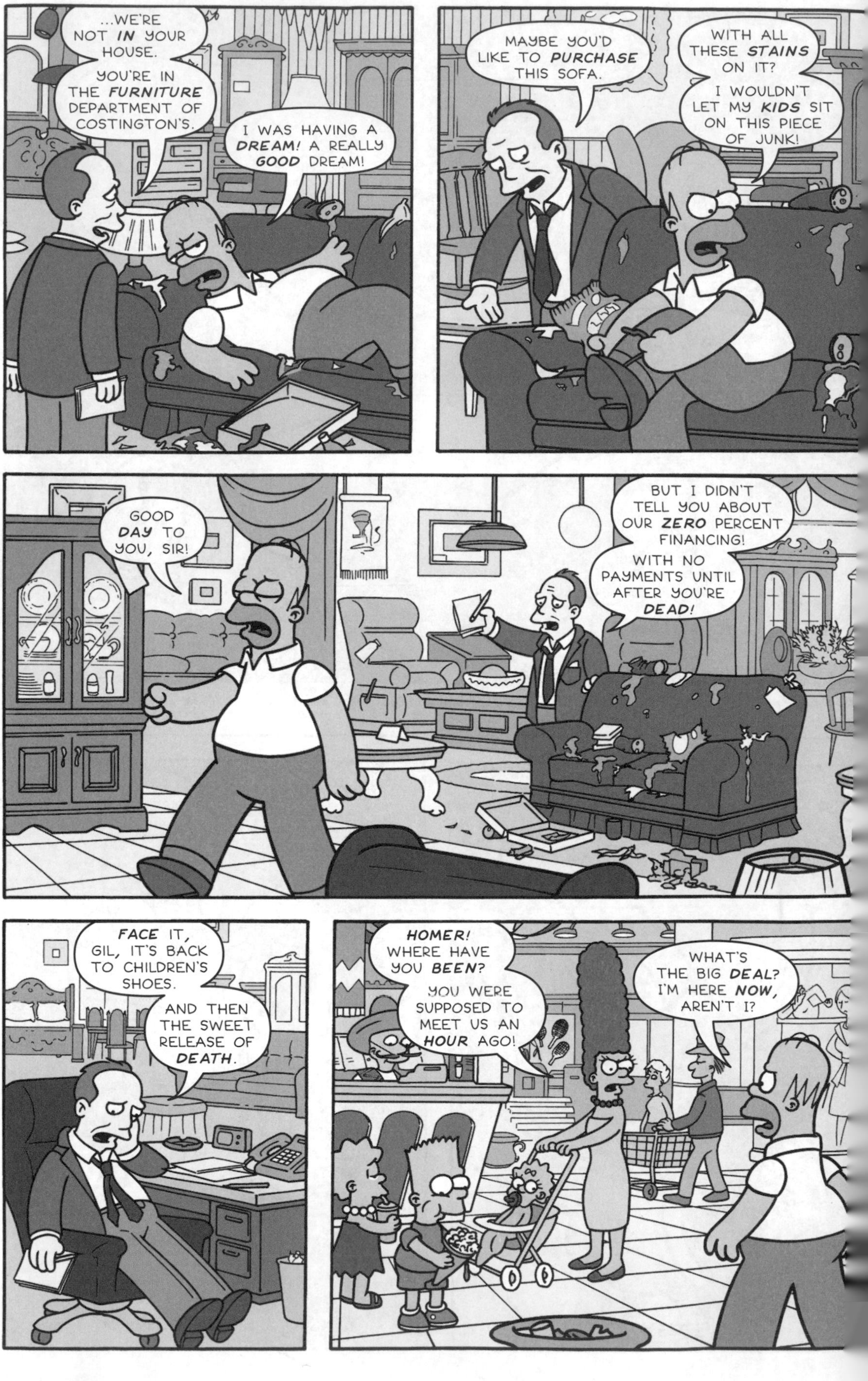
...WE'RE NOT IN YOUR HOUSE.
YOU'RE IN THE FURNITURE DEPARTMENT OF COSTINGTON'S.
I WAS HAVING A DREAM! A REALLY GOOD DREAM!
MAYBE YOU'D LIKE TO PURCHASE THIS SOFA.
WITH ALL THESE STAINS ON IT?
I WOULDN'T LET MY KIDS SIT ON THIS PIECE OF JUNK!
GOOD DAY TO YOU, SIR!
BUT I DIDN'T TELL YOU ABOUT OUR ZERO PERCENT FINANCING!
WITH NO PAYMENTS UNTIL AFTER YOU'RE DEAD!
FACE IT, GIL, IT'S BACK TO CHILDREN'S SHOES.
AND THEN THE SWEET RELEASE OF DEATH.
HOMER! WHERE HAVE YOU BEEN?
YOU WERE SUPPOSED TO MEET US AN HOUR AGO!
WHAT'S THE BIG DEAL? I'M HERE NOW, AREN'T I?

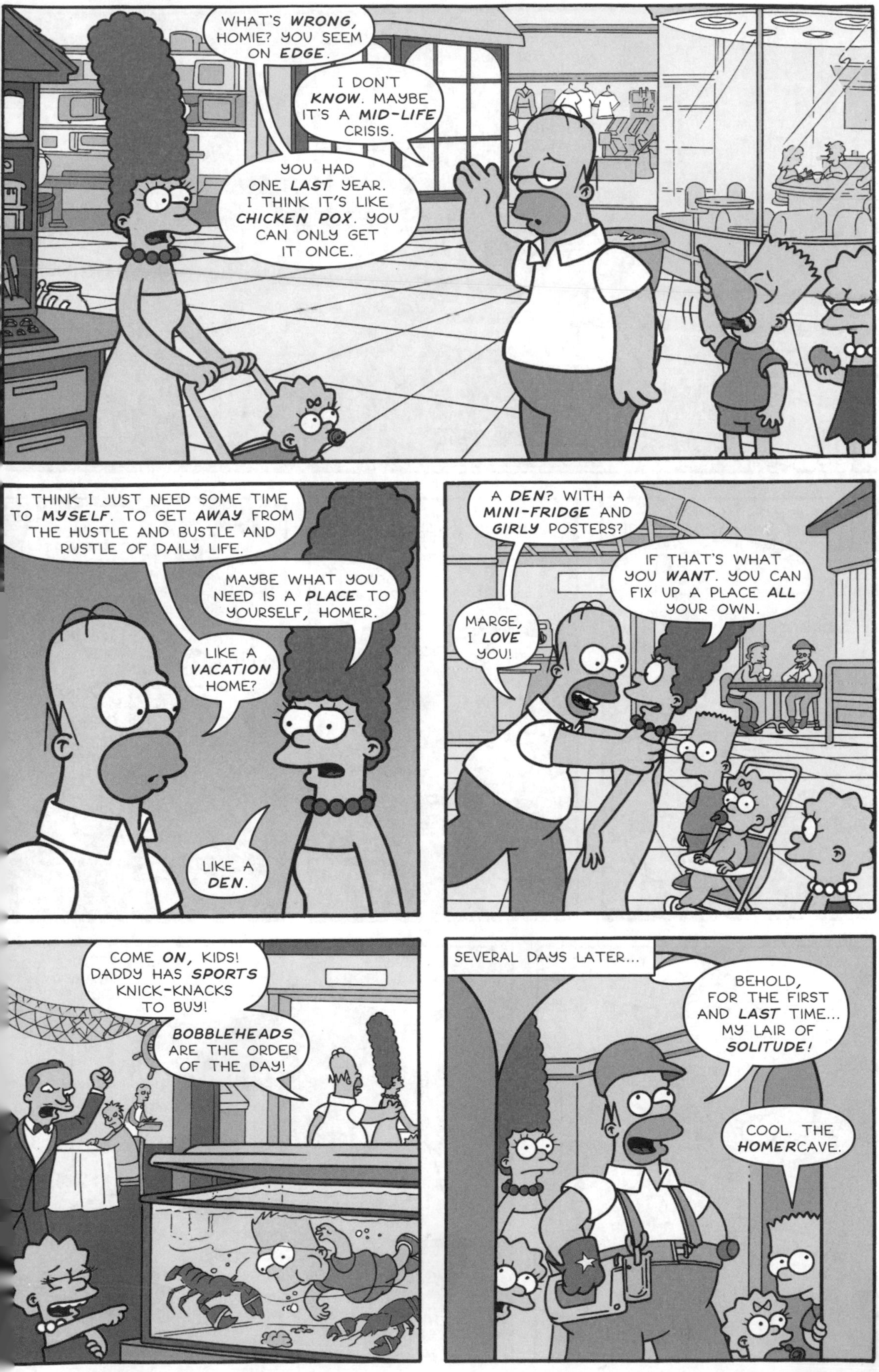

WHAT'S WRONG, HOMIE? YOU SEEM ON EDGE.
I DON'T KNOW. MAYBE IT'S A MID-LIFE CRISIS.
YOU HAD ONE LAST YEAR. I THINK IT'S LIKE CHICKEN POX. YOU CAN ONLY GET IT ONCE.
I THINK I JUST NEED SOME TIME TO MYSELF. TO GET AWAY FROM THE HUSTLE AND BUSTLE AND RUSTLE OF DAILY LIFE.
MAYBE WHAT YOU NEED IS A PLACE TO YOURSELF, HOMER.
LIKE A VACATION HOME?
LIKE A DEN.
A DEN? WITH A MINI-FRIDGE AND GIRLY POSTERS?
IF THAT'S WHAT YOU WANT. YOU CAN FIX UP A PLACE ALL YOUR OWN.
MARGE, I LOVE YOU!
COME ON, KIDS! DADDY HAS SPORTS KNICK-KNACKS TO BUY!
BOBBLEHEADS ARE THE ORDER OF THE DAY!
SEVERAL DAYS LATER...
BEHOLD, FOR THE FIRST AND LAST TIME... MY LAIR OF SOLITUDE!
COOL. THE HOMERCAVE.

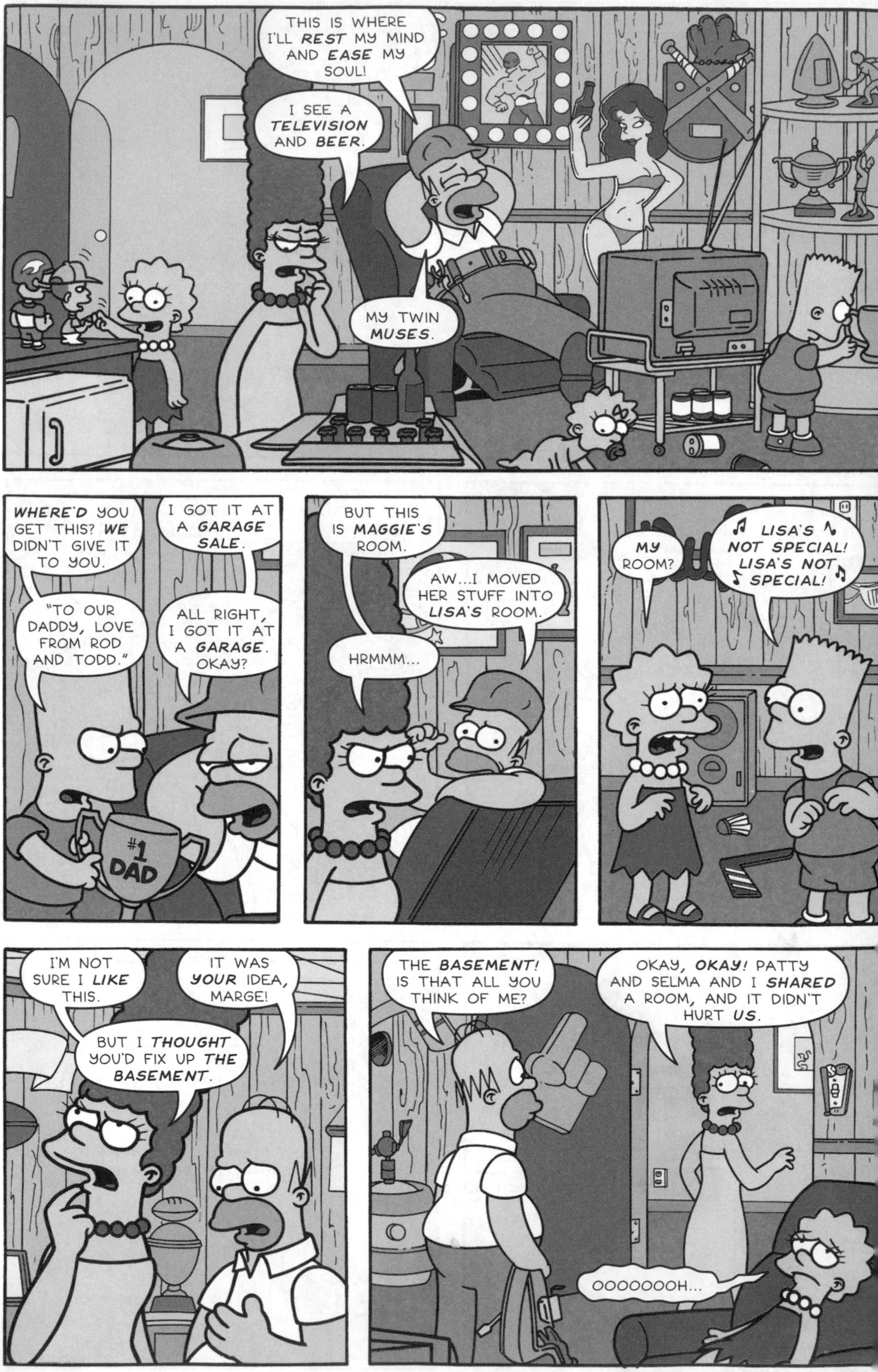
THIS IS WHERE I'LL REST MY MIND AND EASE MY SOUL!
I SEE A TELEVISION AND BEER.
MY TWIN MUSES.
WHERE'D YOU GET THIS? WE DIDN'T GIVE IT TO YOU.
I GOT IT AT A GARAGE SALE.
"TO OUR DADDY, LOVE FROM ROD AND TODD."
ALL RIGHT, I GOT IT AT A GARAGE. OKAY?
#1 DAD
BUT THIS IS MAGGIE'S ROOM.
AW...I MOVED HER STUFF INTO LISA'S ROOM.
HRMMM...
MY ROOM?
♫ LISA'S NOT SPECIAL! LISA'S NOT SPECIAL! ♫
I'M NOT SURE I LIKE THIS.
IT WAS YOUR IDEA, MARGE!
BUT I THOUGHT YOU'D FIX UP THE BASEMENT.
THE BASEMENT! IS THAT ALL YOU THINK OF ME?
OKAY, OKAY! PATTY AND SELMA AND I SHARED A ROOM, AND IT DIDN'T HURT US.
OOOOOOOH...

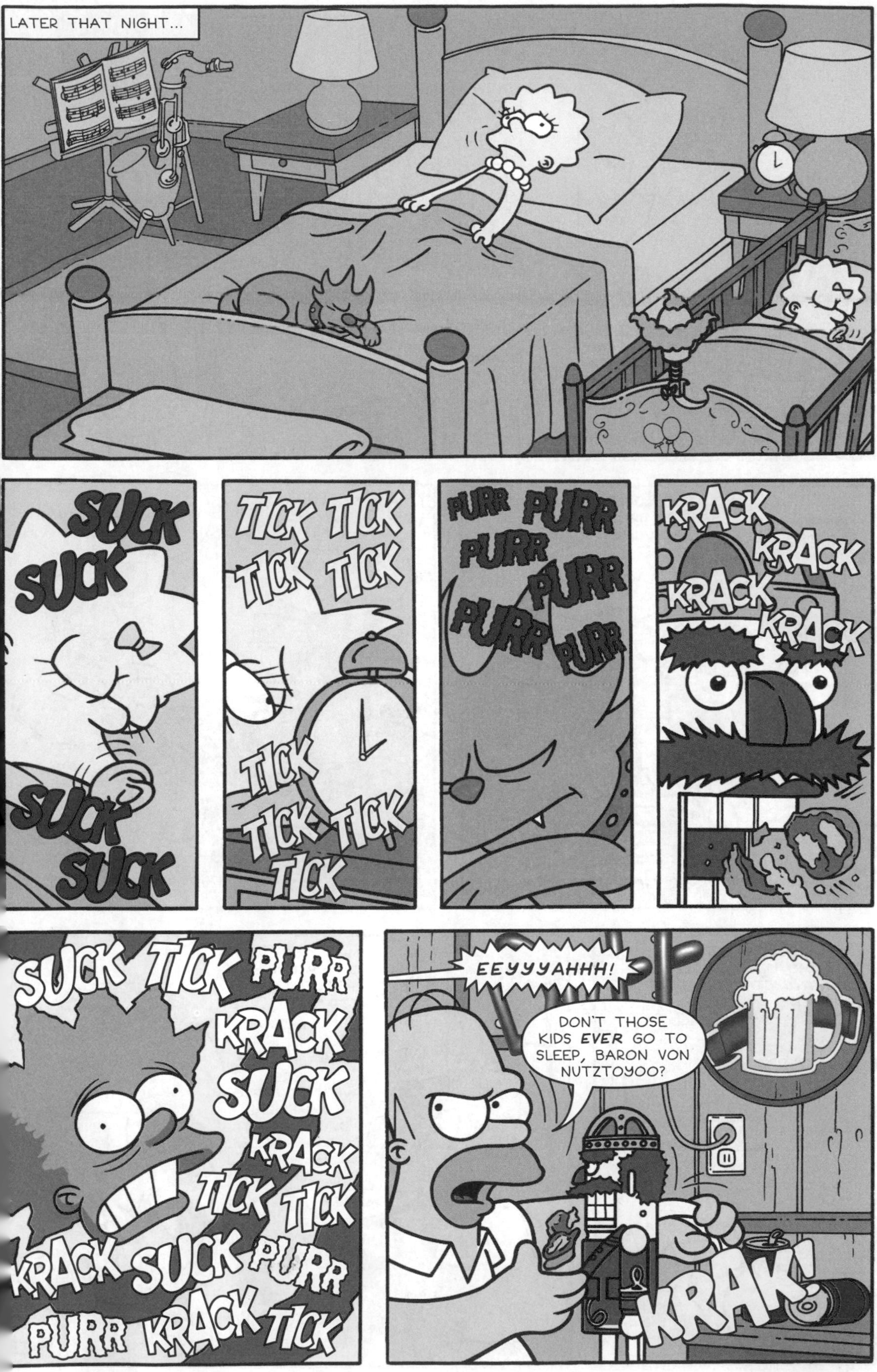
LATER THAT NIGHT...
SUCK
SUCK
SUCK
SUCK
TICK TICK
TICK TICK
TICK
TICK TICK
TICK
PURR PURR
PURR
PURR
PURR PURR
KRACK
KRACK
KRACK
KRACK
SUCK TICK PURR
KRACK
SUCK
KRACK
TICK TICK
KRACK SUCK PURR
PURR KRACK TICK
EEYYYAHHH!
DON'T THOSE KIDS *EVER* GO TO SLEEP, BARON VON NUTZTOYOO?
KRAK!

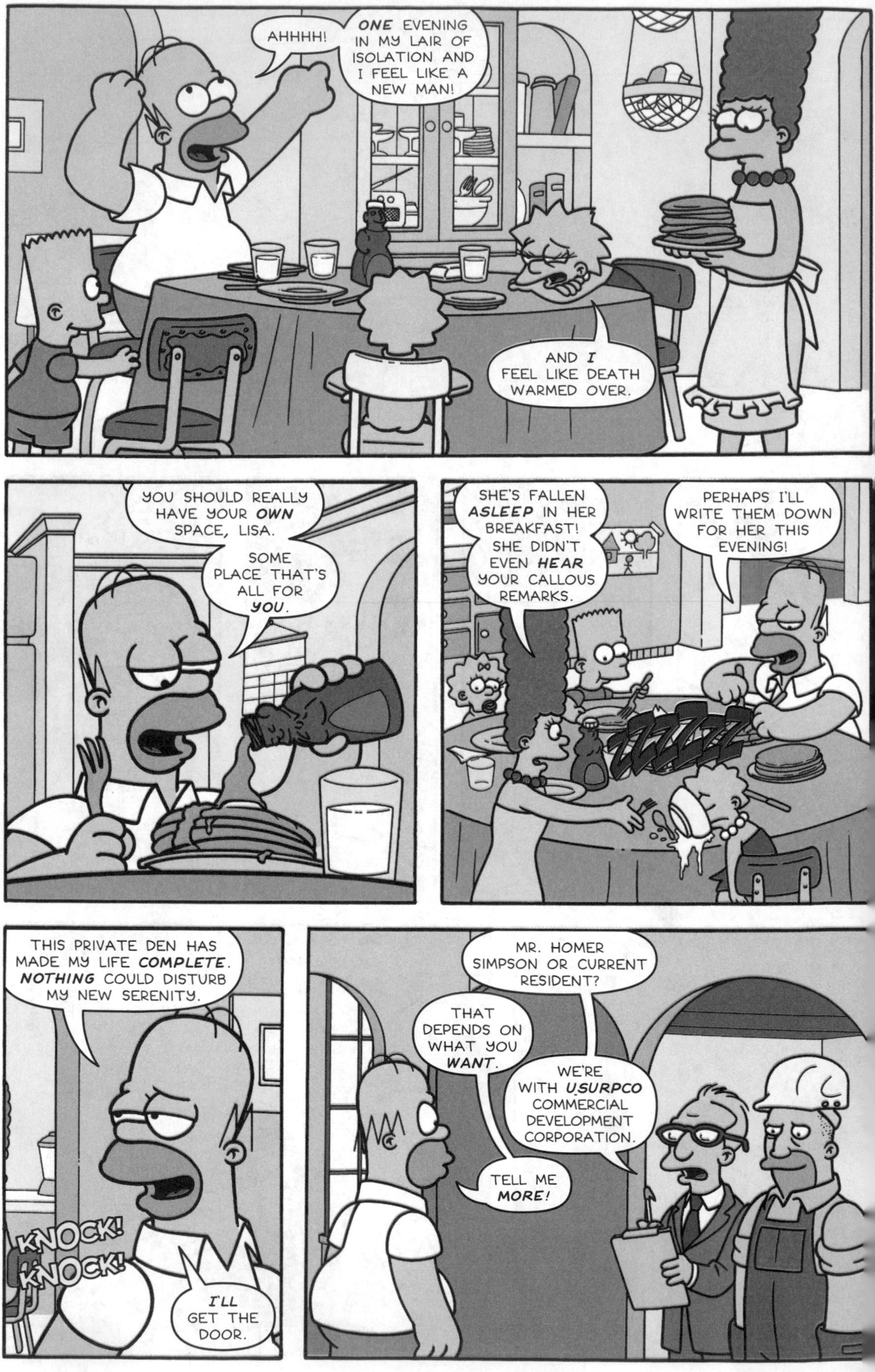
AHHHH!
ONE EVENING IN MY LAIR OF ISOLATION AND I FEEL LIKE A NEW MAN!
AND I FEEL LIKE DEATH WARMED OVER.
YOU SHOULD REALLY HAVE YOUR OWN SPACE, LISA.
SOME PLACE THAT'S ALL FOR YOU.
SHE'S FALLEN ASLEEP IN HER BREAKFAST! SHE DIDN'T EVEN HEAR YOUR CALLOUS REMARKS.
PERHAPS I'LL WRITE THEM DOWN FOR HER THIS EVENING!
THIS PRIVATE DEN HAS MADE MY LIFE COMPLETE. NOTHING COULD DISTURB MY NEW SERENITY.
KNOCK! KNOCK!
I'LL GET THE DOOR.
MR. HOMER SIMPSON OR CURRENT RESIDENT?
THAT DEPENDS ON WHAT YOU WANT.
WE'RE WITH U.SURPCO COMMERCIAL DEVELOPMENT CORPORATION.
TELL ME MORE!

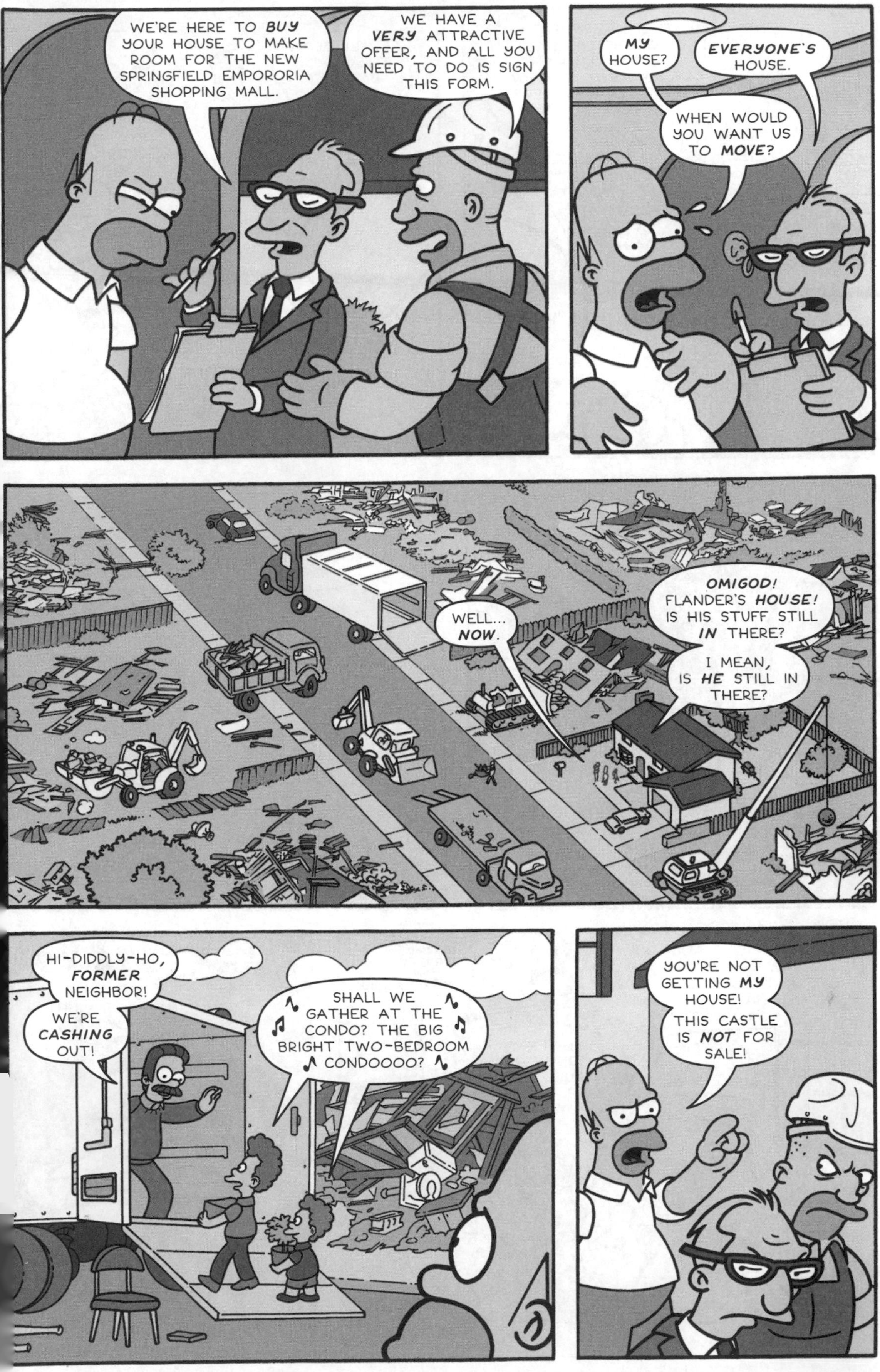

WE'RE HERE TO BUY YOUR HOUSE TO MAKE ROOM FOR THE NEW SPRINGFIELD EMPORORIA SHOPPING MALL.
WE HAVE A VERY ATTRACTIVE OFFER, AND ALL YOU NEED TO DO IS SIGN THIS FORM.
MY HOUSE?
EVERYONE'S HOUSE.
WHEN WOULD YOU WANT US TO MOVE?
WELL... NOW.
OMIGOD! FLANDER'S HOUSE! IS HIS STUFF STILL IN THERE?
I MEAN, IS HE STILL IN THERE?
HI-DIDDLY-HO, FORMER NEIGHBOR!
WE'RE CASHING OUT!
SHALL WE GATHER AT THE CONDO? THE BIG BRIGHT TWO-BEDROOM CONDOOOOO?
YOU'RE NOT GETTING MY HOUSE!
THIS CASTLE IS NOT FOR SALE!

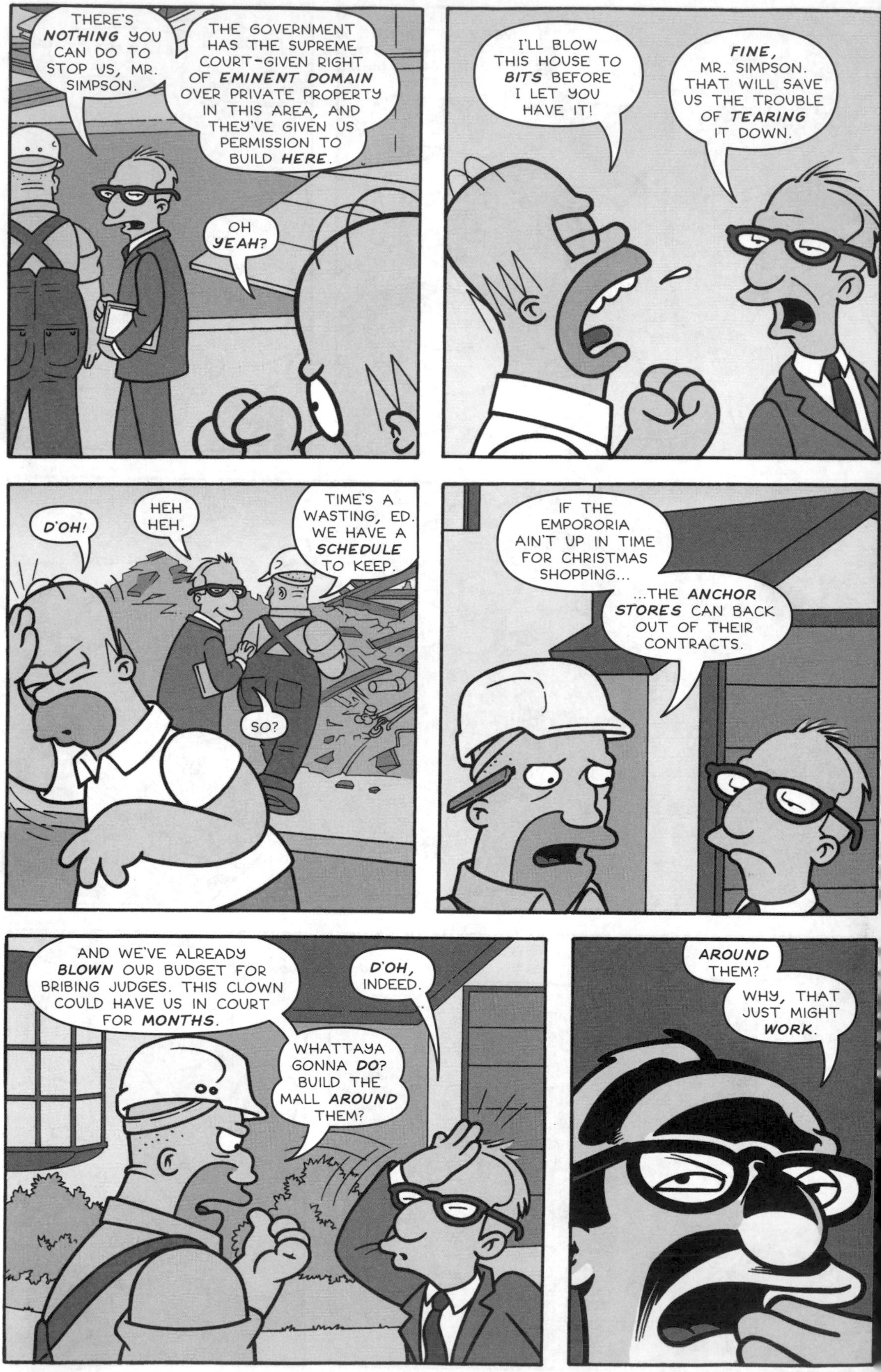
THERE'S NOTHING YOU CAN DO TO STOP US, MR. SIMPSON.
THE GOVERNMENT HAS THE SUPREME COURT-GIVEN RIGHT OF EMINENT DOMAIN OVER PRIVATE PROPERTY IN THIS AREA, AND THEY'VE GIVEN US PERMISSION TO BUILD HERE.
OH YEAH?
I'LL BLOW THIS HOUSE TO BITS BEFORE I LET YOU HAVE IT!
FINE, MR. SIMPSON. THAT WILL SAVE US THE TROUBLE OF TEARING IT DOWN.
D'OH!
HEH HEH.
TIME'S A WASTING, ED. WE HAVE A SCHEDULE TO KEEP.
SO?
IF THE EMPORORIA AIN'T UP IN TIME FOR CHRISTMAS SHOPPING...
...THE ANCHOR STORES CAN BACK OUT OF THEIR CONTRACTS.
AND WE'VE ALREADY BLOWN OUR BUDGET FOR BRIBING JUDGES. THIS CLOWN COULD HAVE US IN COURT FOR MONTHS.
D'OH, INDEED.
WHATTAYA GONNA DO? BUILD THE MALL AROUND THEM?
AROUND THEM?
WHY, THAT JUST MIGHT WORK.

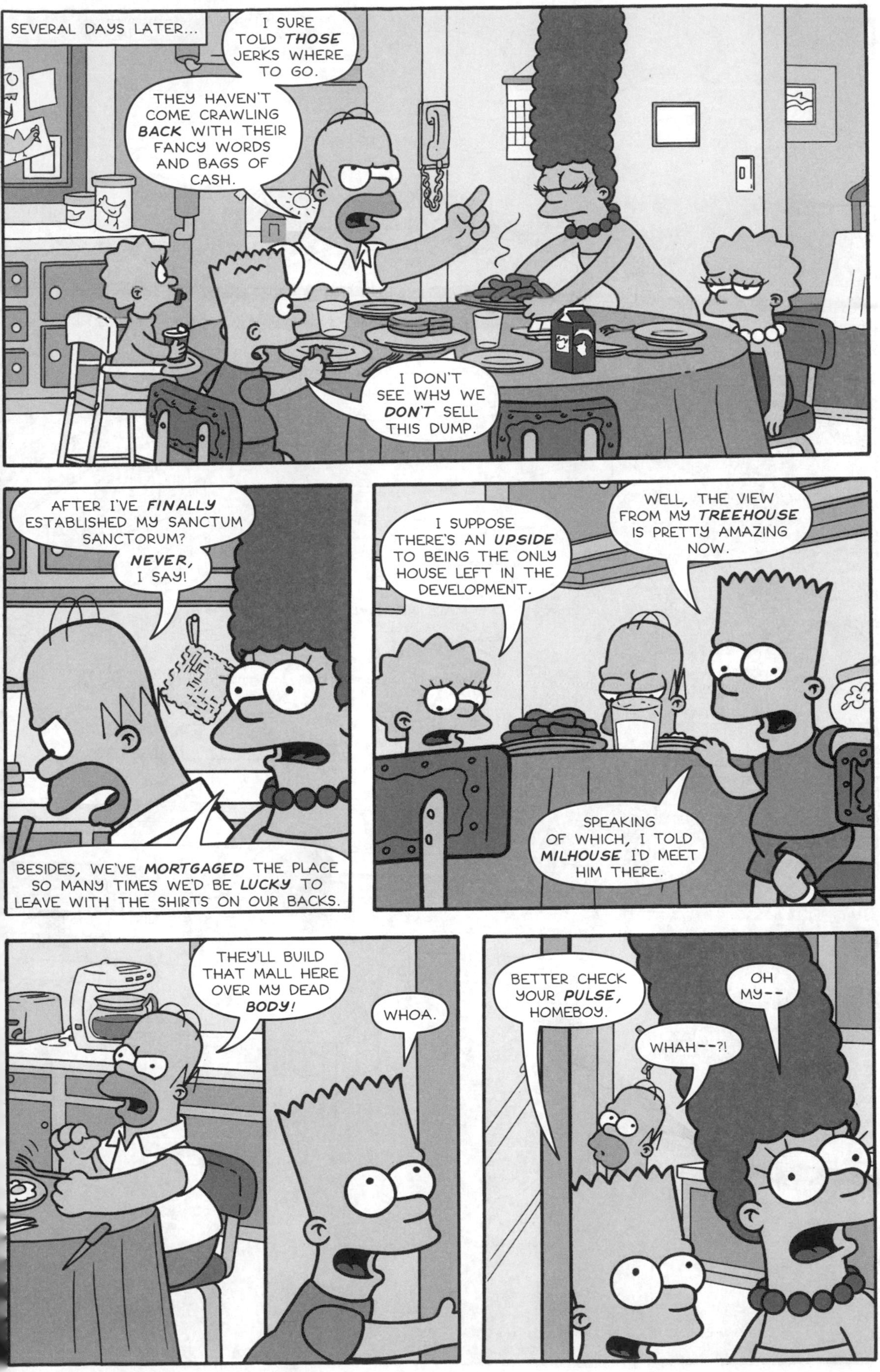
SEVERAL DAYS LATER...
I SURE TOLD THOSE JERKS WHERE TO GO.
THEY HAVEN'T COME CRAWLING BACK WITH THEIR FANCY WORDS AND BAGS OF CASH.
I DON'T SEE WHY WE DON'T SELL THIS DUMP.
AFTER I'VE FINALLY ESTABLISHED MY SANCTUM SANCTORUM?
NEVER, I SAY!
BESIDES, WE'VE MORTGAGED THE PLACE SO MANY TIMES WE'D BE LUCKY TO LEAVE WITH THE SHIRTS ON OUR BACKS.
I SUPPOSE THERE'S AN UPSIDE TO BEING THE ONLY HOUSE LEFT IN THE DEVELOPMENT.
WELL, THE VIEW FROM MY TREEHOUSE IS PRETTY AMAZING NOW.
SPEAKING OF WHICH, I TOLD MILHOUSE I'D MEET HIM THERE.
THEY'LL BUILD THAT MALL HERE OVER MY DEAD BODY!
WHOA.
BETTER CHECK YOUR PULSE, HOMEBOY.
OH MY--
WHAH--?!

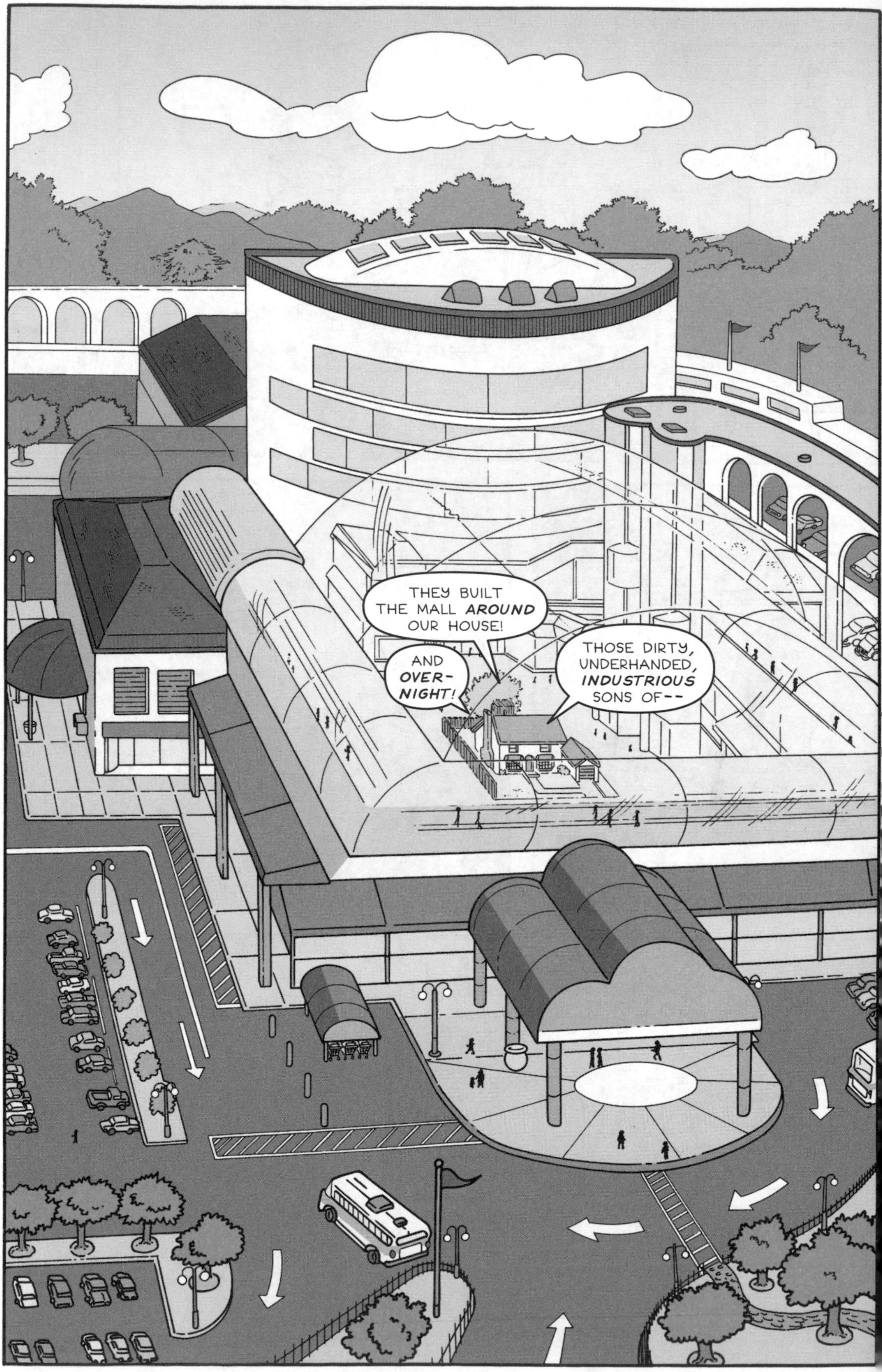
THEY BUILT THE MALL AROUND OUR HOUSE!
AND OVER-NIGHT!
THOSE DIRTY, UNDERHANDED, INDUSTRIOUS SONS OF--

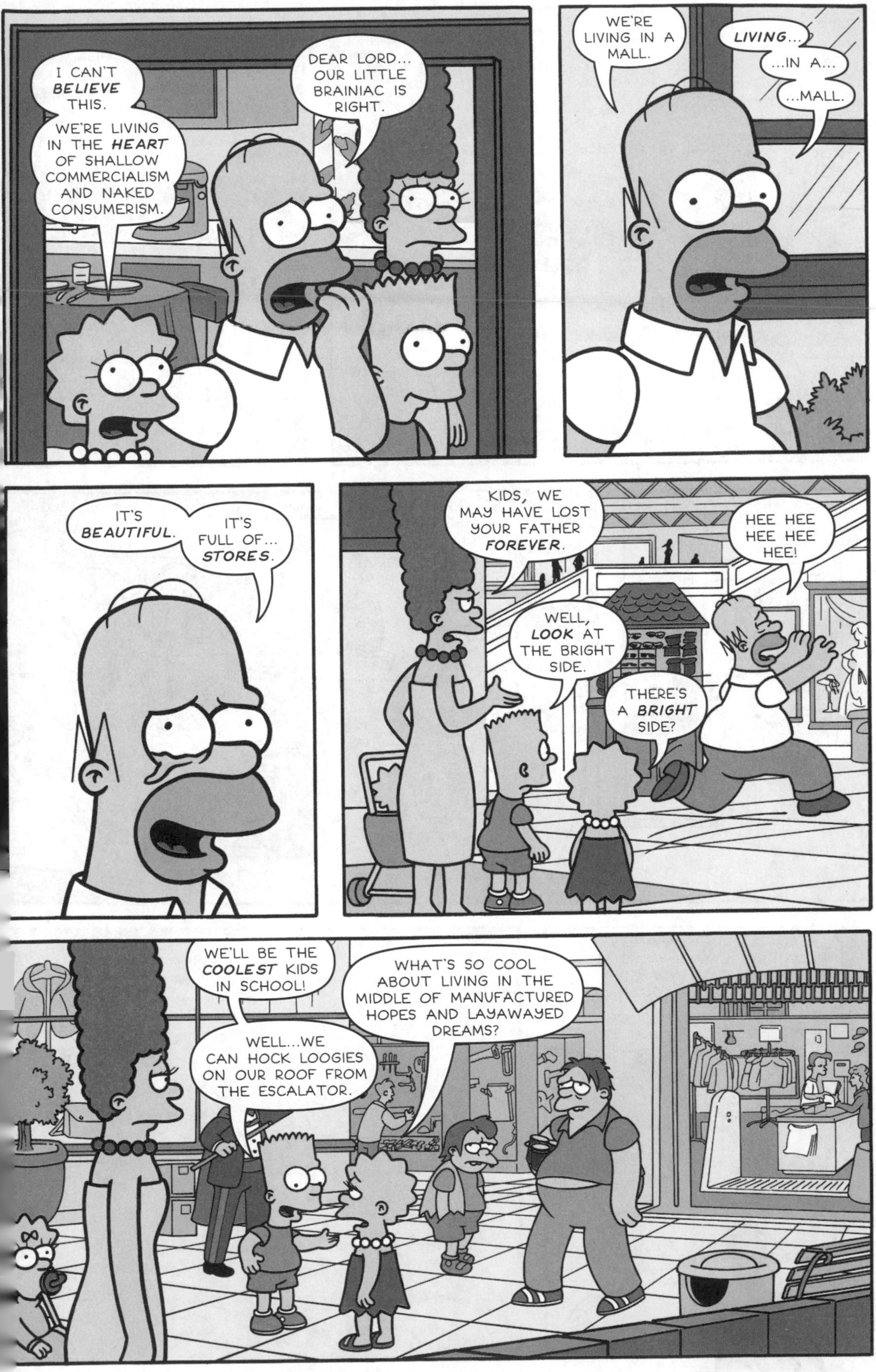
I CAN'T BELIEVE THIS.
WE'RE LIVING IN THE HEART OF SHALLOW COMMERCIALISM AND NAKED CONSUMERISM.
DEAR LORD... OUR LITTLE BRAINIAC IS RIGHT.
WE'RE LIVING IN A MALL.
LIVING...
...IN A...
...MALL.
IT'S BEAUTIFUL.
IT'S FULL OF... STORES.
KIDS, WE MAY HAVE LOST YOUR FATHER FOREVER.
HEE HEE HEE HEE HEE!
WELL, LOOK AT THE BRIGHT SIDE.
THERE'S A BRIGHT SIDE?
WE'LL BE THE COOLEST KIDS IN SCHOOL!
WHAT'S SO COOL ABOUT LIVING IN THE MIDDLE OF MANUFACTURED HOPES AND LAYAWAYED DREAMS?
WELL...WE CAN HOCK LOOGIES ON OUR ROOF FROM THE ESCALATOR.

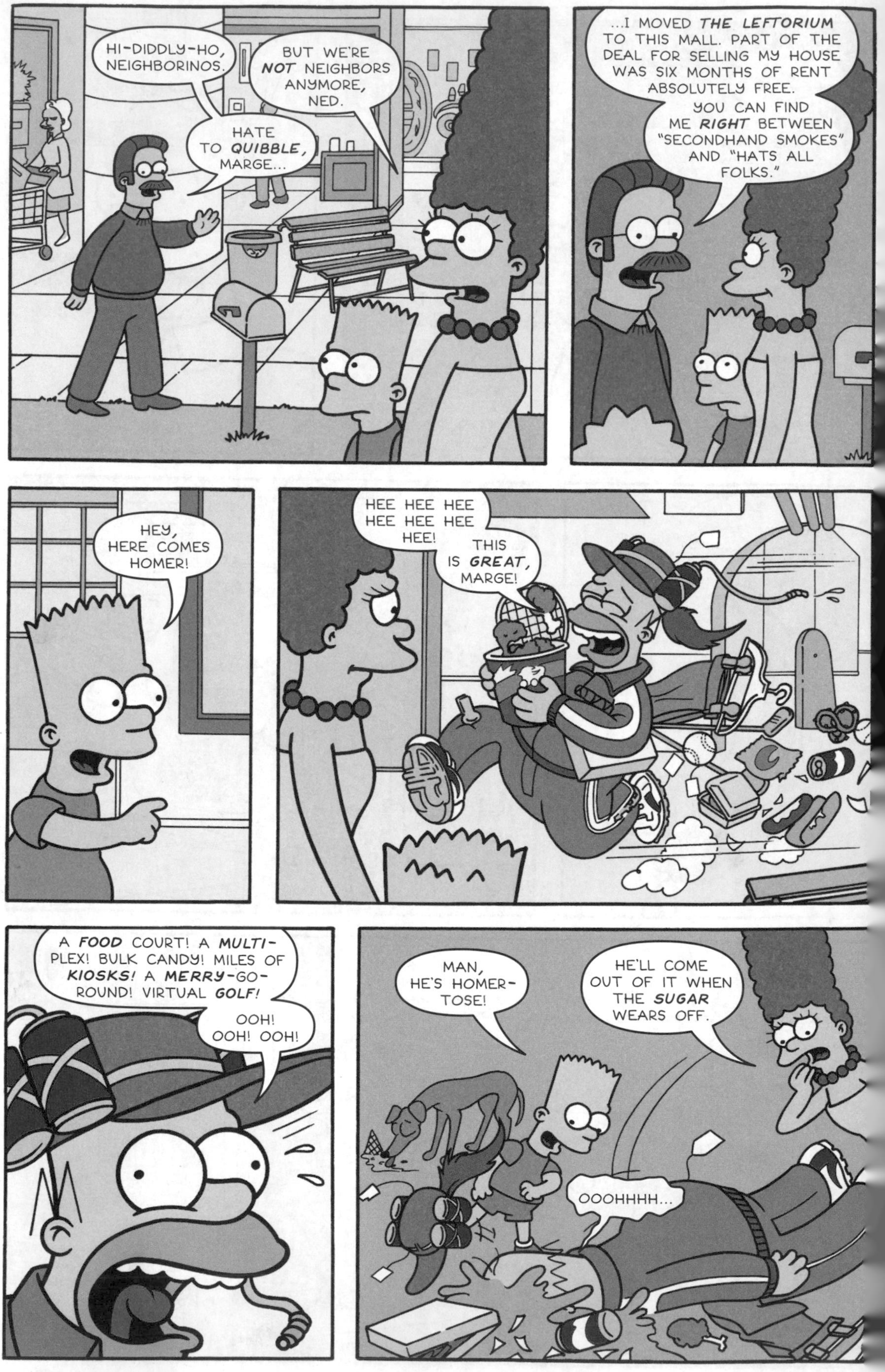
HI-DIDDLY-HO, NEIGHBORINOS.
BUT WE'RE NOT NEIGHBORS ANYMORE, NED.
HATE TO QUIBBLE, MARGE...
...I MOVED THE LEFTORIUM TO THIS MALL. PART OF THE DEAL FOR SELLING MY HOUSE WAS SIX MONTHS OF RENT ABSOLUTELY FREE.
YOU CAN FIND ME RIGHT BETWEEN "SECONDHAND SMOKES" AND "HATS ALL FOLKS."
HEY, HERE COMES HOMER!
HEE HEE HEE HEE HEE HEE HEE!
THIS IS GREAT, MARGE!
A FOOD COURT! A MULTI-PLEX! BULK CANDY! MILES OF KIOSKS! A MERRY-GO-ROUND! VIRTUAL GOLF!
OOH! OOH! OOH!
MAN, HE'S HOMER-TOSE!
HE'LL COME OUT OF IT WHEN THE SUGAR WEARS OFF.
OOOHHHH...

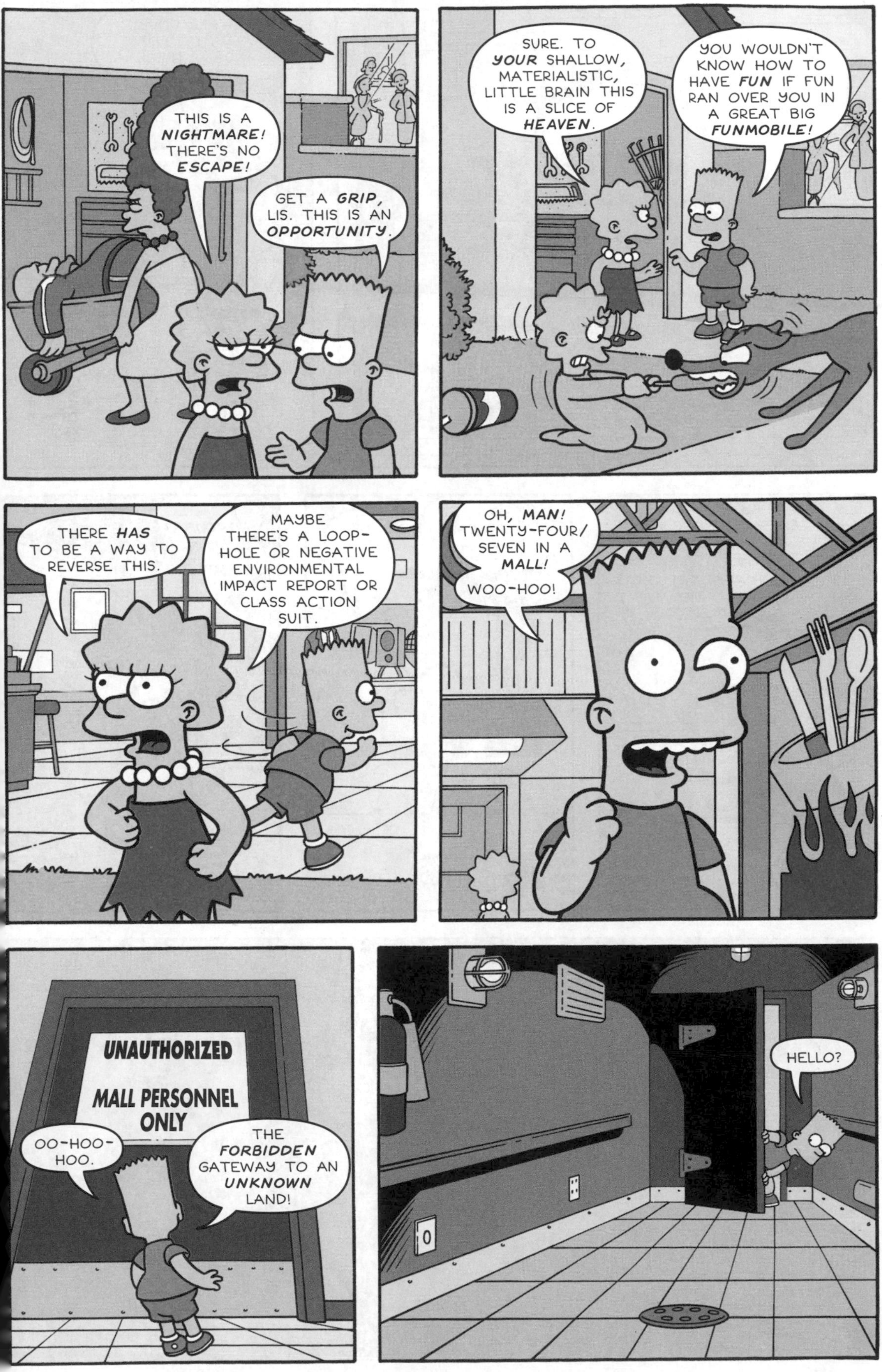
THIS IS A NIGHTMARE! THERE'S NO ESCAPE!
GET A GRIP, LIS. THIS IS AN OPPORTUNITY.
SURE. TO YOUR SHALLOW, MATERIALISTIC, LITTLE BRAIN THIS IS A SLICE OF HEAVEN.
YOU WOULDN'T KNOW HOW TO HAVE FUN IF FUN RAN OVER YOU IN A GREAT BIG FUNMOBILE!
THERE HAS TO BE A WAY TO REVERSE THIS.
MAYBE THERE'S A LOOP-HOLE OR NEGATIVE ENVIRONMENTAL IMPACT REPORT OR CLASS ACTION SUIT.
OH, MAN! TWENTY-FOUR/SEVEN IN A MALL!
WOO-HOO!
UNAUTHORIZED
MALL PERSONNEL ONLY
OO-HOO-HOO.
THE FORBIDDEN GATEWAY TO AN UNKNOWN LAND!
HELLO?

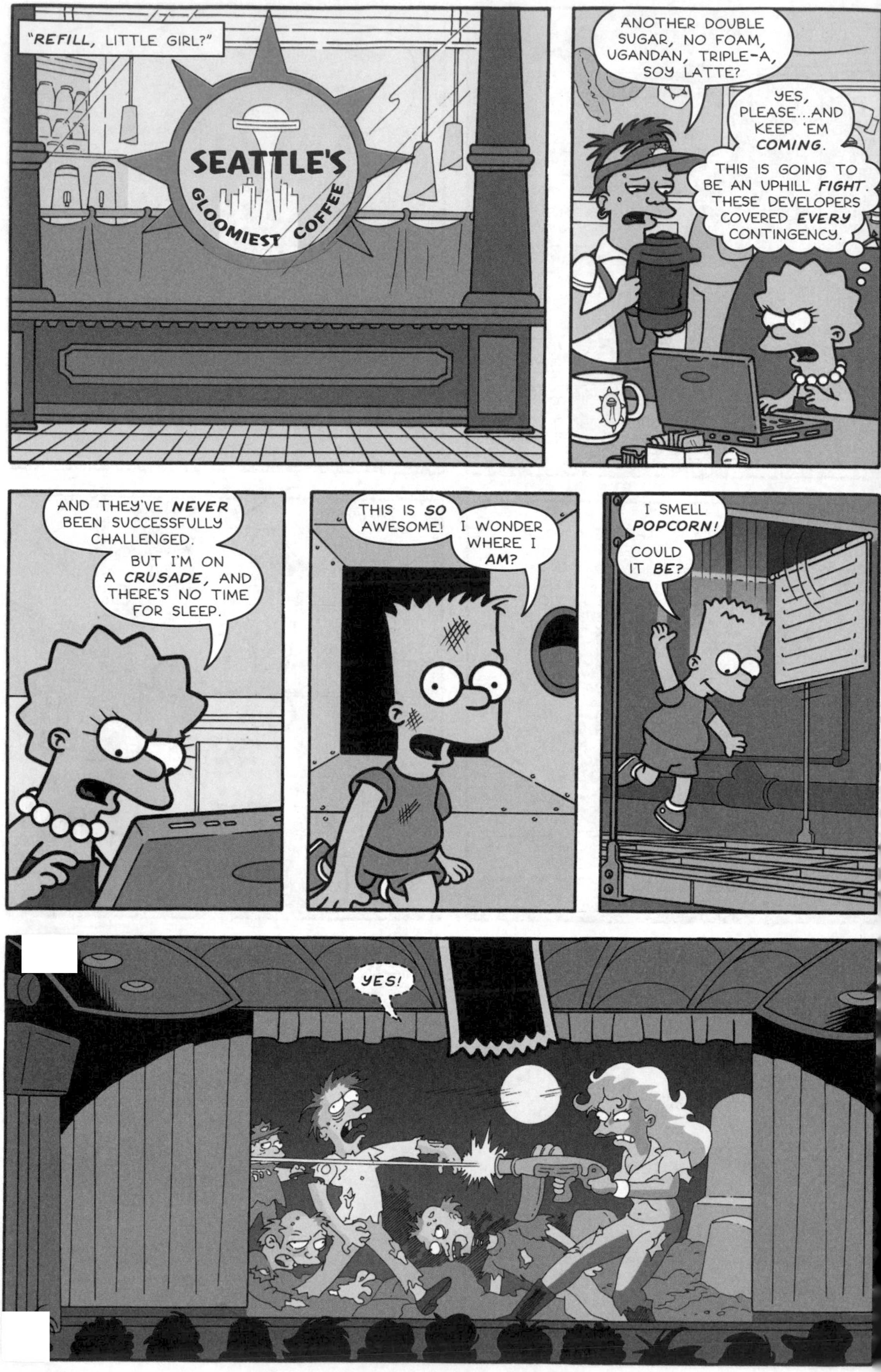
"REFILL, LITTLE GIRL?"
SEATTLE'S GLOOMIEST COFFEE
ANOTHER DOUBLE SUGAR, NO FOAM, UGANDAN, TRIPLE-A, SOY LATTE?
YES, PLEASE...AND KEEP 'EM COMING.
THIS IS GOING TO BE AN UPHILL FIGHT. THESE DEVELOPERS COVERED EVERY CONTINGENCY.
AND THEY'VE NEVER BEEN SUCCESSFULLY CHALLENGED.
BUT I'M ON A CRUSADE, AND THERE'S NO TIME FOR SLEEP.
THIS IS SO AWESOME!
I WONDER WHERE I AM?
I SMELL POPCORN!
COULD IT BE?
YES!

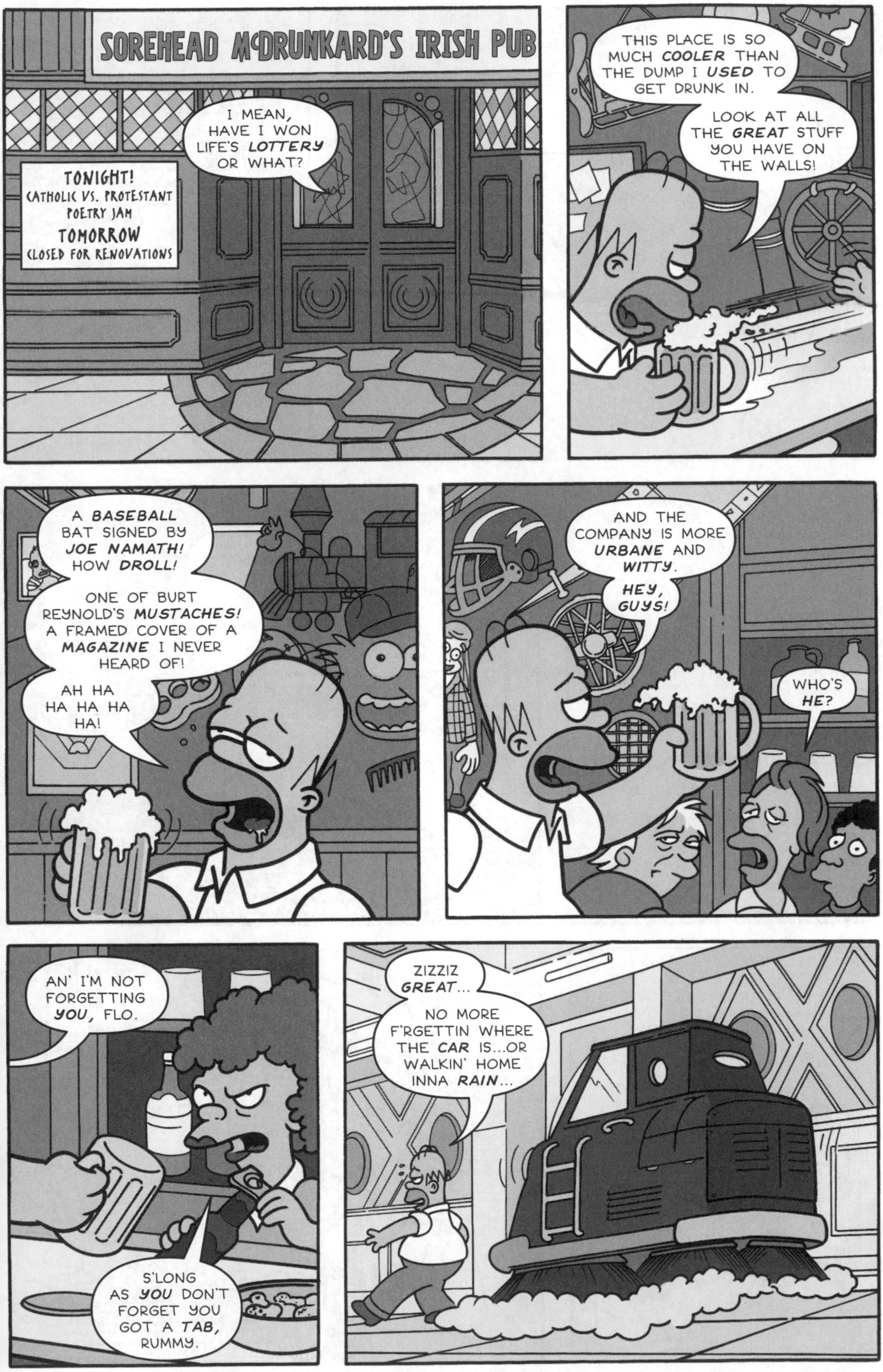

SOREHEAD McDRUNKARD'S IRISH PUB
TONIGHT! CATHOLIC VS. PROTESTANT POETRY JAM
TOMORROW CLOSED FOR RENOVATIONS
I MEAN, HAVE I WON LIFE'S LOTTERY OR WHAT?
THIS PLACE IS SO MUCH COOLER THAN THE DUMP I USED TO GET DRUNK IN.
LOOK AT ALL THE GREAT STUFF YOU HAVE ON THE WALLS!
A BASEBALL BAT SIGNED BY JOE NAMATH! HOW DROLL!
ONE OF BURT REYNOLD'S MUSTACHES! A FRAMED COVER OF A MAGAZINE I NEVER HEARD OF!
AH HA HA HA HA HA!
AND THE COMPANY IS MORE URBANE AND WITTY.
HEY, GUYS!
WHO'S HE?
AN' I'M NOT FORGETTING YOU, FLO.
S'LONG AS YOU DON'T FORGET YOU GOT A TAB, RUMMY.
ZIZZIZ GREAT...
NO MORE F'RGETTIN WHERE THE CAR IS...OR WALKIN' HOME INNA RAIN...

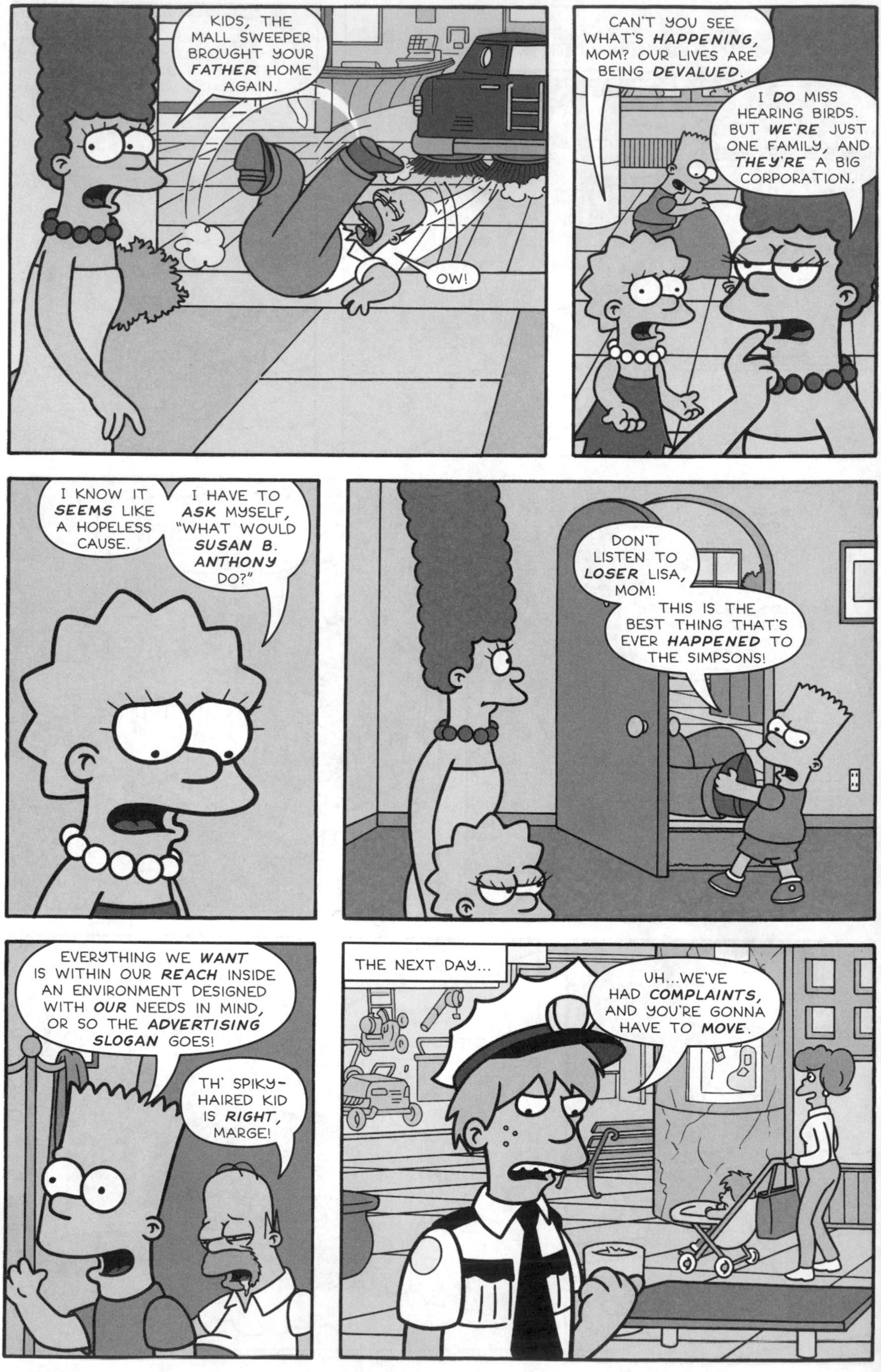
KIDS, THE MALL SWEEPER BROUGHT YOUR FATHER HOME AGAIN.
OW!
CAN'T YOU SEE WHAT'S HAPPENING, MOM? OUR LIVES ARE BEING DEVALUED.
I DO MISS HEARING BIRDS. BUT WE'RE JUST ONE FAMILY, AND THEY'RE A BIG CORPORATION.
I KNOW IT SEEMS LIKE A HOPELESS CAUSE.
I HAVE TO ASK MYSELF, "WHAT WOULD SUSAN B. ANTHONY DO?"
DON'T LISTEN TO LOSER LISA, MOM!
THIS IS THE BEST THING THAT'S EVER HAPPENED TO THE SIMPSONS!
EVERYTHING WE WANT IS WITHIN OUR REACH INSIDE AN ENVIRONMENT DESIGNED WITH OUR NEEDS IN MIND, OR SO THE ADVERTISING SLOGAN GOES!
TH' SPIKY-HAIRED KID IS RIGHT, MARGE!
THE NEXT DAY...
UH...WE'VE HAD COMPLAINTS, AND YOU'RE GONNA HAVE TO MOVE.

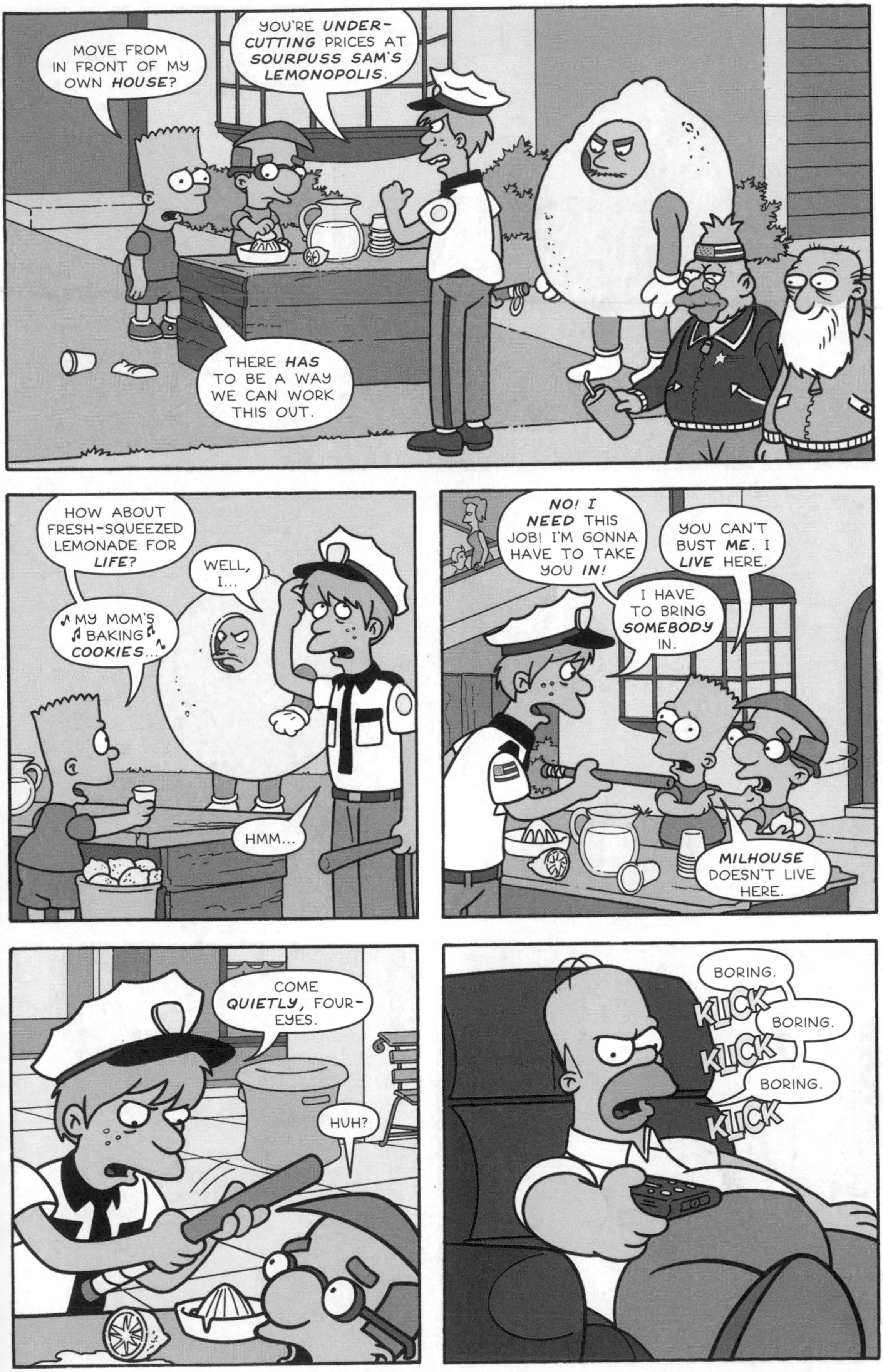

MOVE FROM IN FRONT OF MY OWN HOUSE?
YOU'RE UNDER-CUTTING PRICES AT SOURPUSS SAM'S LEMONOPOLIS.
THERE HAS TO BE A WAY WE CAN WORK THIS OUT.
HOW ABOUT FRESH-SQUEEZED LEMONADE FOR LIFE?
WELL, I...
♪ MY MOM'S BAKING COOKIES... ♪
HMM...
NO! I NEED THIS JOB! I'M GONNA HAVE TO TAKE YOU IN!
YOU CAN'T BUST ME. I LIVE HERE.
I HAVE TO BRING SOMEBODY IN.
MILHOUSE DOESN'T LIVE HERE.
COME QUIETLY, FOUR-EYES.
HUH?
BORING.
KLICK
BORING.
KLICK
BORING.
KLICK

MARGE: HOMER, CAN WE *TALK*?

HOMER: COME *ON*, MARGE. CAN'T I HAVE A MINUTE'S PEACE WHEN I COME HOME FROM WORK?

MARGE: BUT YOU *HAVEN'T* BEEN COMING HOME.

MARGE: HAVE YOU EVEN BEEN GOING TO *WORK*? RECENTLY?

HOMER: HOMIE, THINGS HAVE CHANGED *SO* MUCH SINCE THEY BUILT THE MALL AROUND OUR HOUSE.

HOMER: FOR THE *BETTER*, MARGE! WE LIVE IN A WORLD I COULD NEVER *AFFORD* TO GIVE US!

HOMER: IT'S LIKE THAT *MOVIE* WHERE THE PEOPLE LIVE IN A MALL EXCEPT THERE ARE NO ZOMBIES TRYING TO *EAT* US!

MARGE: THOUGH...HOW COOL WOULD *THAT* BE?

MARGE: I'M WORRIED ABOUT THE *KIDS*. BART IS GETTING INTO WHO KNOWS *WHAT* KIND OF TROUBLE.

MARGE: AND LISA IS LOSING *SLEEP* OVER THIS WHOLE THING.

MARGE: AND *YOU'VE* MAXED OUT OUR CREDIT CARDS PAYING OFF THE *OTHER* CREDIT CARDS YOU'VE MAXED OUT.

HOMER: *BAM!* THERE GOES ZOMBIE FLANDERS! *POW!* ZOMBIE GRAMPA BITES THE DUST!

MARGE: YOU'RE *NOT* LISTENING TO ME. WHY DO I *BOTHER*?

HOMER: *BOOM!* ZOMBIE PATTY! *KA-BLAM!* ZOMBIE SELMA!

MARGE: HRMMM...

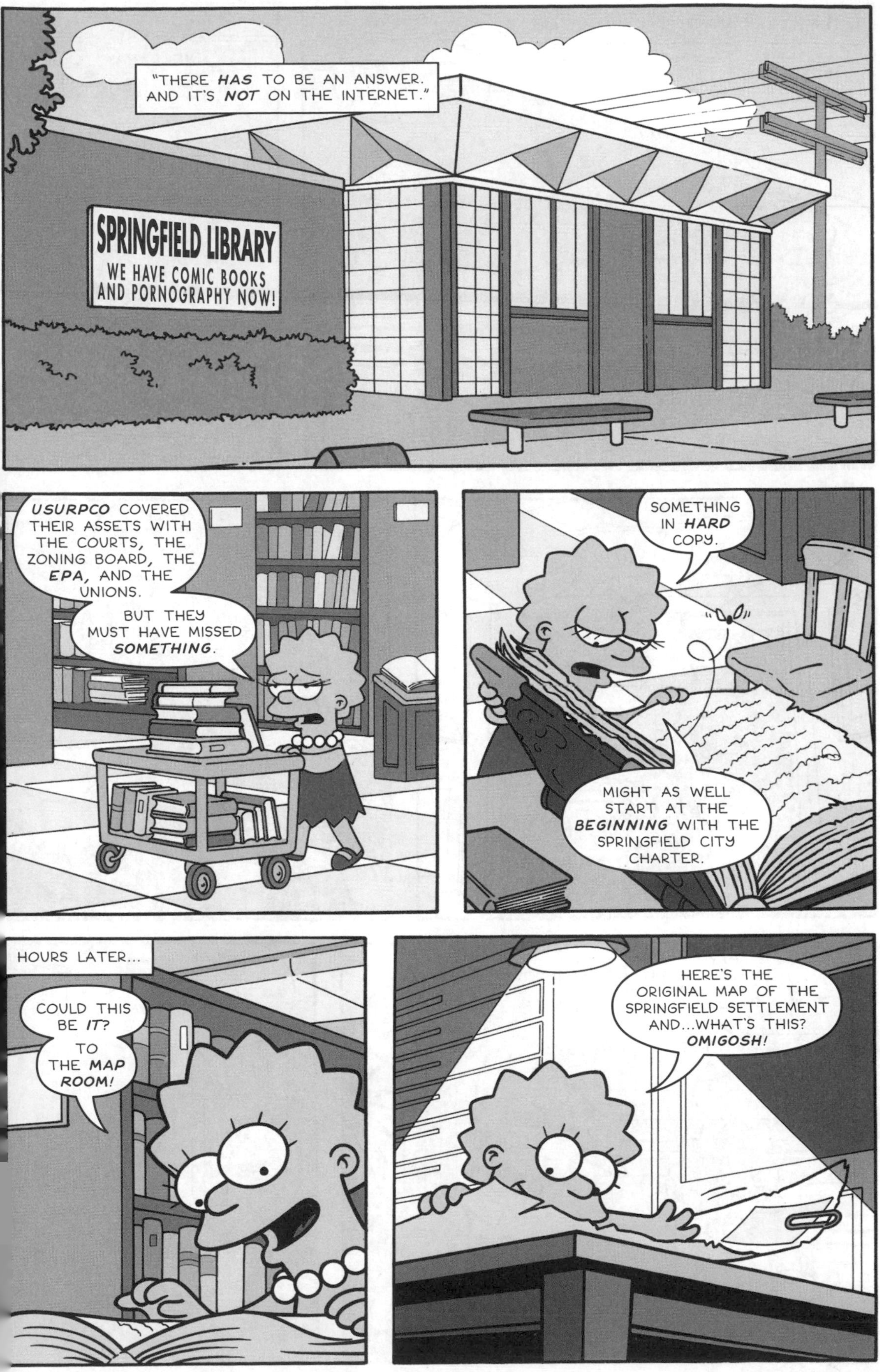

"THERE HAS TO BE AN ANSWER. AND IT'S NOT ON THE INTERNET."
SPRINGFIELD LIBRARY
WE HAVE COMIC BOOKS AND PORNOGRAPHY NOW!
USURPCO COVERED THEIR ASSETS WITH THE COURTS, THE ZONING BOARD, THE EPA, AND THE UNIONS.
BUT THEY MUST HAVE MISSED SOMETHING.
SOMETHING IN HARD COPY.
MIGHT AS WELL START AT THE BEGINNING WITH THE SPRINGFIELD CITY CHARTER.
HOURS LATER...
COULD THIS BE IT?
TO THE MAP ROOM!
HERE'S THE ORIGINAL MAP OF THE SPRINGFIELD SETTLEMENT AND...WHAT'S THIS? OMIGOSH!

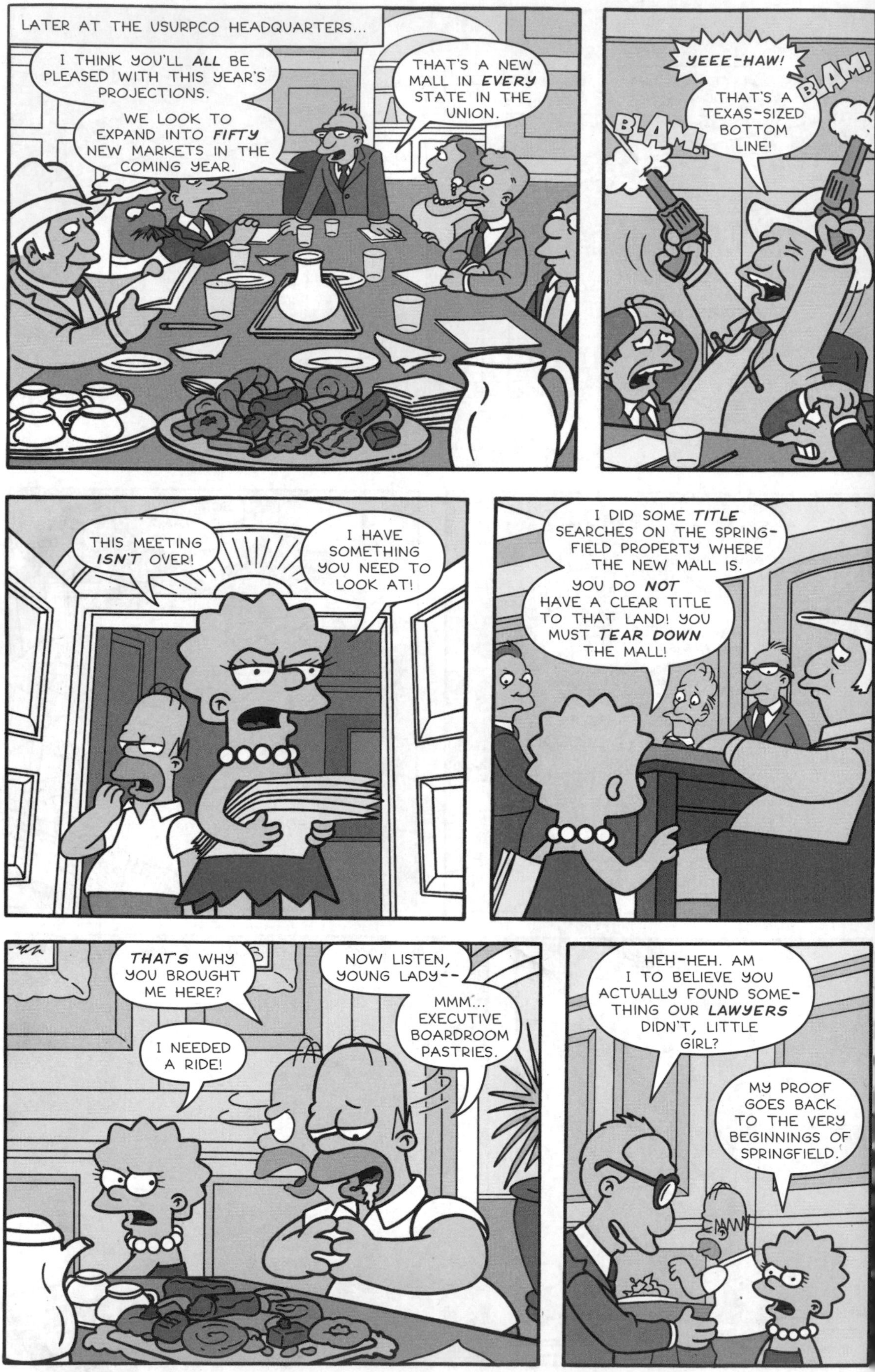
LATER AT THE USURPCO HEADQUARTERS...
I THINK YOU'LL ALL BE PLEASED WITH THIS YEAR'S PROJECTIONS.
WE LOOK TO EXPAND INTO FIFTY NEW MARKETS IN THE COMING YEAR.
THAT'S A NEW MALL IN EVERY STATE IN THE UNION.
YEEE-HAW!
BLAM!
BLAM!
THAT'S A TEXAS-SIZED BOTTOM LINE!
THIS MEETING ISN'T OVER!
I HAVE SOMETHING YOU NEED TO LOOK AT!
I DID SOME TITLE SEARCHES ON THE SPRING-FIELD PROPERTY WHERE THE NEW MALL IS.
YOU DO NOT HAVE A CLEAR TITLE TO THAT LAND! YOU MUST TEAR DOWN THE MALL!
THAT'S WHY YOU BROUGHT ME HERE?
I NEEDED A RIDE!
NOW LISTEN, YOUNG LADY--
MMM... EXECUTIVE BOARDROOM PASTRIES.
HEH-HEH. AM I TO BELIEVE YOU ACTUALLY FOUND SOME-THING OUR LAWYERS DIDN'T, LITTLE GIRL?
MY PROOF GOES BACK TO THE VERY BEGINNINGS OF SPRINGFIELD.

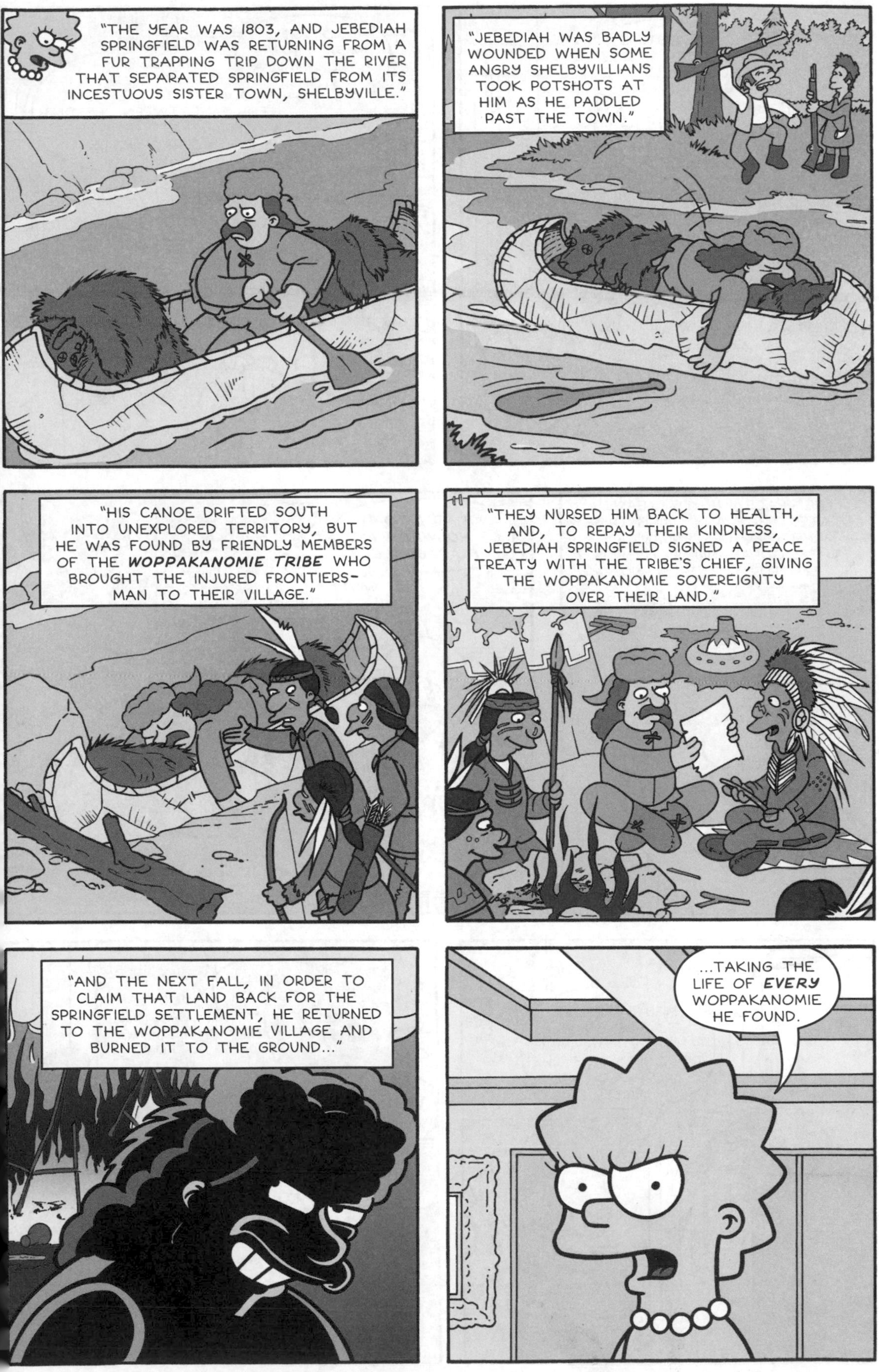
"THE YEAR WAS 1803, AND JEBEDIAH SPRINGFIELD WAS RETURNING FROM A FUR TRAPPING TRIP DOWN THE RIVER THAT SEPARATED SPRINGFIELD FROM ITS INCESTUOUS SISTER TOWN, SHELBYVILLE."
"JEBEDIAH WAS BADLY WOUNDED WHEN SOME ANGRY SHELBYVILLIANS TOOK POTSHOTS AT HIM AS HE PADDLED PAST THE TOWN."
"HIS CANOE DRIFTED SOUTH INTO UNEXPLORED TERRITORY, BUT HE WAS FOUND BY FRIENDLY MEMBERS OF THE **WOPPAKANOMIE TRIBE** WHO BROUGHT THE INJURED FRONTIERSMAN TO THEIR VILLAGE."
"THEY NURSED HIM BACK TO HEALTH, AND, TO REPAY THEIR KINDNESS, JEBEDIAH SPRINGFIELD SIGNED A PEACE TREATY WITH THE TRIBE'S CHIEF, GIVING THE WOPPAKANOMIE SOVEREIGNTY OVER THEIR LAND."
"AND THE NEXT FALL, IN ORDER TO CLAIM THAT LAND BACK FOR THE SPRINGFIELD SETTLEMENT, HE RETURNED TO THE WOPPAKANOMIE VILLAGE AND BURNED IT TO THE GROUND..."
...TAKING THE LIFE OF ***EVERY*** WOPPAKANOMIE HE FOUND.

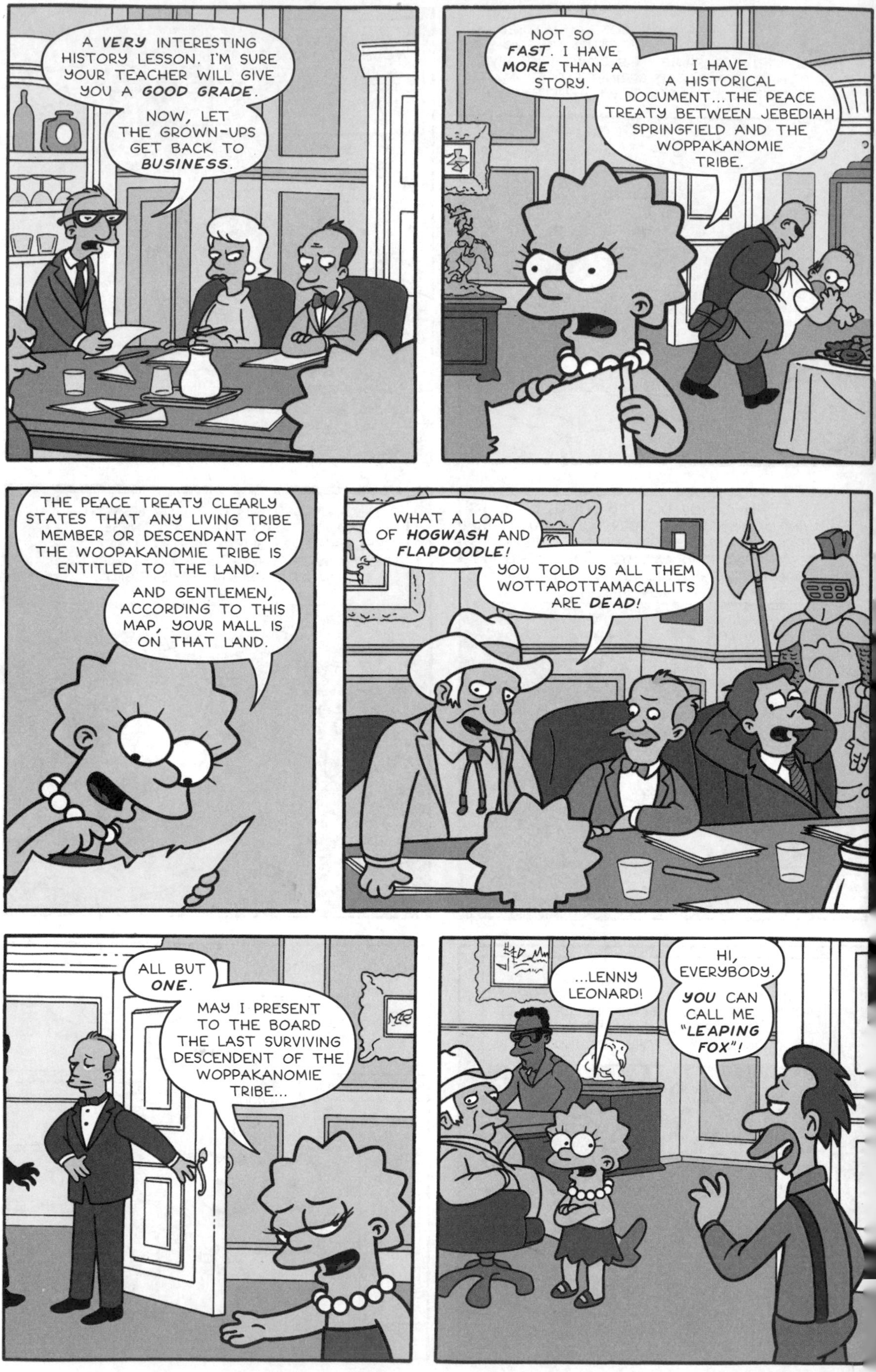
A VERY INTERESTING HISTORY LESSON. I'M SURE YOUR TEACHER WILL GIVE YOU A GOOD GRADE.
NOW, LET THE GROWN-UPS GET BACK TO BUSINESS.
NOT SO FAST. I HAVE MORE THAN A STORY.
I HAVE A HISTORICAL DOCUMENT...THE PEACE TREATY BETWEEN JEBEDIAH SPRINGFIELD AND THE WOPPAKANOMIE TRIBE.
THE PEACE TREATY CLEARLY STATES THAT ANY LIVING TRIBE MEMBER OR DESCENDANT OF THE WOOPAKANOMIE TRIBE IS ENTITLED TO THE LAND.
AND GENTLEMEN, ACCORDING TO THIS MAP, YOUR MALL IS ON THAT LAND.
WHAT A LOAD OF HOGWASH AND FLAPDOODLE!
YOU TOLD US ALL THEM WOTTAPOTTAMACALLITS ARE DEAD!
ALL BUT ONE.
MAY I PRESENT TO THE BOARD THE LAST SURVIVING DESCENDENT OF THE WOPPAKANOMIE TRIBE...
...LENNY LEONARD!
HI, EVERYBODY. YOU CAN CALL ME "LEAPING FOX"!

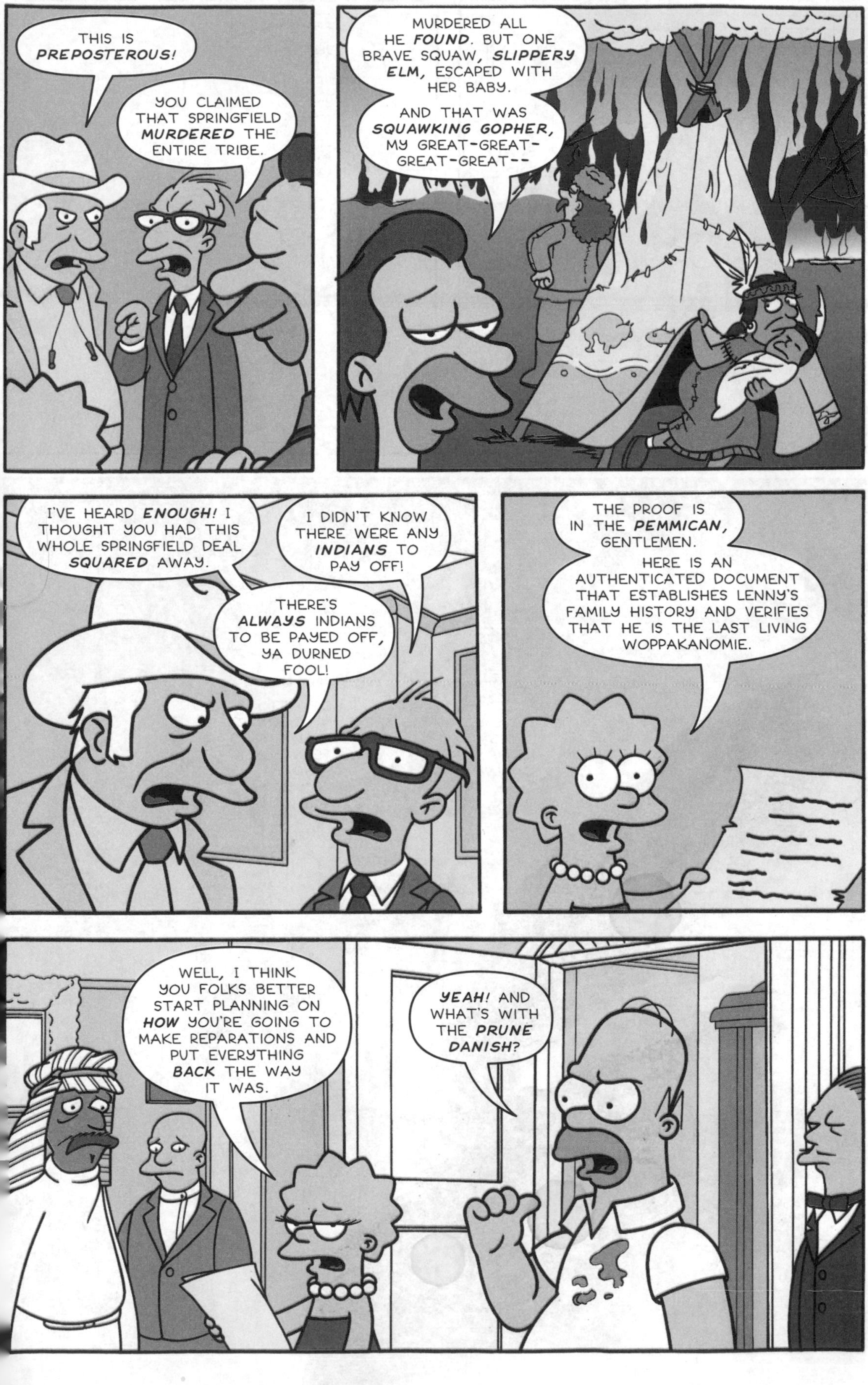
THIS IS PREPOSTEROUS!
YOU CLAIMED THAT SPRINGFIELD MURDERED THE ENTIRE TRIBE.
MURDERED ALL HE FOUND. BUT ONE BRAVE SQUAW, SLIPPERY ELM, ESCAPED WITH HER BABY.
AND THAT WAS SQUAWKING GOPHER, MY GREAT-GREAT-GREAT-GREAT--
I'VE HEARD ENOUGH! I THOUGHT YOU HAD THIS WHOLE SPRINGFIELD DEAL SQUARED AWAY.
I DIDN'T KNOW THERE WERE ANY INDIANS TO PAY OFF!
THERE'S ALWAYS INDIANS TO BE PAYED OFF, YA DURNED FOOL!
THE PROOF IS IN THE PEMMICAN, GENTLEMEN.
HERE IS AN AUTHENTICATED DOCUMENT THAT ESTABLISHES LENNY'S FAMILY HISTORY AND VERIFIES THAT HE IS THE LAST LIVING WOPPAKANOMIE.
WELL, I THINK YOU FOLKS BETTER START PLANNING ON HOW YOU'RE GOING TO MAKE REPARATIONS AND PUT EVERYTHING BACK THE WAY IT WAS.
YEAH! AND WHAT'S WITH THE PRUNE DANISH?

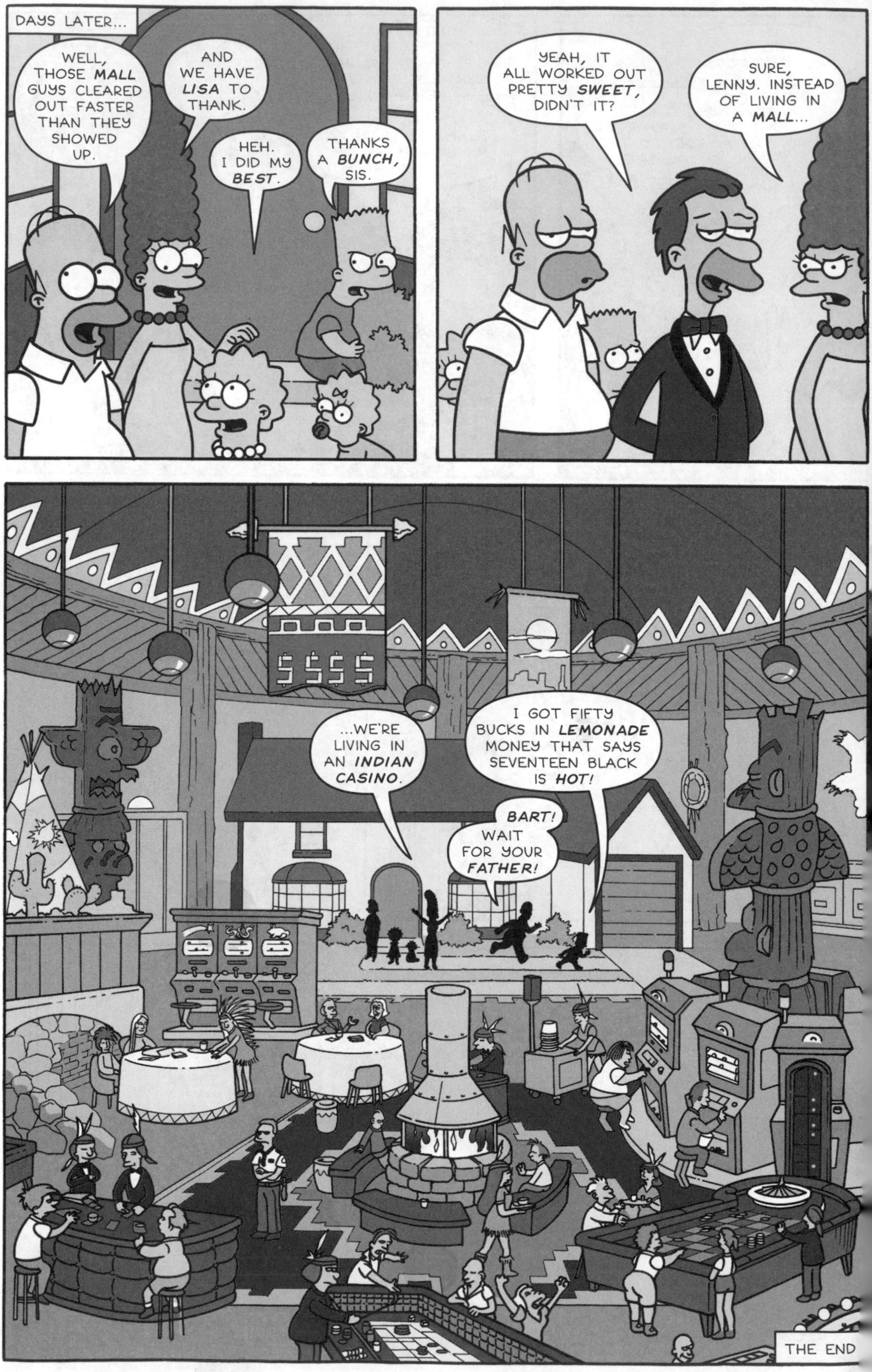
DAYS LATER...
WELL, THOSE MALL GUYS CLEARED OUT FASTER THAN THEY SHOWED UP.
AND WE HAVE LISA TO THANK.
HEH. I DID MY BEST.
THANKS A BUNCH, SIS.
YEAH, IT ALL WORKED OUT PRETTY SWEET, DIDN'T IT?
SURE, LENNY. INSTEAD OF LIVING IN A MALL...
...WE'RE LIVING IN AN INDIAN CASINO.
I GOT FIFTY BUCKS IN LEMONADE MONEY THAT SAYS SEVENTEEN BLACK IS HOT!
BART! WAIT FOR YOUR FATHER!
$ $ $ $
THE END

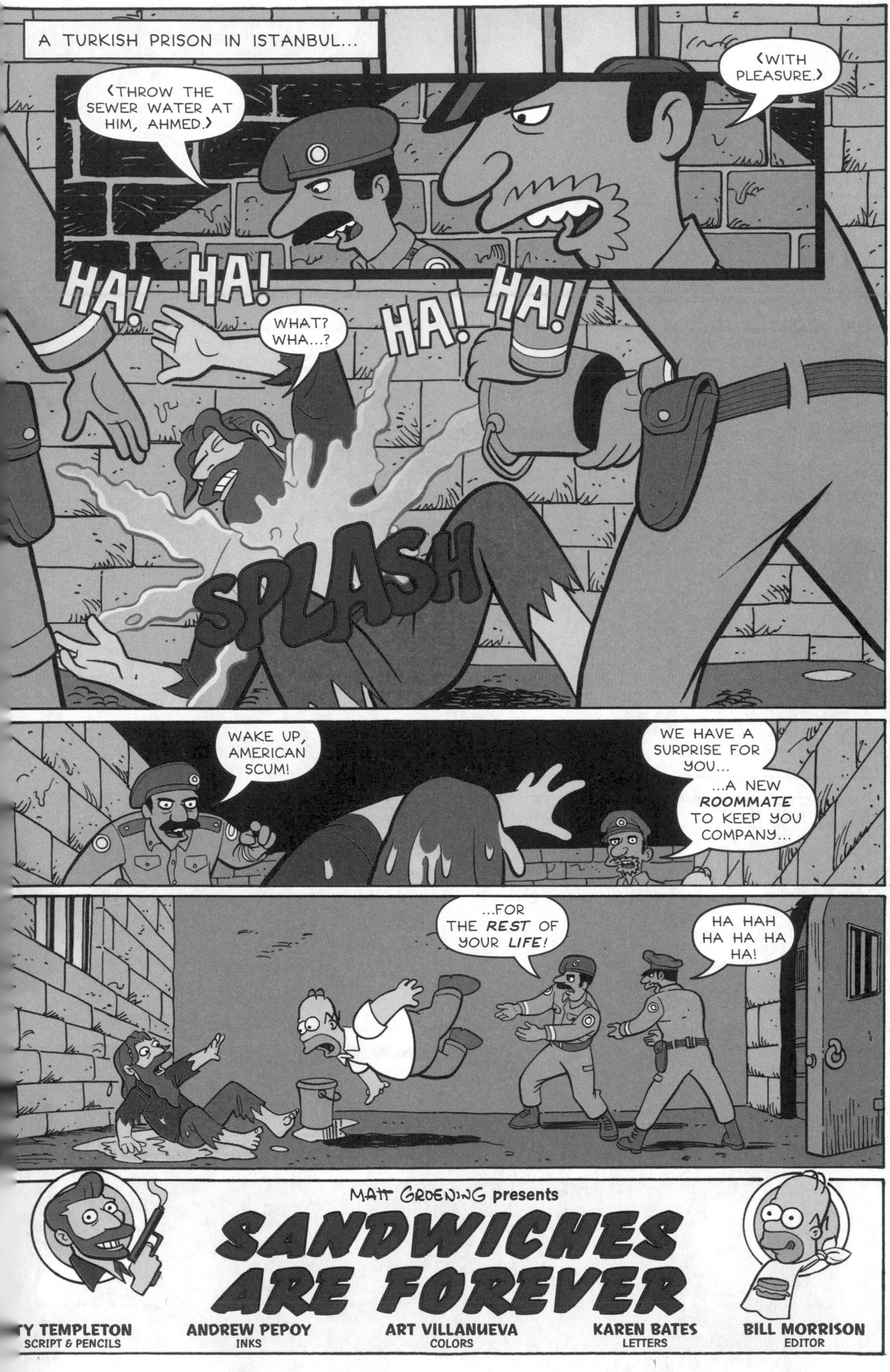

A TURKISH PRISON IN ISTANBUL...
‹THROW THE SEWER WATER AT HIM, AHMED.›
‹WITH PLEASURE.›
HA! HA!
WHAT? WHA...?
HA! HA!
SPLASH
WAKE UP, AMERICAN SCUM!
WE HAVE A SURPRISE FOR YOU...
...A NEW ROOMMATE TO KEEP YOU COMPANY...
...FOR THE REST OF YOUR LIFE!
HA HAH HA HA HA HA!
MATT GROENING presents
SANDWICHES ARE FOREVER
TY TEMPLETON
SCRIPT & PENCILS
ANDREW PEPOY
INKS
ART VILLANUEVA
COLORS
KAREN BATES
LETTERS
BILL MORRISON
EDITOR

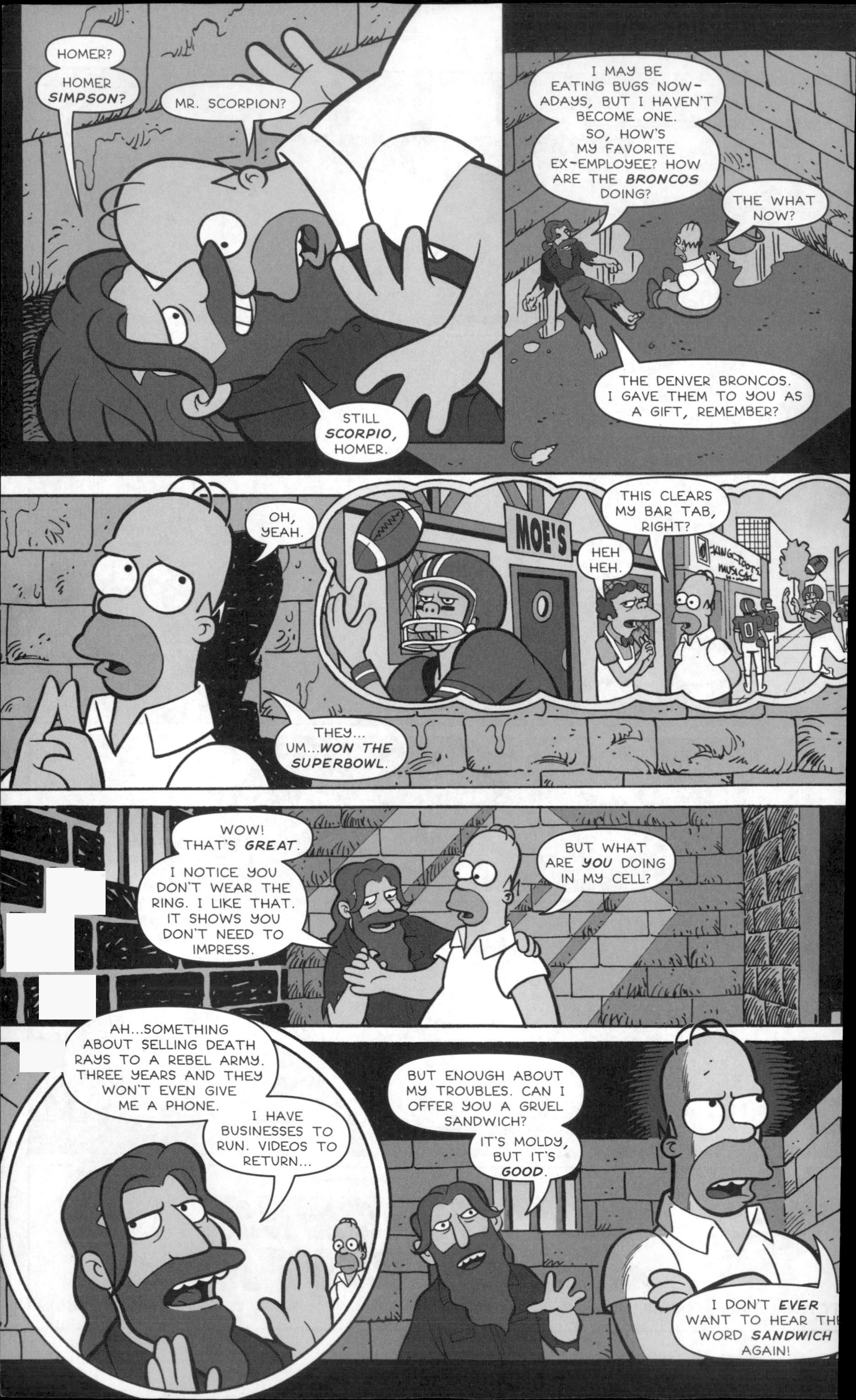
HOMER? HOMER SIMPSON?
MR. SCORPION?
STILL SCORPIO, HOMER.
I MAY BE EATING BUGS NOW-ADAYS, BUT I HAVEN'T BECOME ONE.
SO, HOW'S MY FAVORITE EX-EMPLOYEE? HOW ARE THE BRONCOS DOING?
THE WHAT NOW?
THE DENVER BRONCOS. I GAVE THEM TO YOU AS A GIFT, REMEMBER?
OH, YEAH.
MOE'S
HEH HEH.
THIS CLEARS MY BAR TAB, RIGHT?
THEY... UM...WON THE SUPERBOWL.
WOW! THAT'S GREAT.
I NOTICE YOU DON'T WEAR THE RING. I LIKE THAT. IT SHOWS YOU DON'T NEED TO IMPRESS.
BUT WHAT ARE YOU DOING IN MY CELL?
AH...SOMETHING ABOUT SELLING DEATH RAYS TO A REBEL ARMY. THREE YEARS AND THEY WON'T EVEN GIVE ME A PHONE.
I HAVE BUSINESSES TO RUN. VIDEOS TO RETURN...
BUT ENOUGH ABOUT MY TROUBLES. CAN I OFFER YOU A GRUEL SANDWICH?
IT'S MOLDY, BUT IT'S GOOD.
I DON'T EVER WANT TO HEAR THE WORD SANDWICH AGAIN!

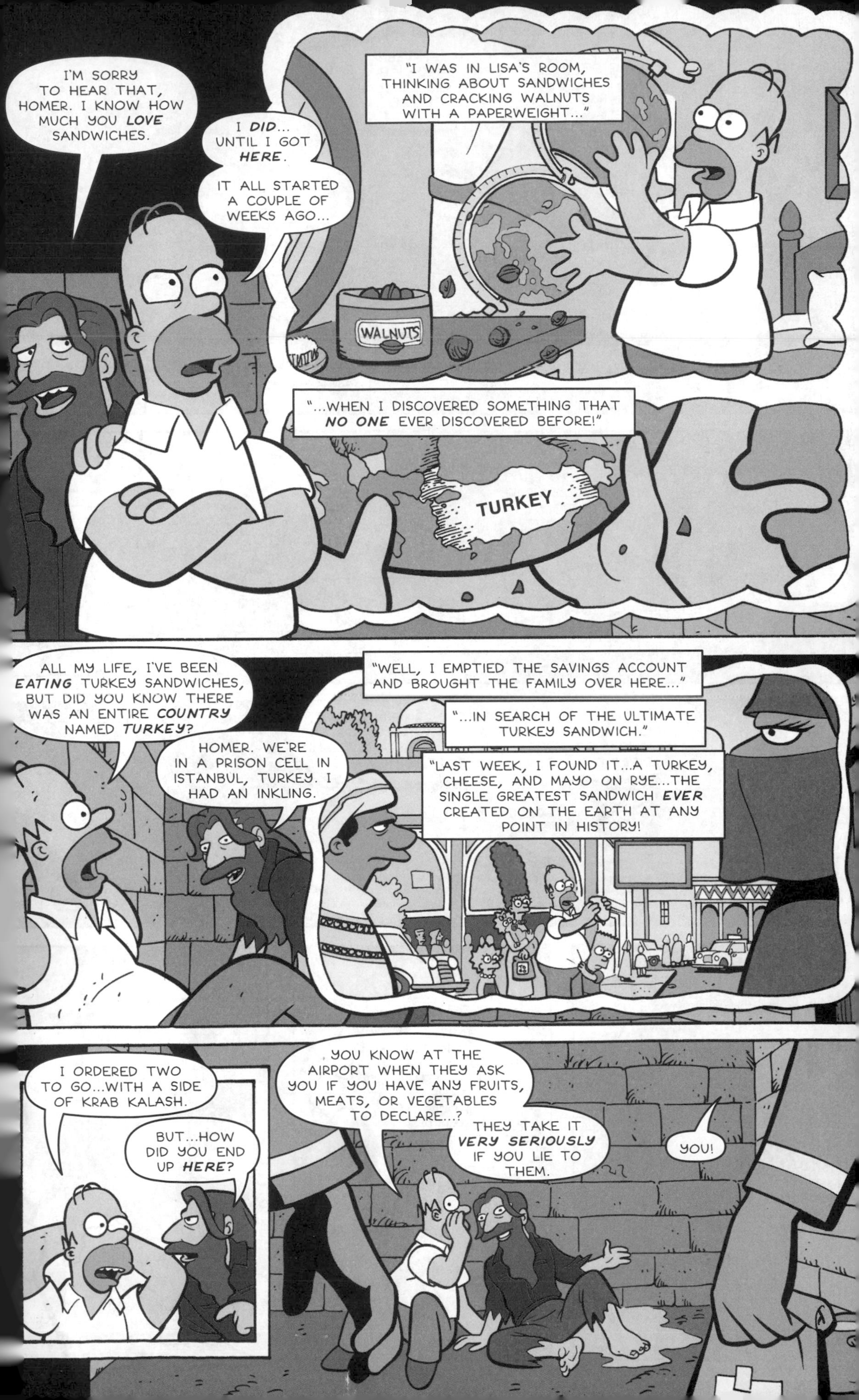
I'M SORRY TO HEAR THAT, HOMER. I KNOW HOW MUCH YOU LOVE SANDWICHES.
I DID... UNTIL I GOT HERE.
IT ALL STARTED A COUPLE OF WEEKS AGO...
"I WAS IN LISA'S ROOM, THINKING ABOUT SANDWICHES AND CRACKING WALNUTS WITH A PAPERWEIGHT..."
WALNUTS
"...WHEN I DISCOVERED SOMETHING THAT NO ONE EVER DISCOVERED BEFORE!"
TURKEY
ALL MY LIFE, I'VE BEEN EATING TURKEY SANDWICHES, BUT DID YOU KNOW THERE WAS AN ENTIRE COUNTRY NAMED TURKEY?
HOMER. WE'RE IN A PRISON CELL IN ISTANBUL, TURKEY. I HAD AN INKLING.
"WELL, I EMPTIED THE SAVINGS ACCOUNT AND BROUGHT THE FAMILY OVER HERE..."
"...IN SEARCH OF THE ULTIMATE TURKEY SANDWICH."
"LAST WEEK, I FOUND IT...A TURKEY, CHEESE, AND MAYO ON RYE...THE SINGLE GREATEST SANDWICH EVER CREATED ON THE EARTH AT ANY POINT IN HISTORY!
I ORDERED TWO TO GO...WITH A SIDE OF KRAB KALASH.
BUT...HOW DID YOU END UP HERE?
...YOU KNOW AT THE AIRPORT WHEN THEY ASK YOU IF YOU HAVE ANY FRUITS, MEATS, OR VEGETABLES TO DECLARE...?
THEY TAKE IT VERY SERIOUSLY IF YOU LIE TO THEM.
YOU!

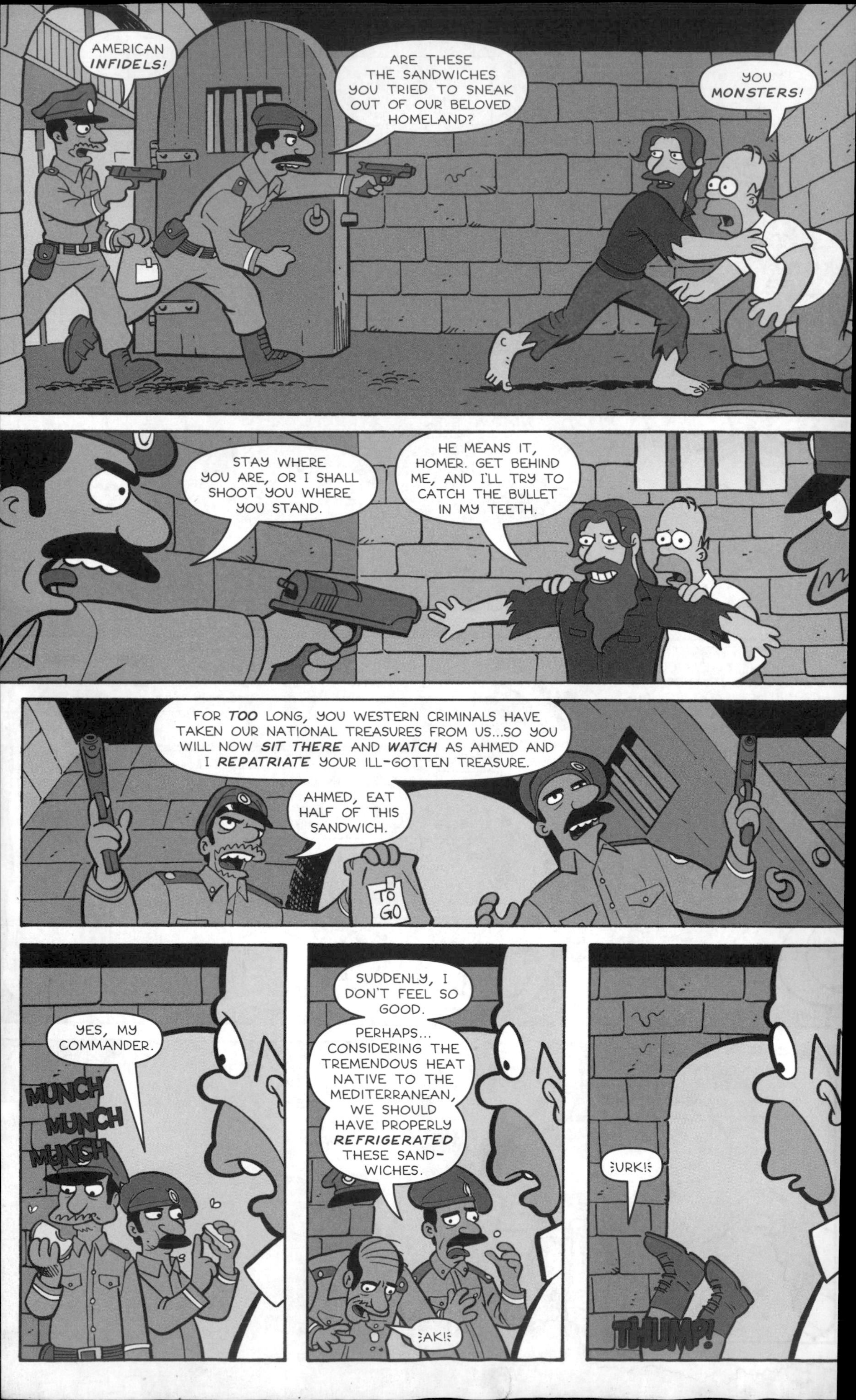
AMERICAN INFIDELS!
ARE THESE THE SANDWICHES YOU TRIED TO SNEAK OUT OF OUR BELOVED HOMELAND?
YOU MONSTERS!
STAY WHERE YOU ARE, OR I SHALL SHOOT YOU WHERE YOU STAND.
HE MEANS IT, HOMER. GET BEHIND ME, AND I'LL TRY TO CATCH THE BULLET IN MY TEETH.
FOR TOO LONG, YOU WESTERN CRIMINALS HAVE TAKEN OUR NATIONAL TREASURES FROM US...SO YOU WILL NOW SIT THERE AND WATCH AS AHMED AND I REPATRIATE YOUR ILL-GOTTEN TREASURE.
AHMED, EAT HALF OF THIS SANDWICH.
TO GO
YES, MY COMMANDER.
MUNCH MUNCH MUNCH
SUDDENLY, I DON'T FEEL SO GOOD.
PERHAPS... CONSIDERING THE TREMENDOUS HEAT NATIVE TO THE MEDITERRANEAN, WE SHOULD HAVE PROPERLY REFRIGERATED THESE SAND-WICHES.
AK!
URK!
THUMP!

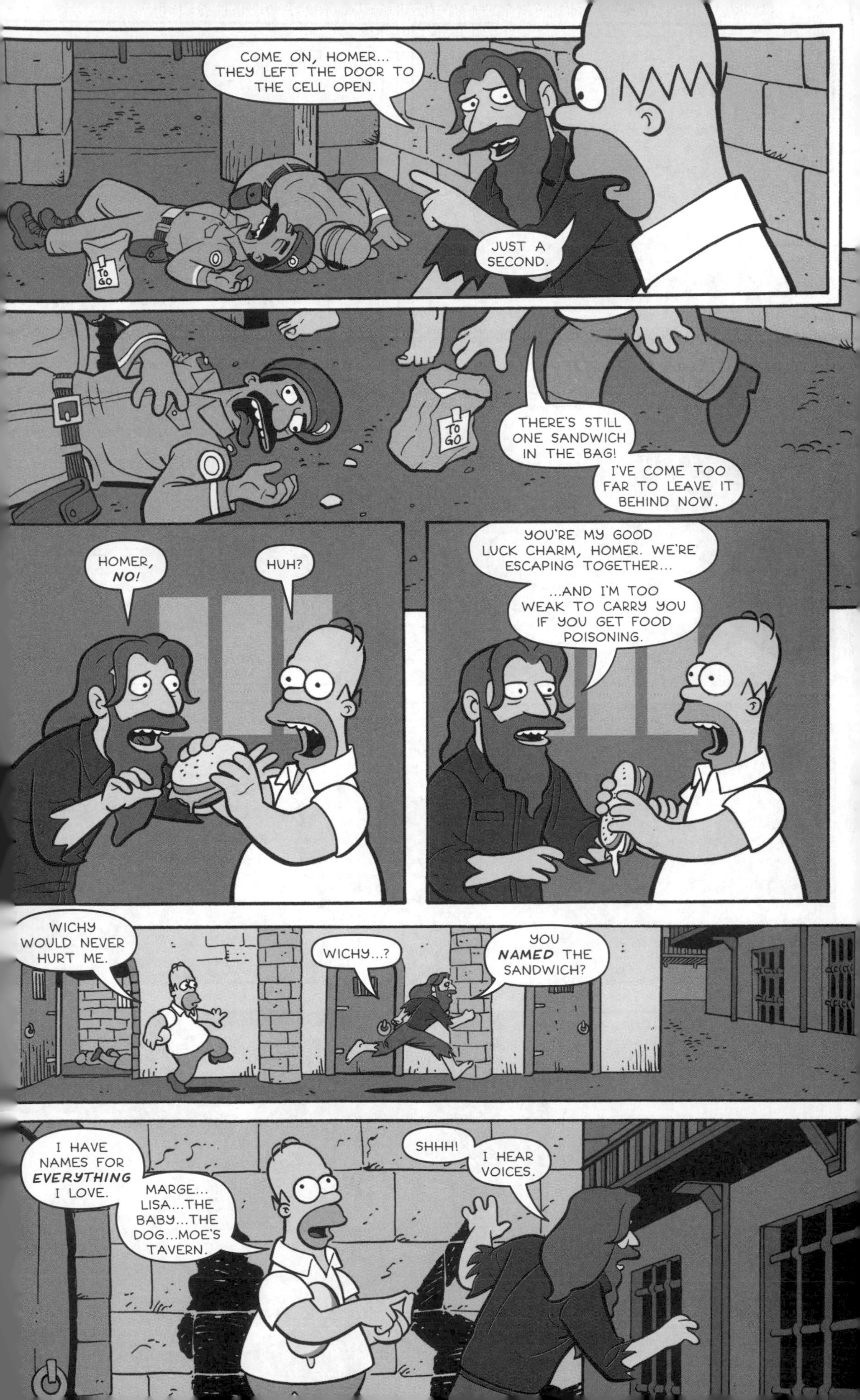
COME ON, HOMER... THEY LEFT THE DOOR TO THE CELL OPEN.
JUST A SECOND.
TO GO
TO GO
THERE'S STILL ONE SANDWICH IN THE BAG!
I'VE COME TOO FAR TO LEAVE IT BEHIND NOW.
HOMER, NO!
HUH?
YOU'RE MY GOOD LUCK CHARM, HOMER. WE'RE ESCAPING TOGETHER...
...AND I'M TOO WEAK TO CARRY YOU IF YOU GET FOOD POISONING.
WICHY WOULD NEVER HURT ME.
WICHY...?
YOU NAMED THE SANDWICH?
I HAVE NAMES FOR EVERYTHING I LOVE.
MARGE... LISA...THE BABY...THE DOG...MOE'S TAVERN.
SHHH!
I HEAR VOICES.

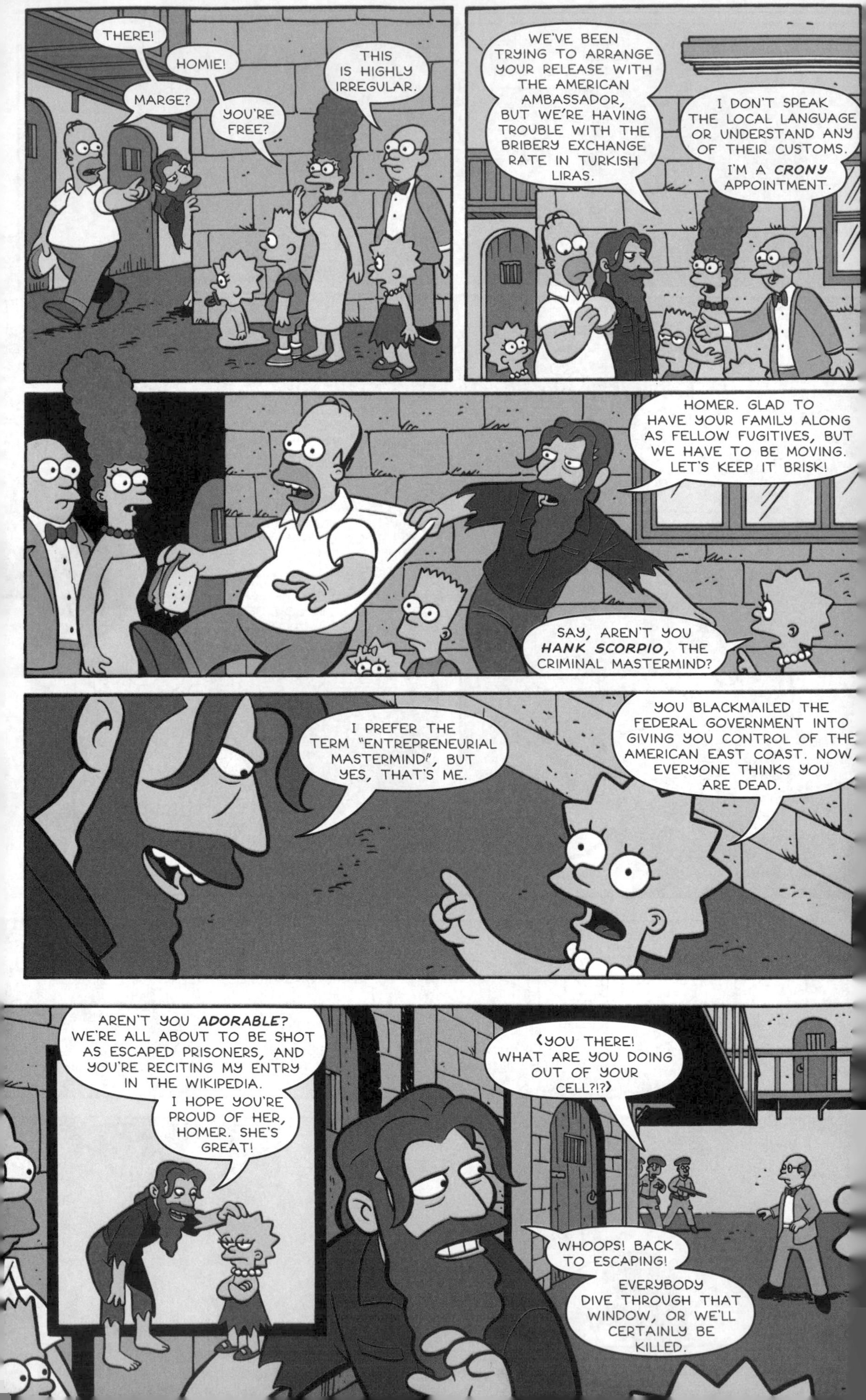

THERE!
MARGE?
HOMIE!
YOU'RE FREE?
THIS IS HIGHLY IRREGULAR.
WE'VE BEEN TRYING TO ARRANGE YOUR RELEASE WITH THE AMERICAN AMBASSADOR, BUT WE'RE HAVING TROUBLE WITH THE BRIBERY EXCHANGE RATE IN TURKISH LIRAS.
I DON'T SPEAK THE LOCAL LANGUAGE OR UNDERSTAND ANY OF THEIR CUSTOMS.
I'M A **CRONY** APPOINTMENT.
HOMER. GLAD TO HAVE YOUR FAMILY ALONG AS FELLOW FUGITIVES, BUT WE HAVE TO BE MOVING. LET'S KEEP IT BRISK!
SAY, AREN'T YOU **HANK SCORPIO,** THE CRIMINAL MASTERMIND?
I PREFER THE TERM "ENTREPRENEURIAL MASTERMIND", BUT YES, THAT'S ME.
YOU BLACKMAILED THE FEDERAL GOVERNMENT INTO GIVING YOU CONTROL OF THE AMERICAN EAST COAST. NOW, EVERYONE THINKS YOU ARE DEAD.
AREN'T YOU **ADORABLE**? WE'RE ALL ABOUT TO BE SHOT AS ESCAPED PRISONERS, AND YOU'RE RECITING MY ENTRY IN THE WIKIPEDIA.
I HOPE YOU'RE PROUD OF HER, HOMER. SHE'S GREAT!
‹YOU THERE! WHAT ARE YOU DOING OUT OF YOUR CELL?!?›
WHOOPS! BACK TO ESCAPING!
EVERYBODY DIVE THROUGH THAT WINDOW, OR WE'LL CERTAINLY BE KILLED.

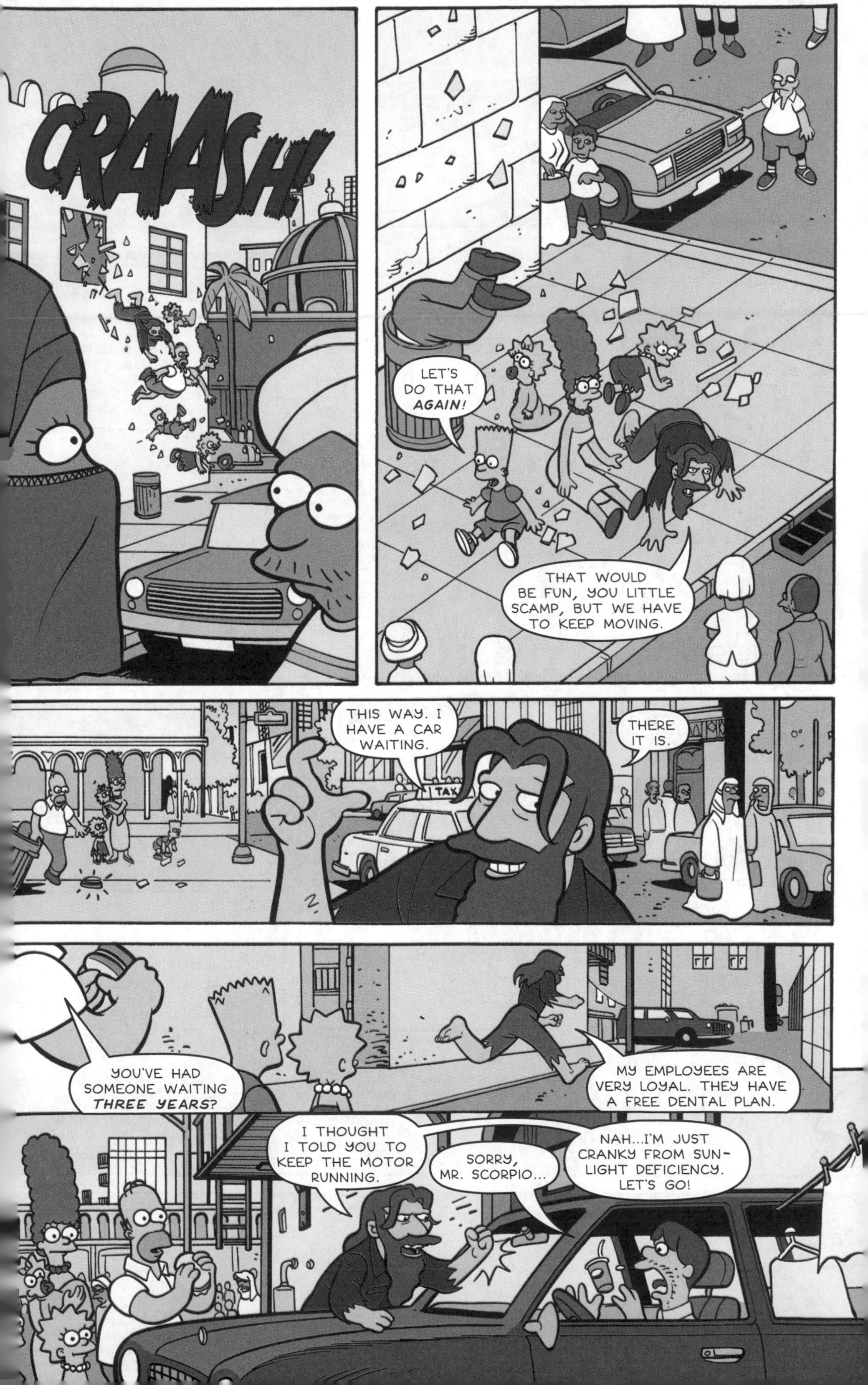

CRAASH!
LET'S DO THAT AGAIN!
THAT WOULD BE FUN, YOU LITTLE SCAMP, BUT WE HAVE TO KEEP MOVING.
THIS WAY. I HAVE A CAR WAITING.
TAXI
THERE IT IS.
YOU'VE HAD SOMEONE WAITING THREE YEARS?
MY EMPLOYEES ARE VERY LOYAL. THEY HAVE A FREE DENTAL PLAN.
I THOUGHT I TOLD YOU TO KEEP THE MOTOR RUNNING.
SORRY, MR. SCORPIO...
NAH...I'M JUST CRANKY FROM SUN-LIGHT DEFICIENCY. LET'S GO!

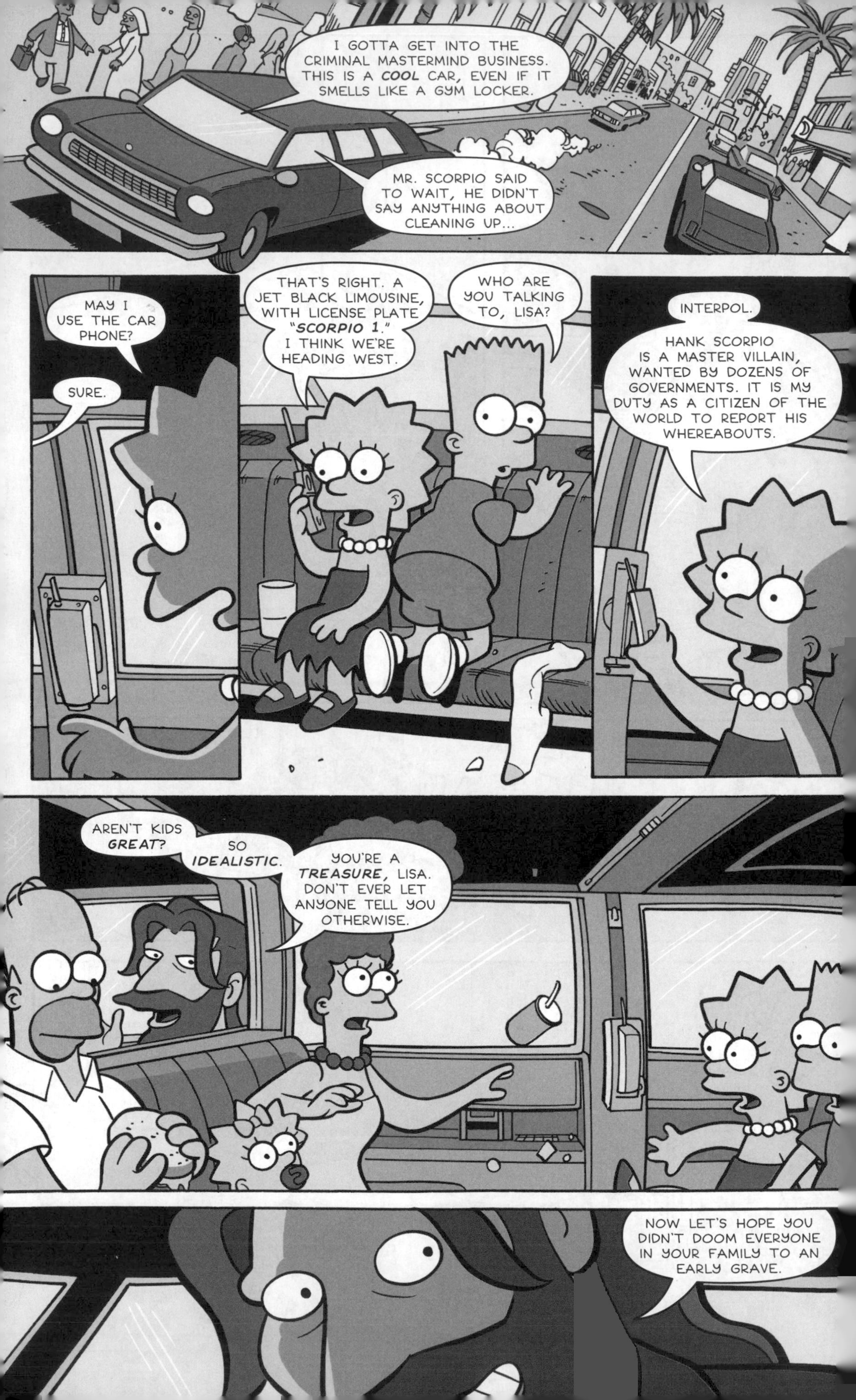
I GOTTA GET INTO THE CRIMINAL MASTERMIND BUSINESS. THIS IS A **COOL** CAR, EVEN IF IT SMELLS LIKE A GYM LOCKER.
MR. SCORPIO SAID TO WAIT, HE DIDN'T SAY ANYTHING ABOUT CLEANING UP...
MAY I USE THE CAR PHONE?
SURE.
THAT'S RIGHT. A JET BLACK LIMOUSINE, WITH LICENSE PLATE "**SCORPIO 1**." I THINK WE'RE HEADING WEST.
WHO ARE YOU TALKING TO, LISA?
INTERPOL.
HANK SCORPIO IS A MASTER VILLAIN, WANTED BY DOZENS OF GOVERNMENTS. IT IS MY DUTY AS A CITIZEN OF THE WORLD TO REPORT HIS WHEREABOUTS.
AREN'T KIDS **GREAT**?
SO **IDEALISTIC**.
YOU'RE A **TREASURE**, LISA. DON'T EVER LET ANYONE TELL YOU OTHERWISE.
NOW LET'S HOPE YOU DIDN'T DOOM EVERYONE IN YOUR FAMILY TO AN EARLY GRAVE.

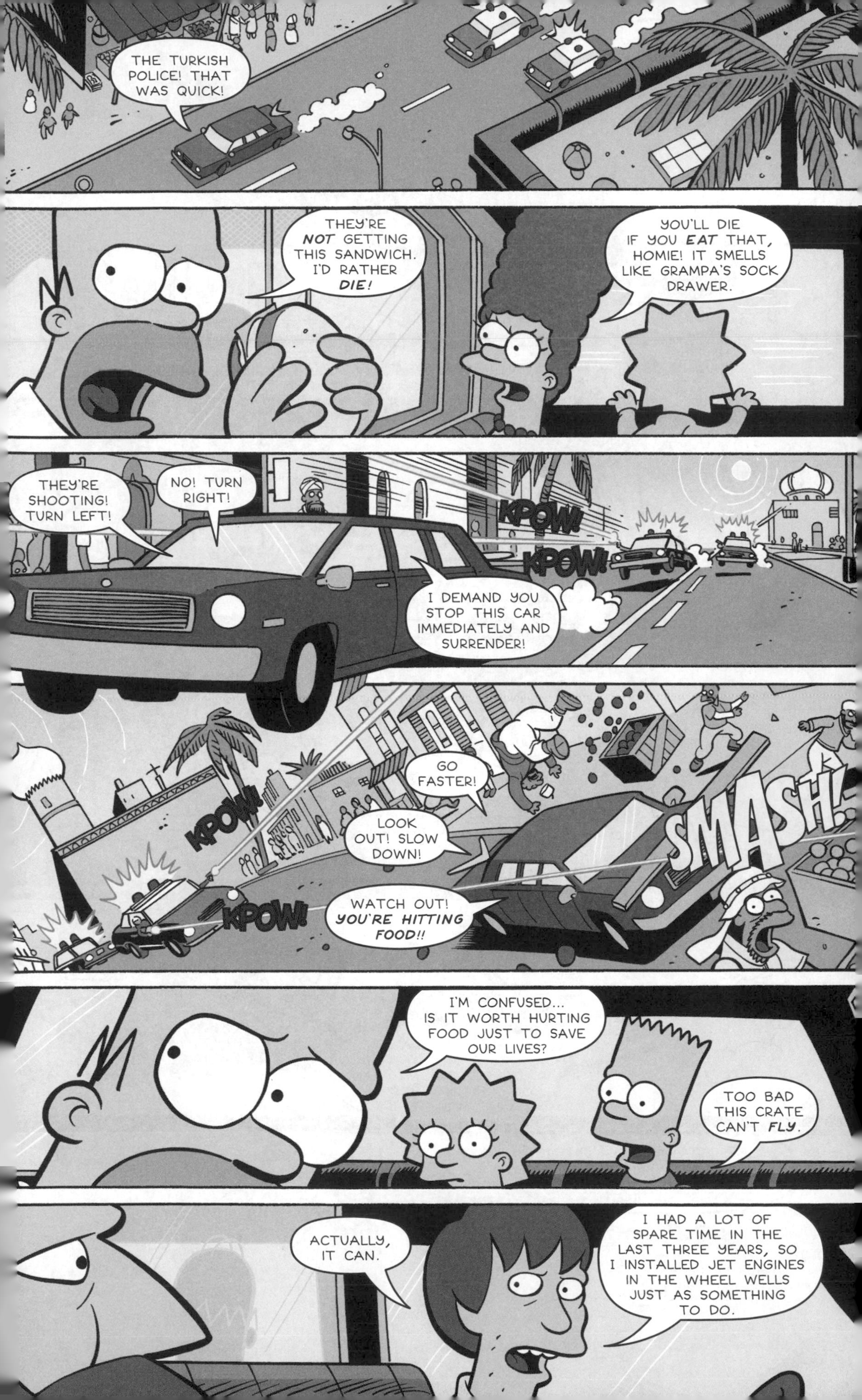
THE TURKISH POLICE! THAT WAS QUICK!
THEY'RE *NOT* GETTING THIS SANDWICH. I'D RATHER *DIE!*
YOU'LL DIE IF YOU *EAT* THAT, HOMIE! IT SMELLS LIKE GRAMPA'S SOCK DRAWER.
THEY'RE SHOOTING! TURN LEFT!
NO! TURN RIGHT!
KPOW!
KPOW!
I DEMAND YOU STOP THIS CAR IMMEDIATELY AND SURRENDER!
GO FASTER!
LOOK OUT! SLOW DOWN!
KPOW!
SMASH!
KPOW!
WATCH OUT! *YOU'RE HITTING FOOD!!*
I'M CONFUSED... IS IT WORTH HURTING FOOD JUST TO SAVE OUR LIVES?
TOO BAD THIS CRATE CAN'T *FLY*.
ACTUALLY, IT CAN.
I HAD A LOT OF SPARE TIME IN THE LAST THREE YEARS, SO I INSTALLED JET ENGINES IN THE WHEEL WELLS JUST AS SOMETHING TO DO.

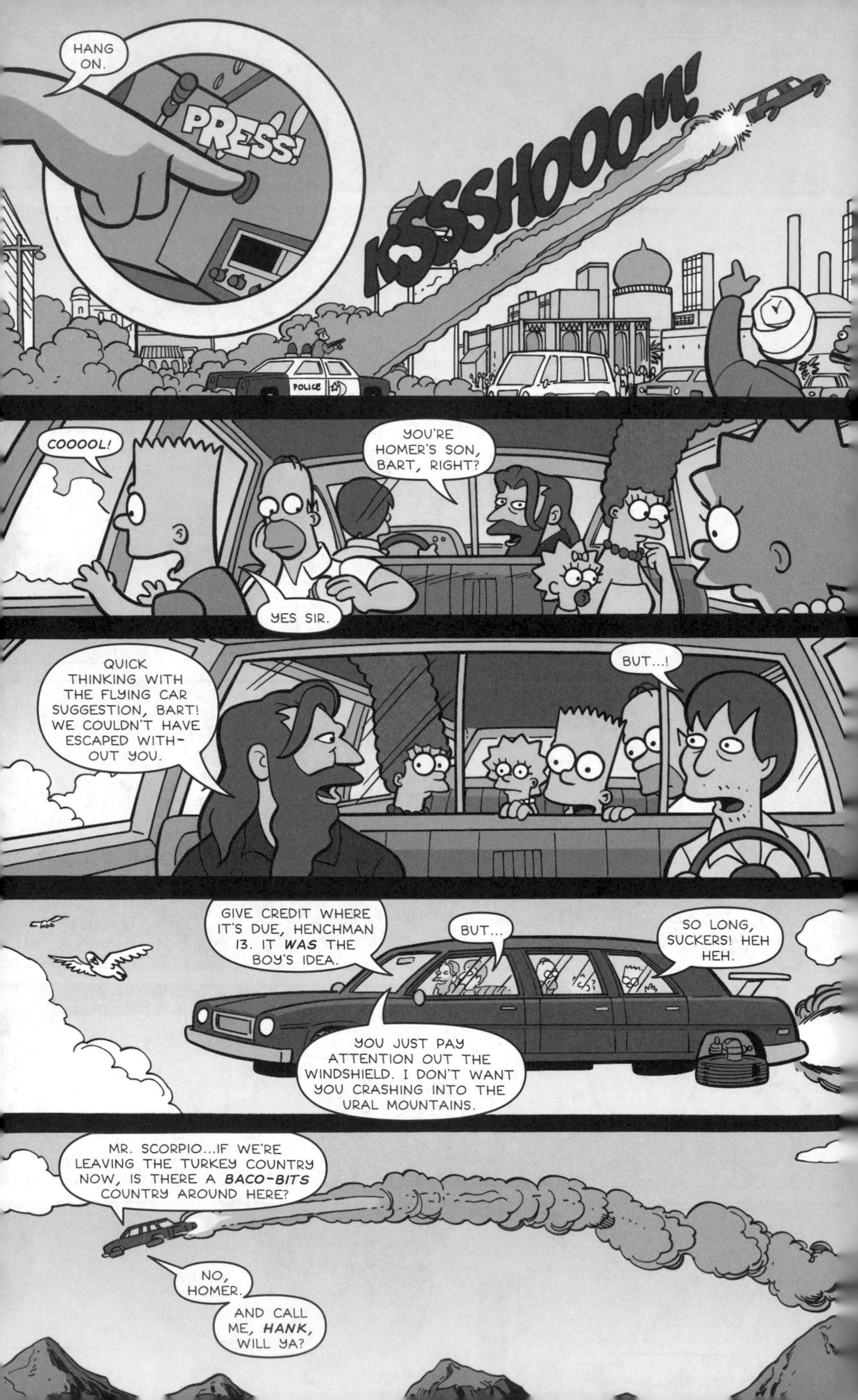

HANG ON.
PRESS!
KSSHOOOM!
POLICE
COOOOL!
YOU'RE HOMER'S SON, BART, RIGHT?
YES SIR.
QUICK THINKING WITH THE FLYING CAR SUGGESTION, BART! WE COULDN'T HAVE ESCAPED WITH-OUT YOU.
BUT...!
GIVE CREDIT WHERE IT'S DUE, HENCHMAN 13. IT *WAS* THE BOY'S IDEA.
BUT...
SO LONG, SUCKERS! HEH HEH.
YOU JUST PAY ATTENTION OUT THE WINDSHIELD. I DON'T WANT YOU CRASHING INTO THE URAL MOUNTAINS.
MR. SCORPIO...IF WE'RE LEAVING THE TURKEY COUNTRY NOW, IS THERE A *BACO-BITS* COUNTRY AROUND HERE?
NO, HOMER.
AND CALL ME, *HANK*, WILL YA?

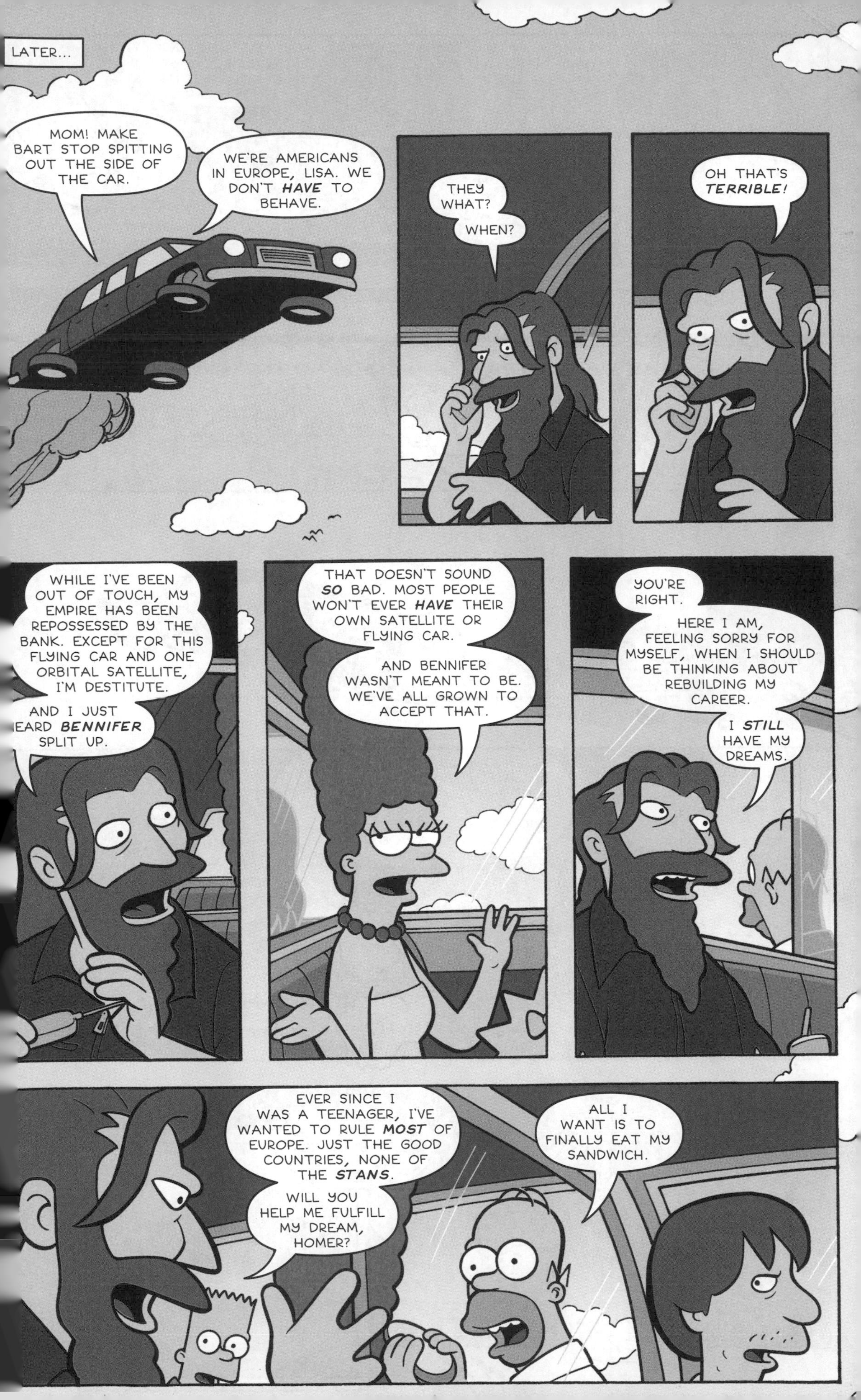
LATER...
MOM! MAKE BART STOP SPITTING OUT THE SIDE OF THE CAR.
WE'RE AMERICANS IN EUROPE, LISA. WE DON'T HAVE TO BEHAVE.
THEY WHAT?
WHEN?
OH THAT'S TERRIBLE!
WHILE I'VE BEEN OUT OF TOUCH, MY EMPIRE HAS BEEN REPOSSESSED BY THE BANK. EXCEPT FOR THIS FLYING CAR AND ONE ORBITAL SATELLITE, I'M DESTITUTE.
AND I JUST EARD BENNIFER SPLIT UP.
THAT DOESN'T SOUND SO BAD. MOST PEOPLE WON'T EVER HAVE THEIR OWN SATELLITE OR FLYING CAR.
AND BENNIFER WASN'T MEANT TO BE. WE'VE ALL GROWN TO ACCEPT THAT.
YOU'RE RIGHT.
HERE I AM, FEELING SORRY FOR MYSELF, WHEN I SHOULD BE THINKING ABOUT REBUILDING MY CAREER.
I STILL HAVE MY DREAMS.
EVER SINCE I WAS A TEENAGER, I'VE WANTED TO RULE MOST OF EUROPE. JUST THE GOOD COUNTRIES, NONE OF THE STANS.
WILL YOU HELP ME FULFILL MY DREAM, HOMER?
ALL I WANT IS TO FINALLY EAT MY SANDWICH.

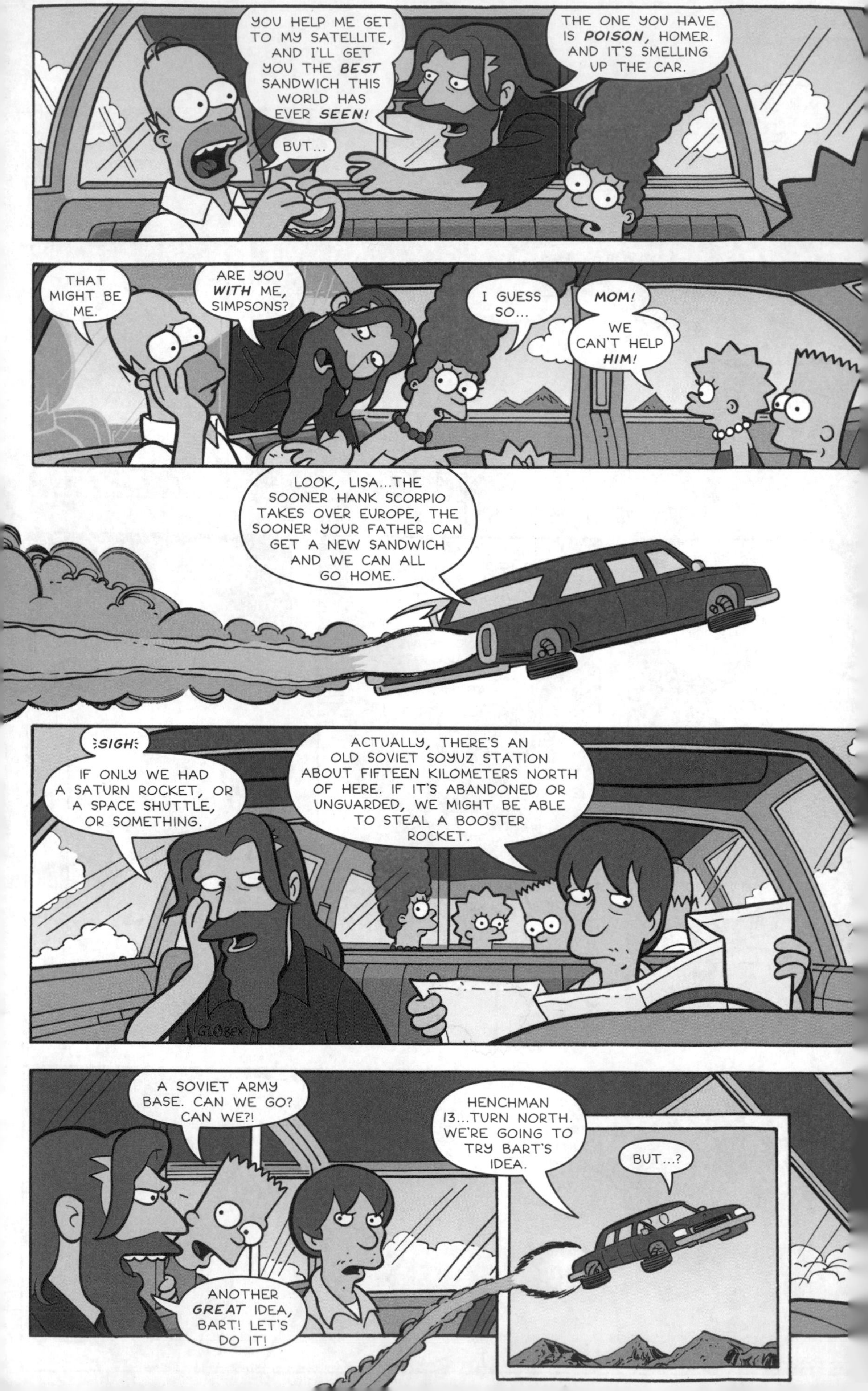
YOU HELP ME GET TO MY SATELLITE, AND I'LL GET YOU THE BEST SANDWICH THIS WORLD HAS EVER SEEN!
BUT...
THE ONE YOU HAVE IS POISON, HOMER. AND IT'S SMELLING UP THE CAR.
THAT MIGHT BE ME.
ARE YOU WITH ME, SIMPSONS?
I GUESS SO...
MOM!
WE CAN'T HELP HIM!
LOOK, LISA...THE SOONER HANK SCORPIO TAKES OVER EUROPE, THE SOONER YOUR FATHER CAN GET A NEW SANDWICH AND WE CAN ALL GO HOME.
SIGH
IF ONLY WE HAD A SATURN ROCKET, OR A SPACE SHUTTLE, OR SOMETHING.
ACTUALLY, THERE'S AN OLD SOVIET SOYUZ STATION ABOUT FIFTEEN KILOMETERS NORTH OF HERE. IF IT'S ABANDONED OR UNGUARDED, WE MIGHT BE ABLE TO STEAL A BOOSTER ROCKET.
GLOBEX
A SOVIET ARMY BASE. CAN WE GO? CAN WE?!
ANOTHER GREAT IDEA, BART! LET'S DO IT!
HENCHMAN 13...TURN NORTH. WE'RE GOING TO TRY BART'S IDEA.
BUT...?

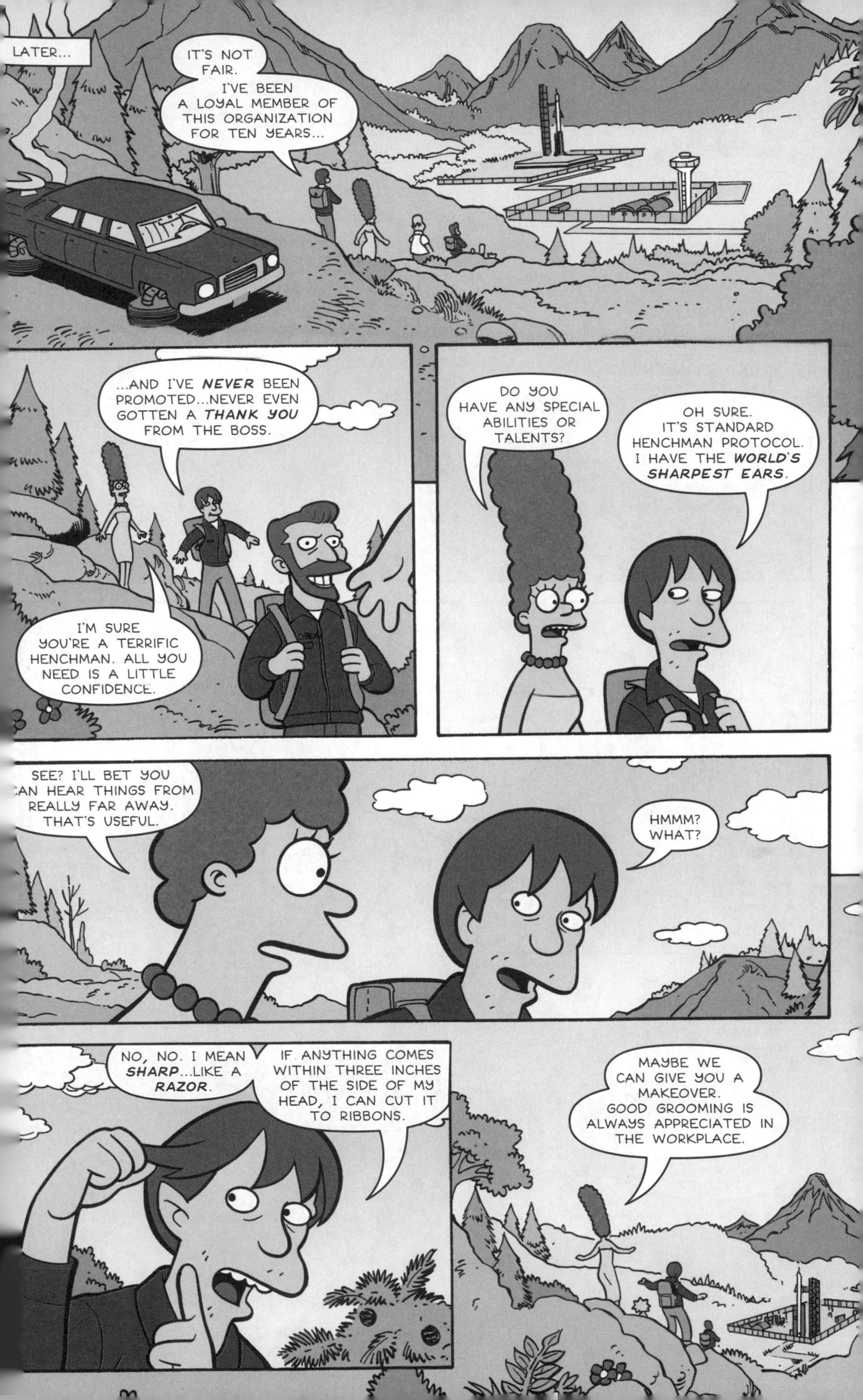
LATER...
IT'S NOT FAIR.
I'VE BEEN A LOYAL MEMBER OF THIS ORGANIZATION FOR TEN YEARS...
...AND I'VE NEVER BEEN PROMOTED...NEVER EVEN GOTTEN A THANK YOU FROM THE BOSS.
I'M SURE YOU'RE A TERRIFIC HENCHMAN. ALL YOU NEED IS A LITTLE CONFIDENCE.
DO YOU HAVE ANY SPECIAL ABILITIES OR TALENTS?
OH SURE. IT'S STANDARD HENCHMAN PROTOCOL. I HAVE THE WORLD'S SHARPEST EARS.
SEE? I'LL BET YOU CAN HEAR THINGS FROM REALLY FAR AWAY. THAT'S USEFUL.
HMMM? WHAT?
NO, NO. I MEAN SHARP...LIKE A RAZOR.
IF ANYTHING COMES WITHIN THREE INCHES OF THE SIDE OF MY HEAD, I CAN CUT IT TO RIBBONS.
MAYBE WE CAN GIVE YOU A MAKEOVER. GOOD GROOMING IS ALWAYS APPRECIATED IN THE WORKPLACE.

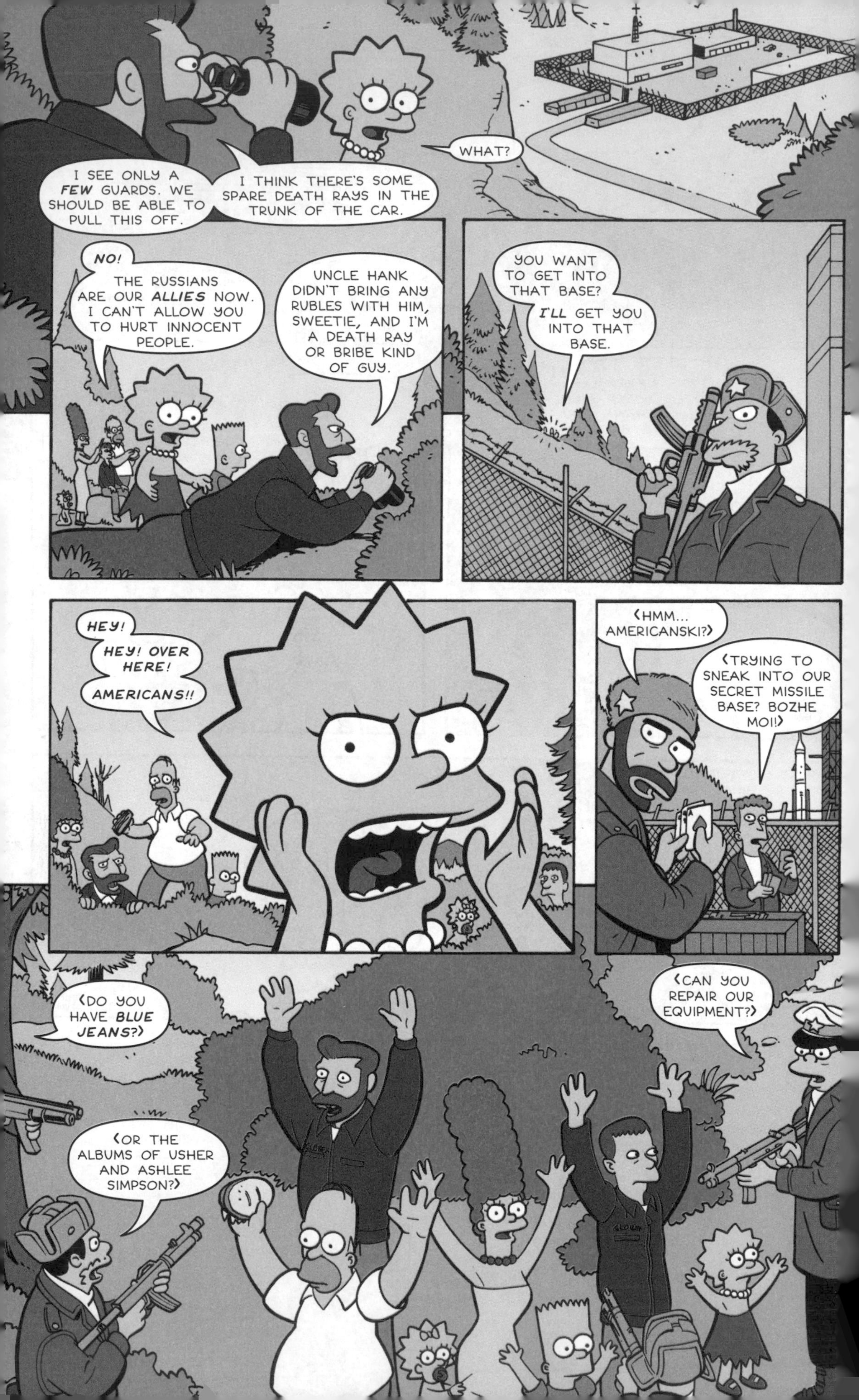
I SEE ONLY A FEW GUARDS. WE SHOULD BE ABLE TO PULL THIS OFF.
I THINK THERE'S SOME SPARE DEATH RAYS IN THE TRUNK OF THE CAR.
WHAT?
NO!
THE RUSSIANS ARE OUR ALLIES NOW. I CAN'T ALLOW YOU TO HURT INNOCENT PEOPLE.
UNCLE HANK DIDN'T BRING ANY RUBLES WITH HIM, SWEETIE, AND I'M A DEATH RAY OR BRIBE KIND OF GUY.
YOU WANT TO GET INTO THAT BASE?
I'LL GET YOU INTO THAT BASE.
HEY!
HEY! OVER HERE!
AMERICANS!!
‹HMM... AMERICANSKI?›
‹TRYING TO SNEAK INTO OUR SECRET MISSILE BASE? BOZHE MOI!›
‹DO YOU HAVE BLUE JEANS?›
‹CAN YOU REPAIR OUR EQUIPMENT?›
‹OR THE ALBUMS OF USHER AND ASHLEE SIMPSON?›

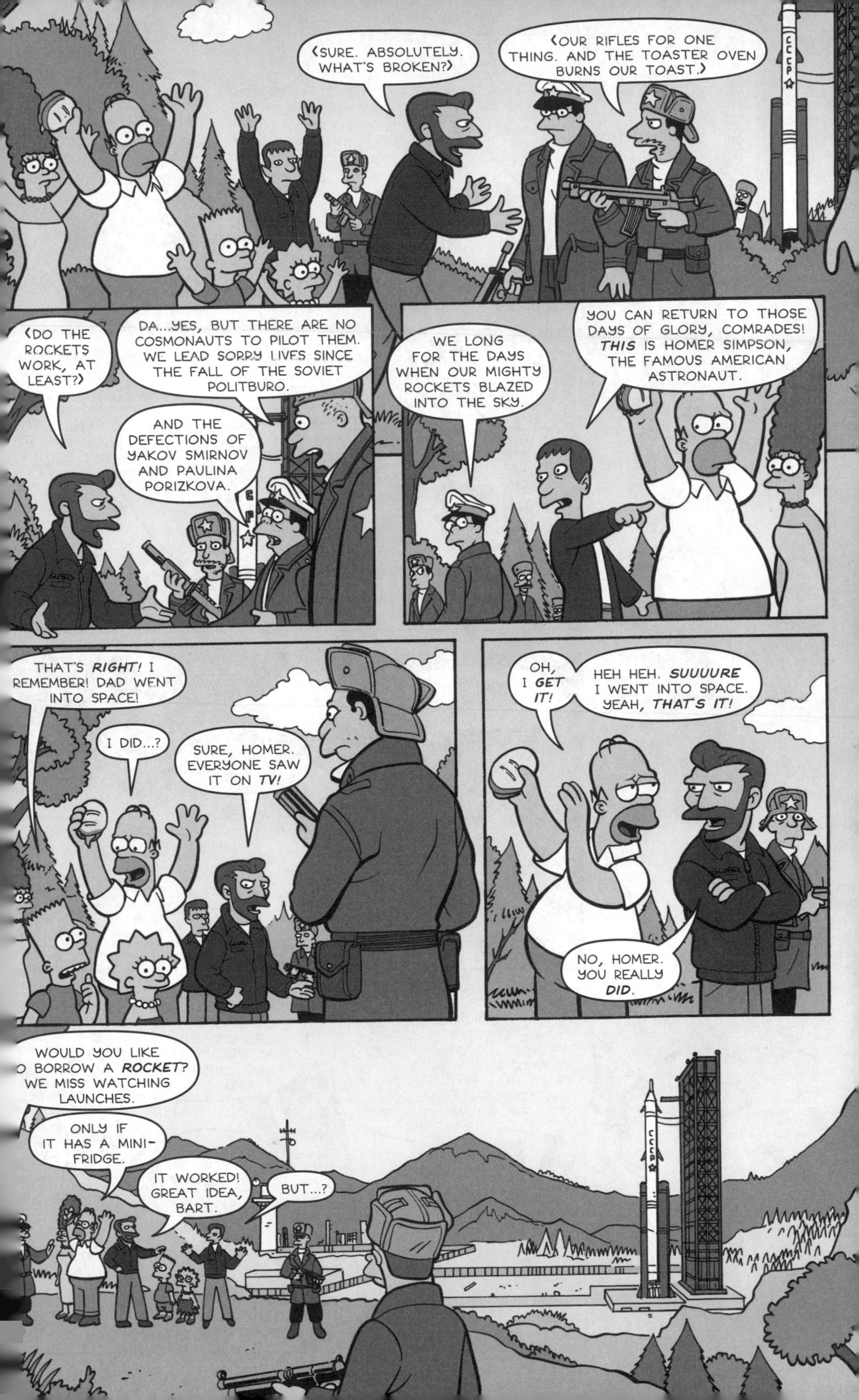
‹SURE. ABSOLUTELY. WHAT'S BROKEN?›
‹OUR RIFLES FOR ONE THING. AND THE TOASTER OVEN BURNS OUR TOAST.›
‹DO THE ROCKETS WORK, AT LEAST?›
DA...YES, BUT THERE ARE NO COSMONAUTS TO PILOT THEM. WE LEAD SORRY LIVES SINCE THE FALL OF THE SOVIET POLITBURO.
AND THE DEFECTIONS OF YAKOV SMIRNOV AND PAULINA PORIZKOVA.
WE LONG FOR THE DAYS WHEN OUR MIGHTY ROCKETS BLAZED INTO THE SKY.
YOU CAN RETURN TO THOSE DAYS OF GLORY, COMRADES! THIS IS HOMER SIMPSON, THE FAMOUS AMERICAN ASTRONAUT.
THAT'S RIGHT! I REMEMBER! DAD WENT INTO SPACE!
I DID...?
SURE, HOMER. EVERYONE SAW IT ON TV!
OH, I GET IT!
HEH HEH. SUUUURE I WENT INTO SPACE. YEAH, THAT'S IT!
NO, HOMER. YOU REALLY DID.
WOULD YOU LIKE TO BORROW A ROCKET? WE MISS WATCHING LAUNCHES.
ONLY IF IT HAS A MINI-FRIDGE.
IT WORKED! GREAT IDEA, BART.
BUT...?

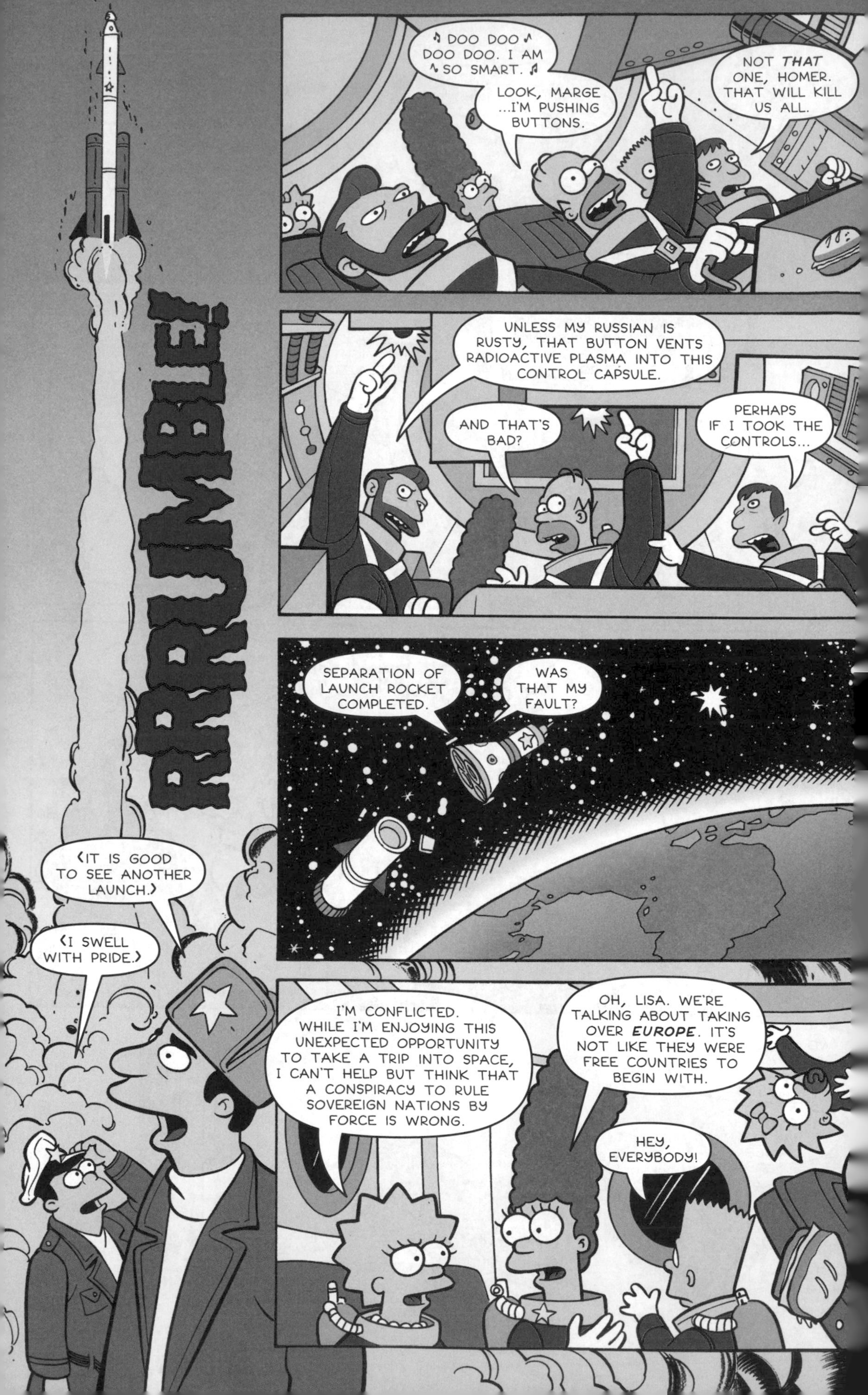

RRRUMBLE!
‹IT IS GOOD TO SEE ANOTHER LAUNCH.›
‹I SWELL WITH PRIDE.›
♪ DOO DOO ♪ DOO DOO. I AM ♪ SO SMART. ♪
LOOK, MARGE ...I'M PUSHING BUTTONS.
NOT THAT ONE, HOMER. THAT WILL KILL US ALL.
UNLESS MY RUSSIAN IS RUSTY, THAT BUTTON VENTS RADIOACTIVE PLASMA INTO THIS CONTROL CAPSULE.
AND THAT'S BAD?
PERHAPS IF I TOOK THE CONTROLS...
SEPARATION OF LAUNCH ROCKET COMPLETED.
WAS THAT MY FAULT?
I'M CONFLICTED. WHILE I'M ENJOYING THIS UNEXPECTED OPPORTUNITY TO TAKE A TRIP INTO SPACE, I CAN'T HELP BUT THINK THAT A CONSPIRACY TO RULE SOVEREIGN NATIONS BY FORCE IS WRONG.
OH, LISA. WE'RE TALKING ABOUT TAKING OVER EUROPE. IT'S NOT LIKE THEY WERE FREE COUNTRIES TO BEGIN WITH.
HEY, EVERYBODY!

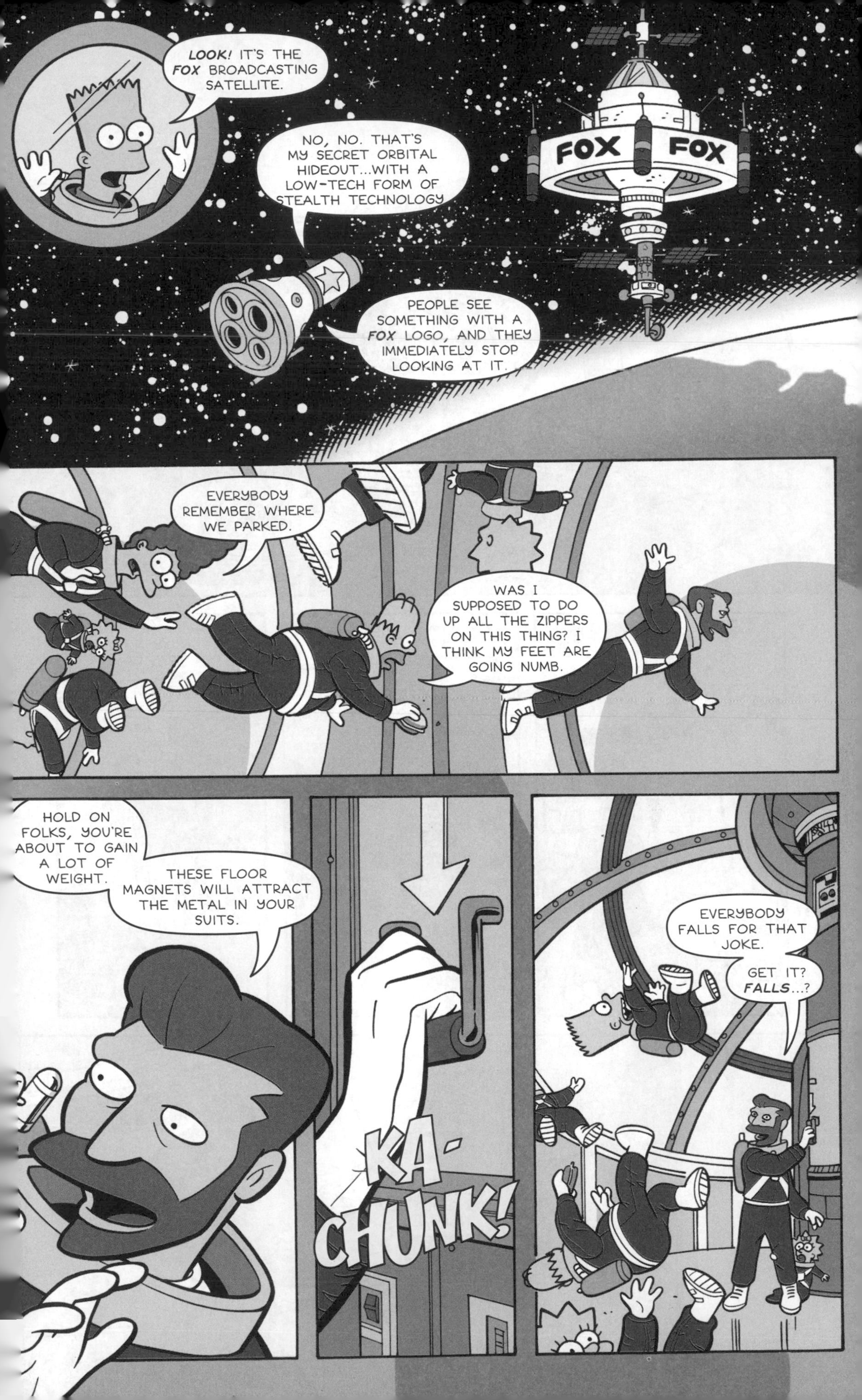
LOOK! IT'S THE FOX BROADCASTING SATELLITE.
NO, NO. THAT'S MY SECRET ORBITAL HIDEOUT...WITH A LOW-TECH FORM OF STEALTH TECHNOLOGY.
FOX
FOX
PEOPLE SEE SOMETHING WITH A FOX LOGO, AND THEY IMMEDIATELY STOP LOOKING AT IT.
EVERYBODY REMEMBER WHERE WE PARKED.
WAS I SUPPOSED TO DO UP ALL THE ZIPPERS ON THIS THING? I THINK MY FEET ARE GOING NUMB.
HOLD ON FOLKS, YOU'RE ABOUT TO GAIN A LOT OF WEIGHT.
THESE FLOOR MAGNETS WILL ATTRACT THE METAL IN YOUR SUITS.
KA-CHUNK!
EVERYBODY FALLS FOR THAT JOKE.
GET IT? FALLS...?

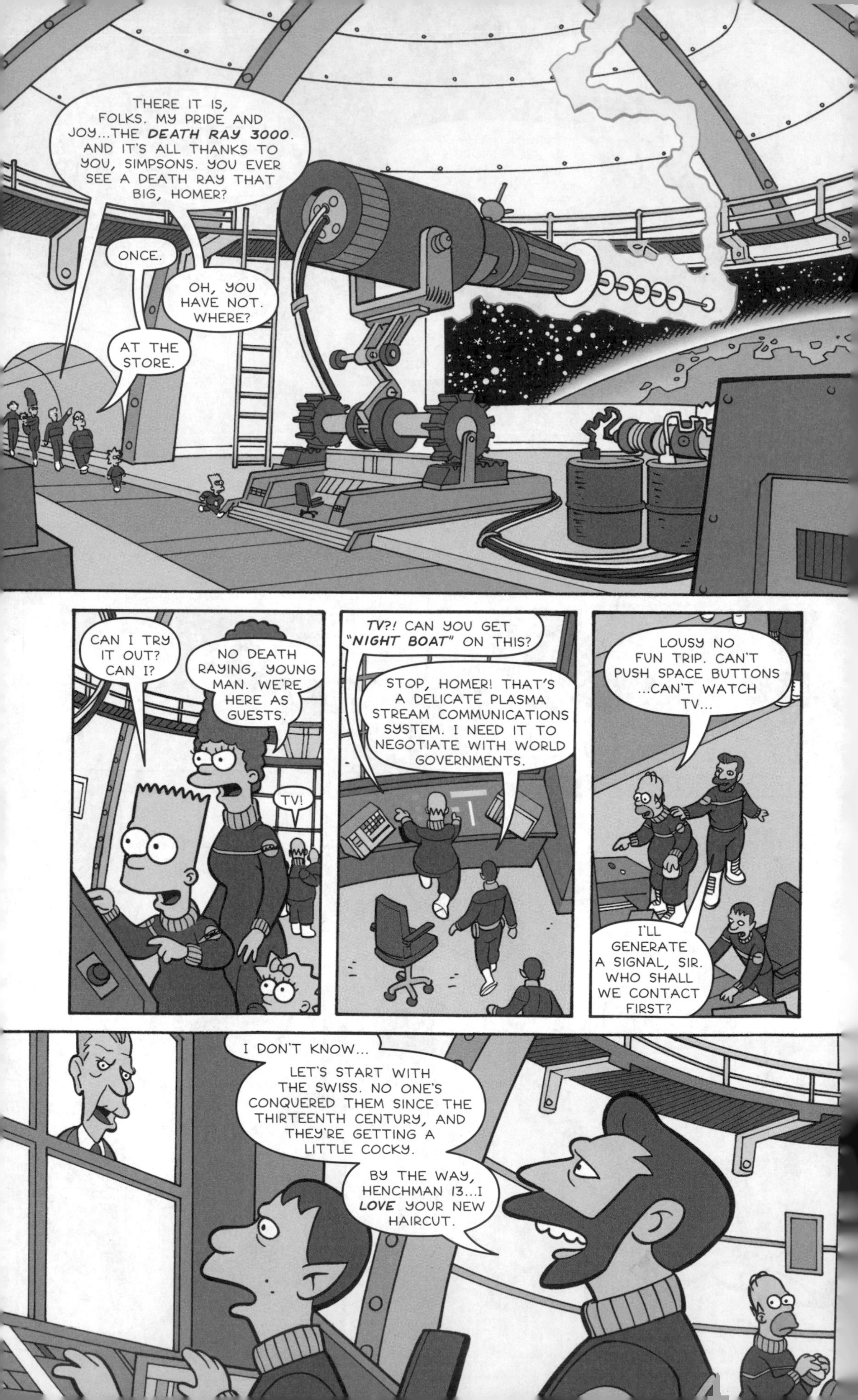

THERE IT IS, FOLKS. MY PRIDE AND JOY...THE *DEATH RAY 3000*. AND IT'S ALL THANKS TO YOU, SIMPSONS. YOU EVER SEE A DEATH RAY THAT BIG, HOMER?
ONCE.
OH, YOU HAVE NOT. WHERE?
AT THE STORE.
CAN I TRY IT OUT? CAN I?
NO DEATH RAYING, YOUNG MAN. WE'RE HERE AS GUESTS.
TV!
TV?! CAN YOU GET "*NIGHT BOAT*" ON THIS?
STOP, HOMER! THAT'S A DELICATE PLASMA STREAM COMMUNICATIONS SYSTEM. I NEED IT TO NEGOTIATE WITH WORLD GOVERNMENTS.
LOUSY NO FUN TRIP. CAN'T PUSH SPACE BUTTONS ...CAN'T WATCH TV...
I'LL GENERATE A SIGNAL, SIR. WHO SHALL WE CONTACT FIRST?
I DON'T KNOW...
LET'S START WITH THE SWISS. NO ONE'S CONQUERED THEM SINCE THE THIRTEENTH CENTURY, AND THEY'RE GETTING A LITTLE COCKY.
BY THE WAY, HENCHMAN 13...I *LOVE* YOUR NEW HAIRCUT.

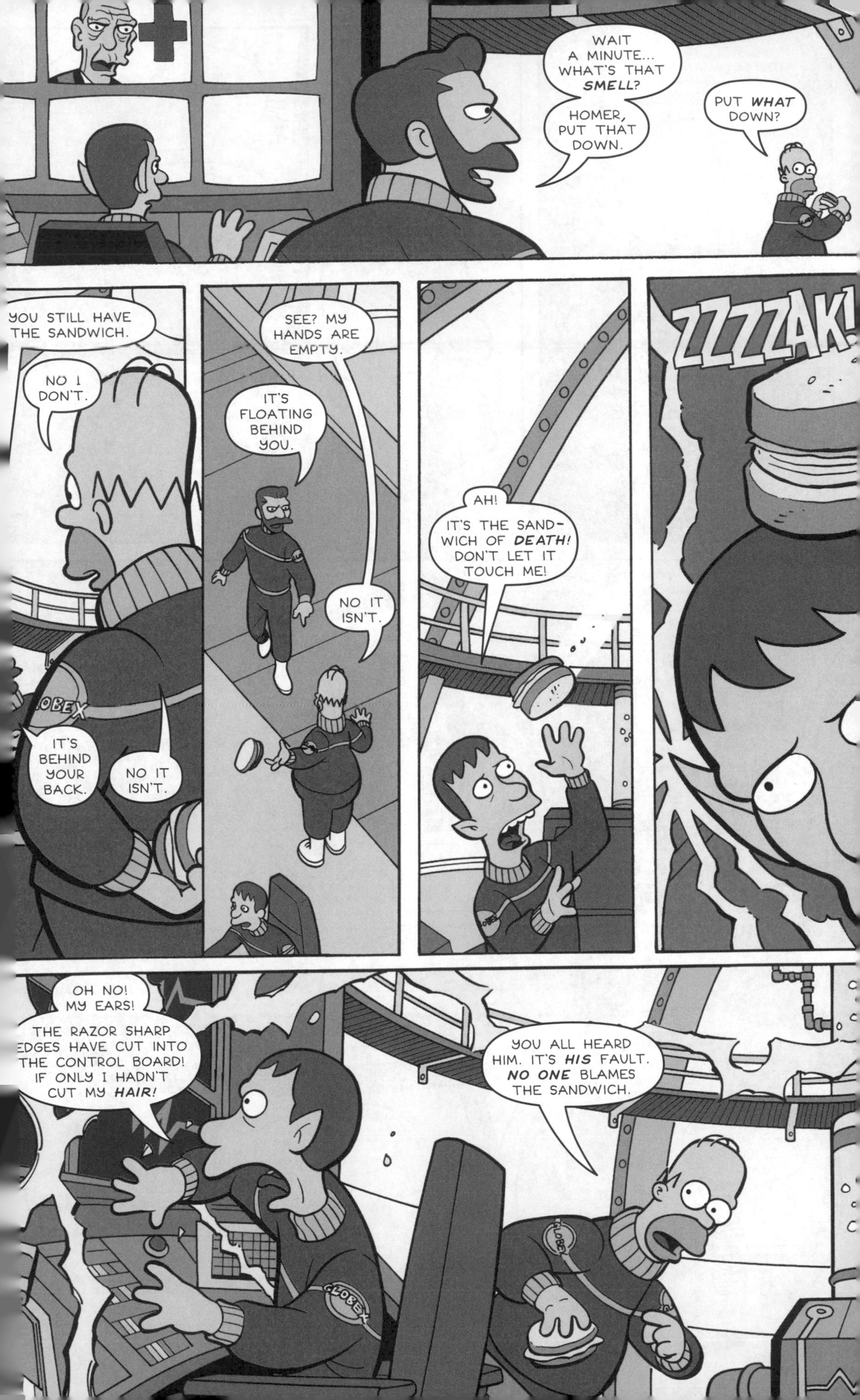
WAIT A MINUTE... WHAT'S THAT SMELL?
HOMER, PUT THAT DOWN.
PUT WHAT DOWN?
YOU STILL HAVE THE SANDWICH.
NO I DON'T.
IT'S BEHIND YOUR BACK.
NO IT ISN'T.
SEE? MY HANDS ARE EMPTY.
IT'S FLOATING BEHIND YOU.
NO IT ISN'T.
AH!
IT'S THE SAND-WICH OF DEATH! DON'T LET IT TOUCH ME!
ZZZZAK!
OH NO! MY EARS!
THE RAZOR SHARP EDGES HAVE CUT INTO THE CONTROL BOARD! IF ONLY I HADN'T CUT MY HAIR!
YOU ALL HEARD HIM. IT'S HIS FAULT. NO ONE BLAMES THE SANDWICH.

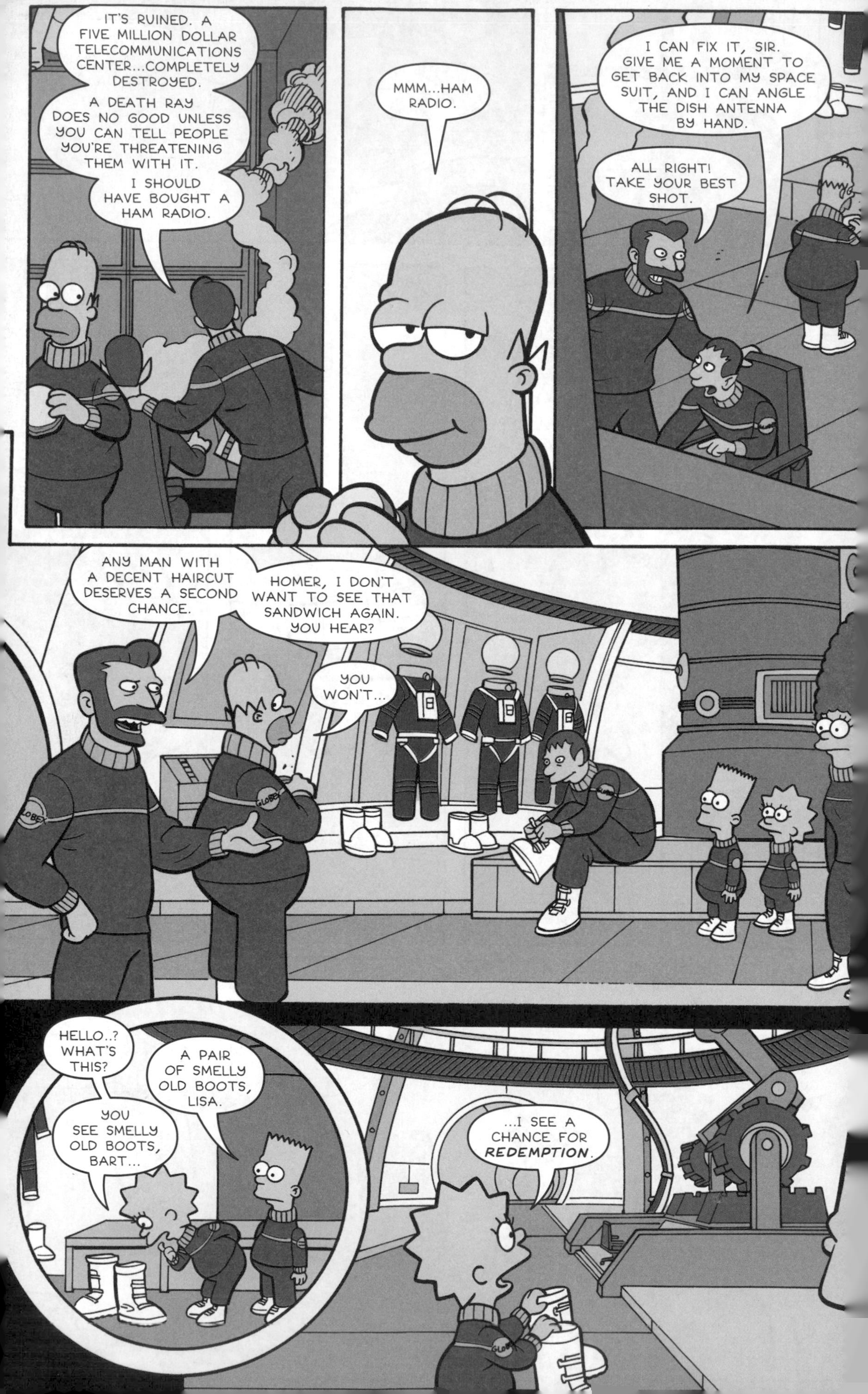
IT'S RUINED. A FIVE MILLION DOLLAR TELECOMMUNICATIONS CENTER...COMPLETELY DESTROYED.
A DEATH RAY DOES NO GOOD UNLESS YOU CAN TELL PEOPLE YOU'RE THREATENING THEM WITH IT.
I SHOULD HAVE BOUGHT A HAM RADIO.
MMM...HAM RADIO.
I CAN FIX IT, SIR. GIVE ME A MOMENT TO GET BACK INTO MY SPACE SUIT, AND I CAN ANGLE THE DISH ANTENNA BY HAND.
ALL RIGHT! TAKE YOUR BEST SHOT.
ANY MAN WITH A DECENT HAIRCUT DESERVES A SECOND CHANCE.
HOMER, I DON'T WANT TO SEE THAT SANDWICH AGAIN. YOU HEAR?
YOU WON'T...
GLOBEX
HELLO..? WHAT'S THIS?
A PAIR OF SMELLY OLD BOOTS, LISA.
YOU SEE SMELLY OLD BOOTS, BART...
...I SEE A CHANCE FOR *REDEMPTION*.

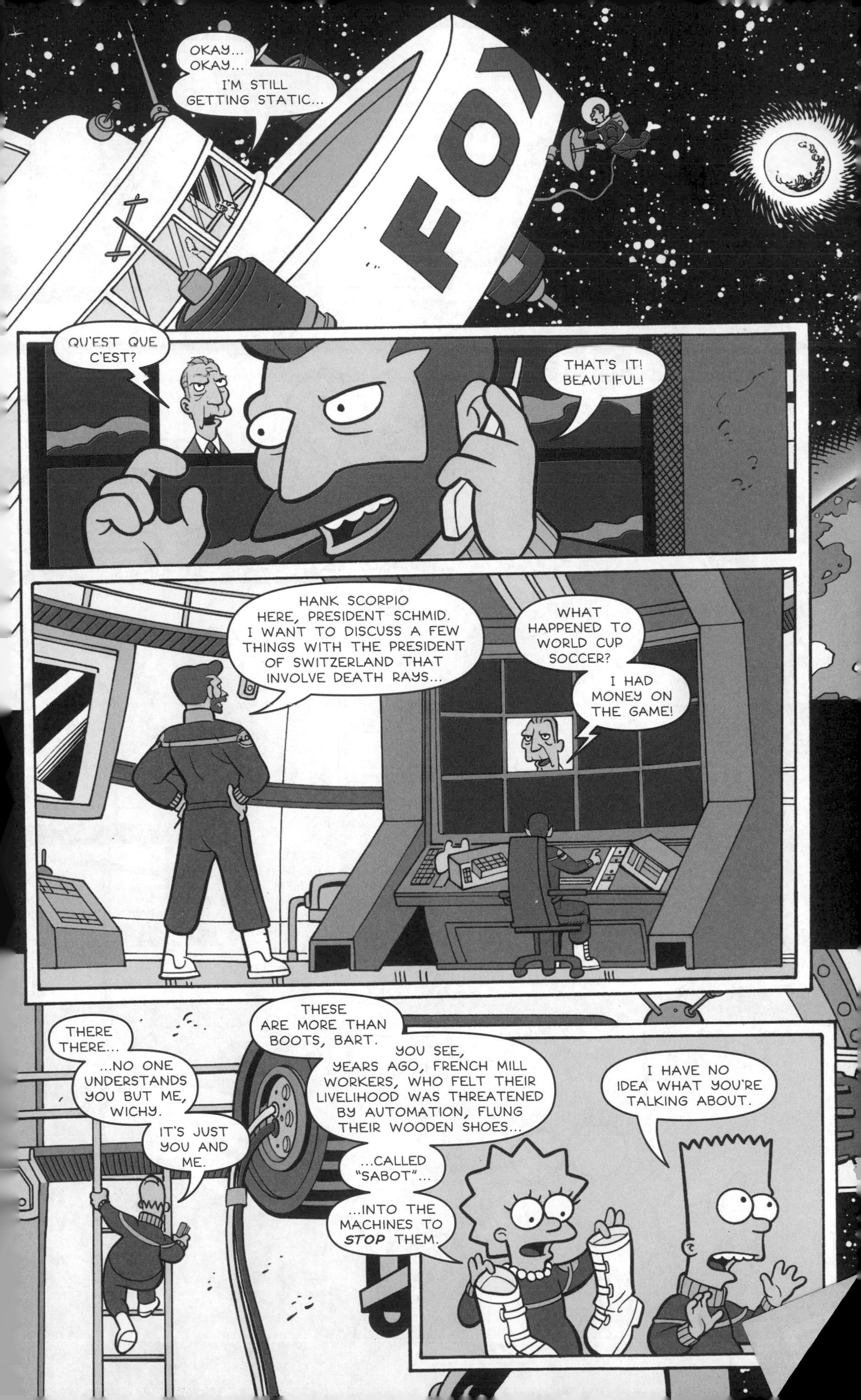

OKAY... OKAY...
I'M STILL GETTING STATIC...
FOX
QU'EST QUE C'EST?
THAT'S IT! BEAUTIFUL!
HANK SCORPIO HERE, PRESIDENT SCHMID. I WANT TO DISCUSS A FEW THINGS WITH THE PRESIDENT OF SWITZERLAND THAT INVOLVE DEATH RAYS...
WHAT HAPPENED TO WORLD CUP SOCCER?
I HAD MONEY ON THE GAME!
THERE THERE...
...NO ONE UNDERSTANDS YOU BUT ME, WICHY.
IT'S JUST YOU AND ME.
THESE ARE MORE THAN BOOTS, BART.
YOU SEE, YEARS AGO, FRENCH MILL WORKERS, WHO FELT THEIR LIVELIHOOD WAS THREATENED BY AUTOMATION, FLUNG THEIR WOODEN SHOES...
...CALLED "SABOT"...
...INTO THE MACHINES TO *STOP* THEM.
I HAVE NO IDEA WHAT YOU'RE TALKING ABOUT.

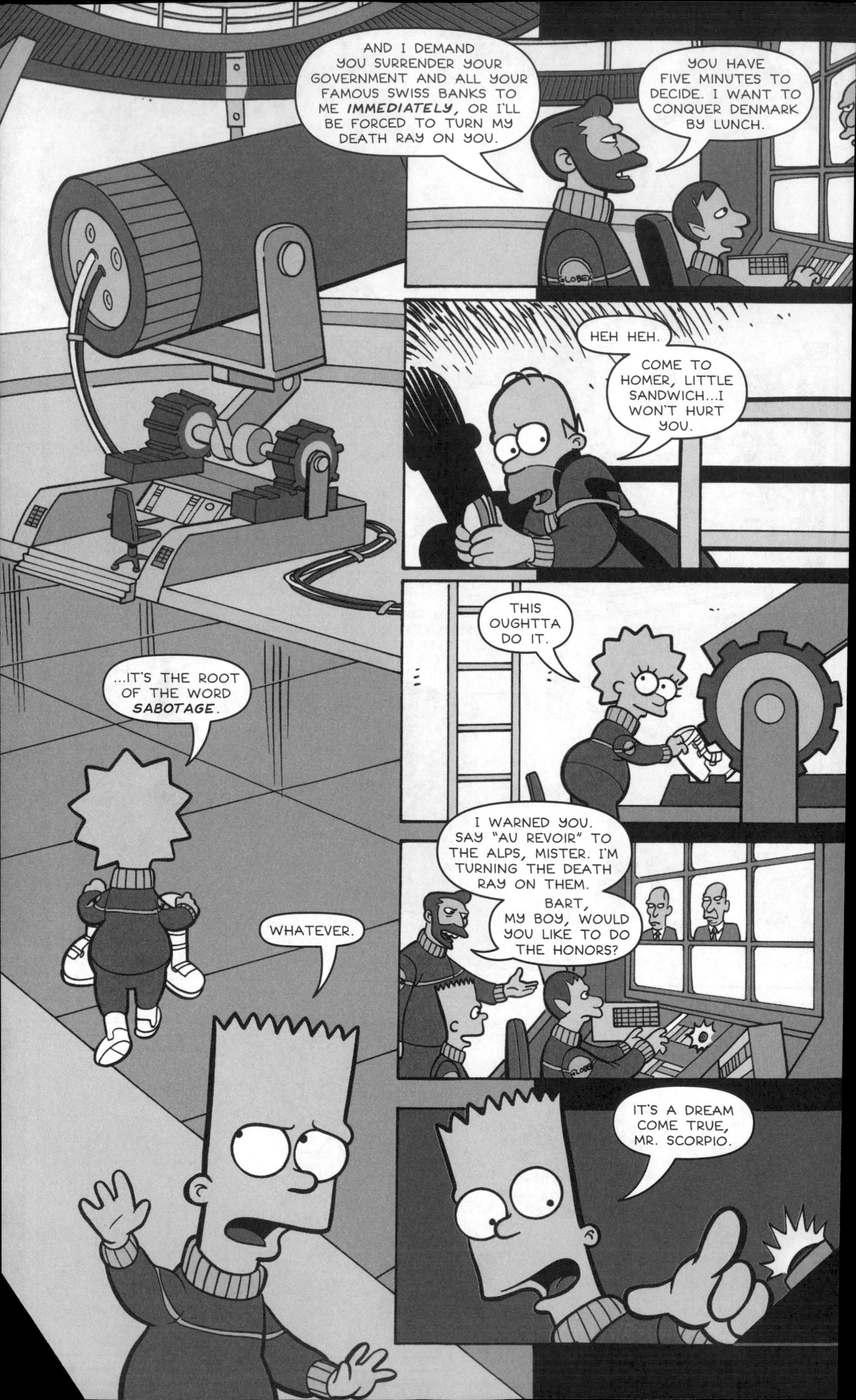
AND I DEMAND YOU SURRENDER YOUR GOVERNMENT AND ALL YOUR FAMOUS SWISS BANKS TO ME **IMMEDIATELY**, OR I'LL BE FORCED TO TURN MY DEATH RAY ON YOU.
YOU HAVE FIVE MINUTES TO DECIDE. I WANT TO CONQUER DENMARK BY LUNCH.
GLOBEX
HEH HEH.
COME TO HOMER, LITTLE SANDWICH...I WON'T HURT YOU.
THIS OUGHTTA DO IT.
...IT'S THE ROOT OF THE WORD **SABOTAGE**.
WHATEVER.
I WARNED YOU. SAY "AU REVOIR" TO THE ALPS, MISTER. I'M TURNING THE DEATH RAY ON THEM.
BART, MY BOY, WOULD YOU LIKE TO DO THE HONORS?
IT'S A DREAM COME TRUE, MR. SCORPIO.

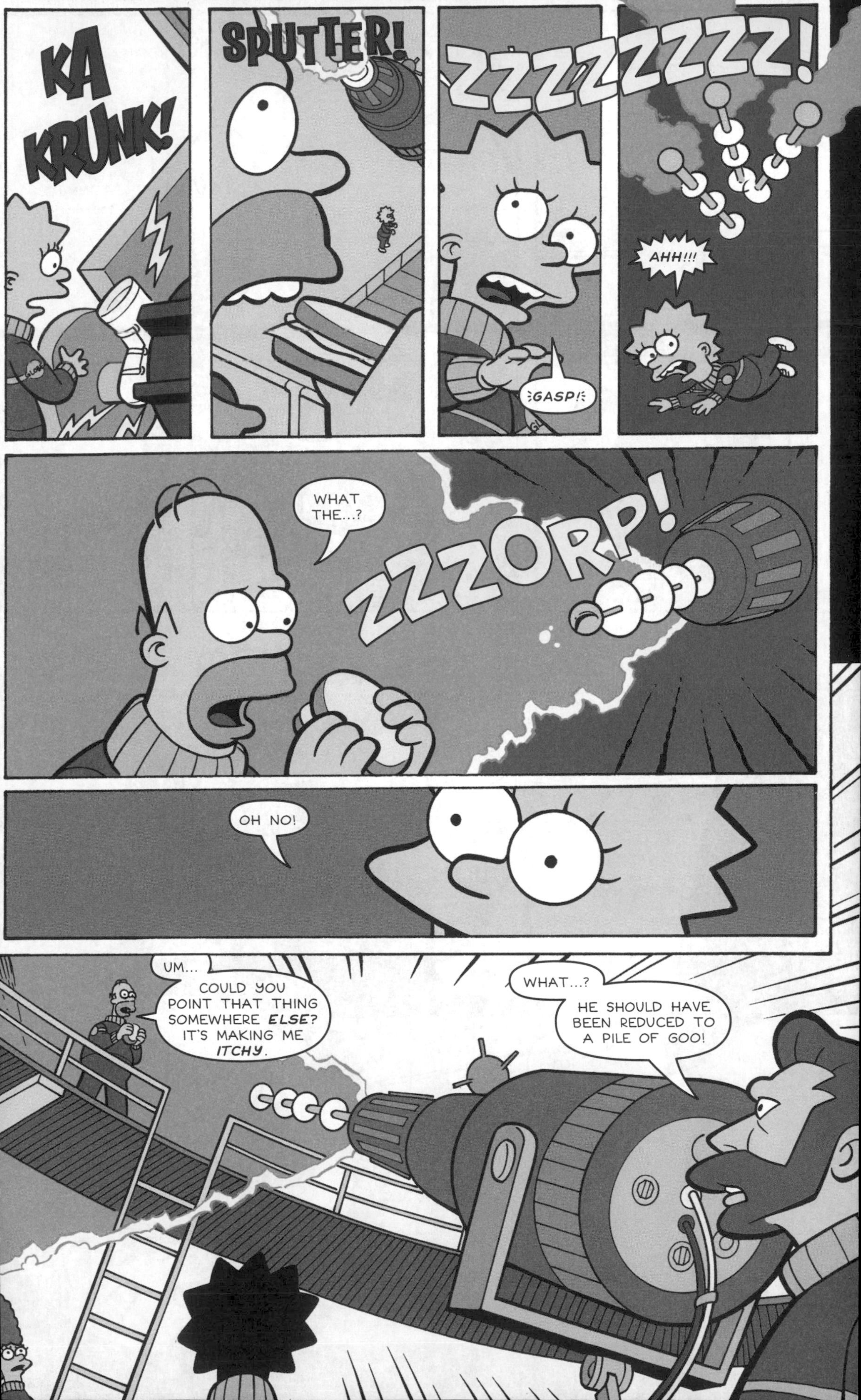

KA KRUNK!
SPUTTER!
ZZZZZZZZZ!
GASP!
AHH!!!
WHAT THE...?
ZZZORP!
OH NO!
UM...
COULD YOU POINT THAT THING SOMEWHERE ELSE? IT'S MAKING ME ITCHY.
WHAT...?
HE SHOULD HAVE BEEN REDUCED TO A PILE OF GOO!

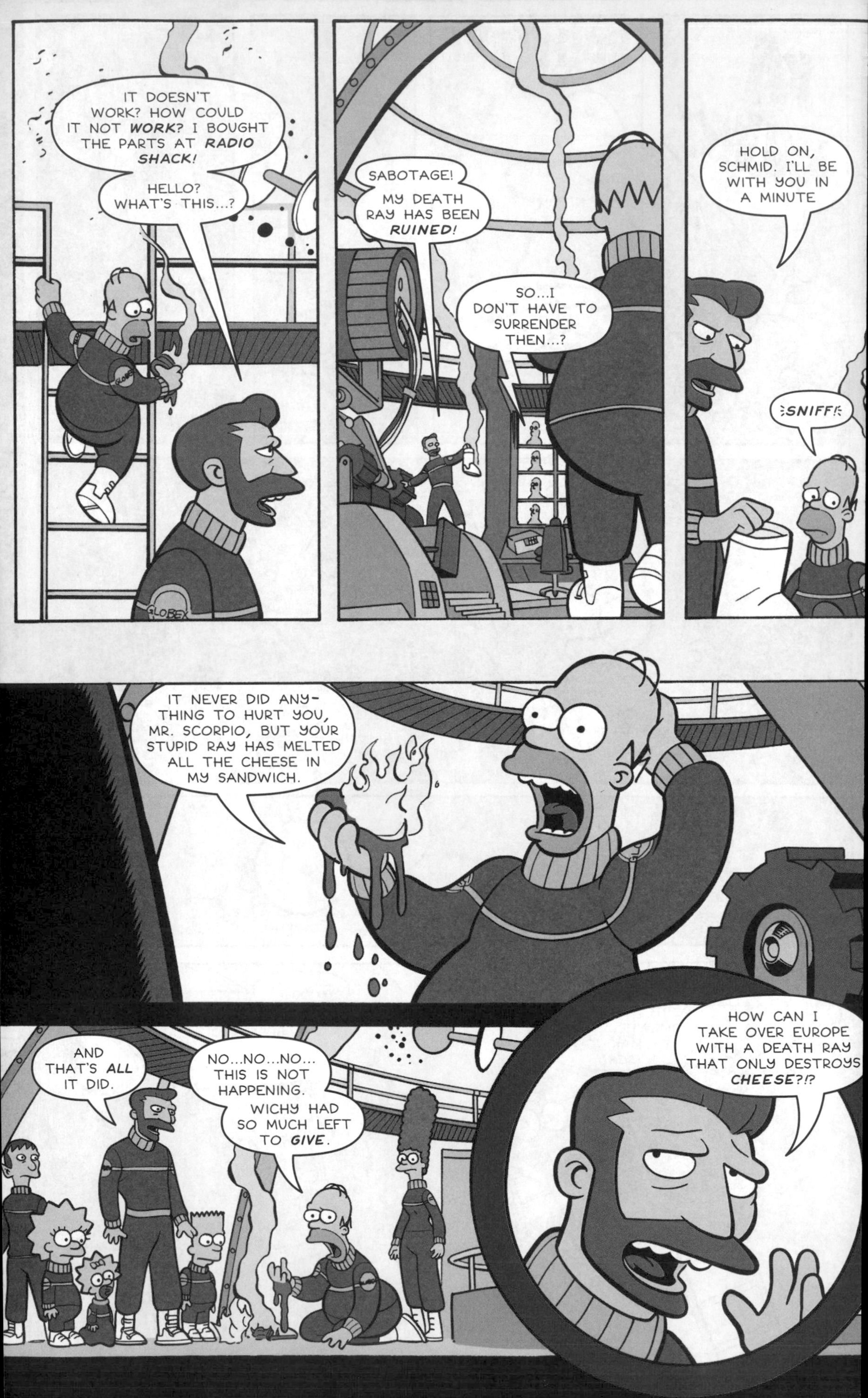
IT DOESN'T WORK? HOW COULD IT NOT WORK? I BOUGHT THE PARTS AT RADIO SHACK!
HELLO? WHAT'S THIS...?
GLOBEX
SABOTAGE!
MY DEATH RAY HAS BEEN RUINED!
SO...I DON'T HAVE TO SURRENDER THEN...?
HOLD ON, SCHMID. I'LL BE WITH YOU IN A MINUTE
SNIFF!
IT NEVER DID ANY-THING TO HURT YOU, MR. SCORPIO, BUT YOUR STUPID RAY HAS MELTED ALL THE CHEESE IN MY SANDWICH.
AND THAT'S ALL IT DID.
NO...NO...NO... THIS IS NOT HAPPENING.
WICHY HAD SO MUCH LEFT TO GIVE.
HOW CAN I TAKE OVER EUROPE WITH A DEATH RAY THAT ONLY DESTROYS CHEESE?!?

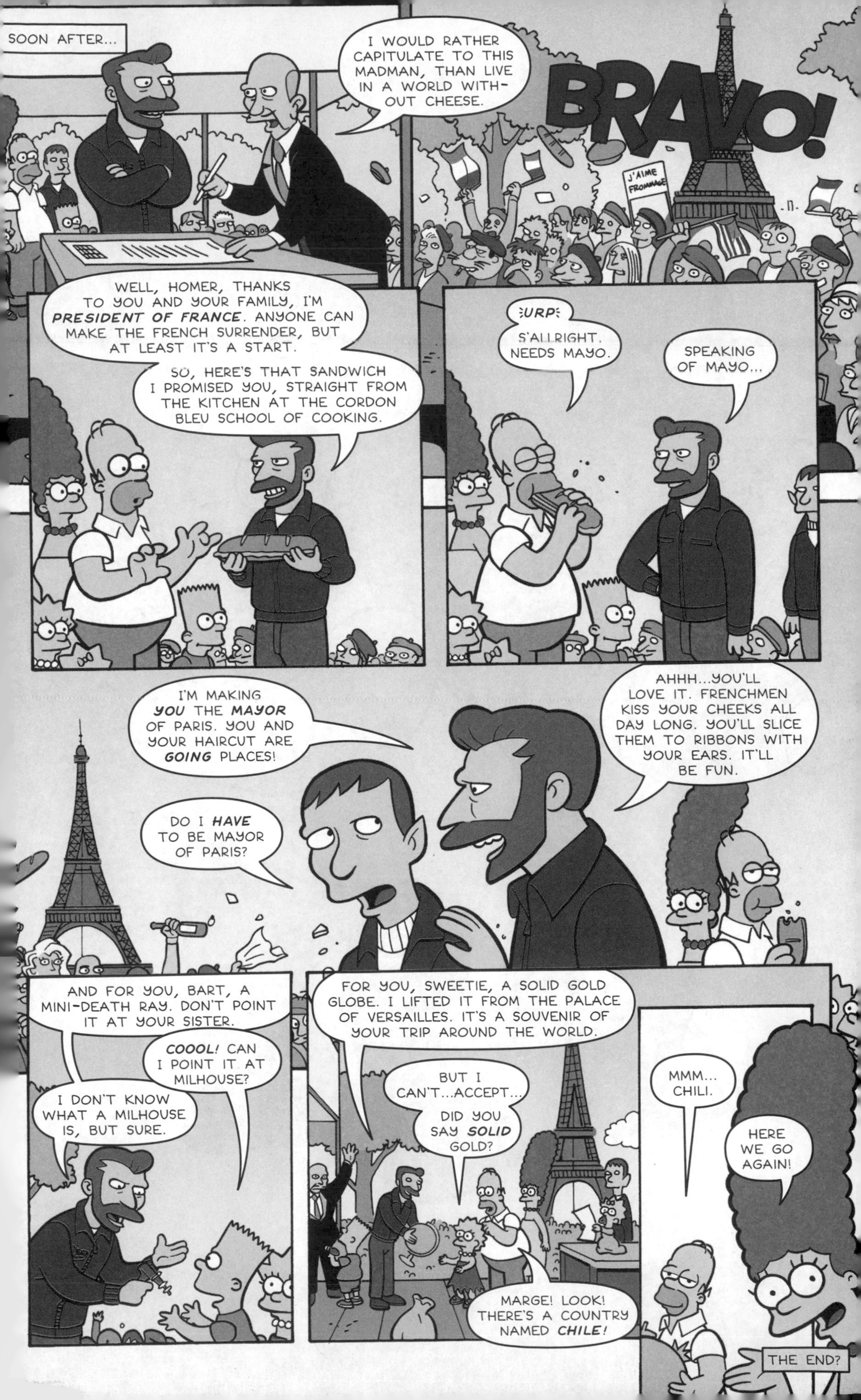
SOON AFTER...
I WOULD RATHER CAPITULATE TO THIS MADMAN, THAN LIVE IN A WORLD WITHOUT CHEESE.
BRAVO!
J'AIME FROMMAGE
WELL, HOMER, THANKS TO YOU AND YOUR FAMILY, I'M PRESIDENT OF FRANCE. ANYONE CAN MAKE THE FRENCH SURRENDER, BUT AT LEAST IT'S A START.
SO, HERE'S THAT SANDWICH I PROMISED YOU, STRAIGHT FROM THE KITCHEN AT THE CORDON BLEU SCHOOL OF COOKING.
URP
S'ALLRIGHT. NEEDS MAYO.
SPEAKING OF MAYO...
I'M MAKING YOU THE MAYOR OF PARIS. YOU AND YOUR HAIRCUT ARE GOING PLACES!
DO I HAVE TO BE MAYOR OF PARIS?
AHHH...YOU'LL LOVE IT. FRENCHMEN KISS YOUR CHEEKS ALL DAY LONG. YOU'LL SLICE THEM TO RIBBONS WITH YOUR EARS. IT'LL BE FUN.
AND FOR YOU, BART, A MINI-DEATH RAY. DON'T POINT IT AT YOUR SISTER.
COOOL! CAN I POINT IT AT MILHOUSE?
I DON'T KNOW WHAT A MILHOUSE IS, BUT SURE.
FOR YOU, SWEETIE, A SOLID GOLD GLOBE. I LIFTED IT FROM THE PALACE OF VERSAILLES. IT'S A SOUVENIR OF YOUR TRIP AROUND THE WORLD.
BUT I CAN'T...ACCEPT...
DID YOU SAY SOLID GOLD?
MARGE! LOOK! THERE'S A COUNTRY NAMED CHILE!
MMM... CHILI.
HERE WE GO AGAIN!
THE END?

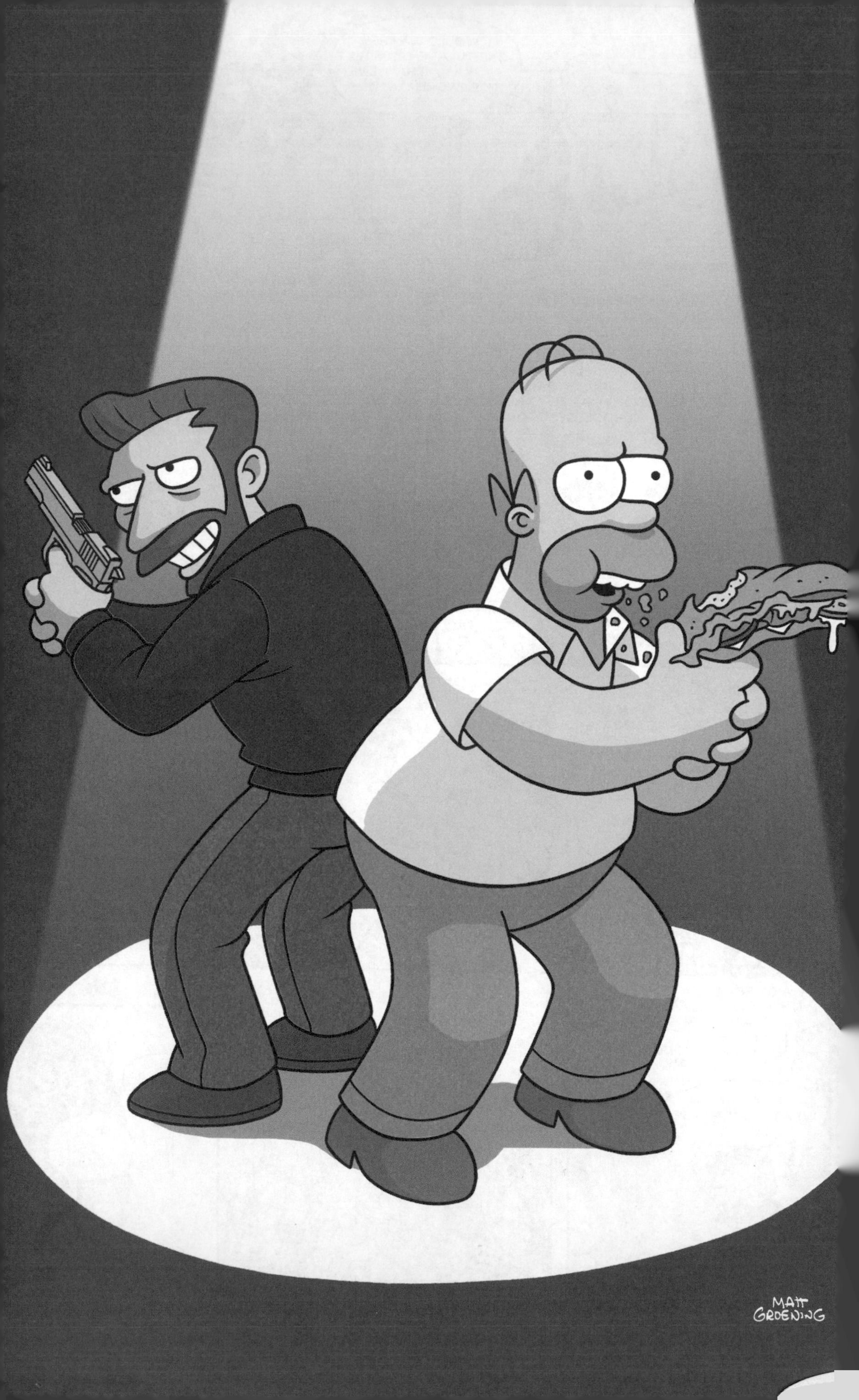
MATT GROENING

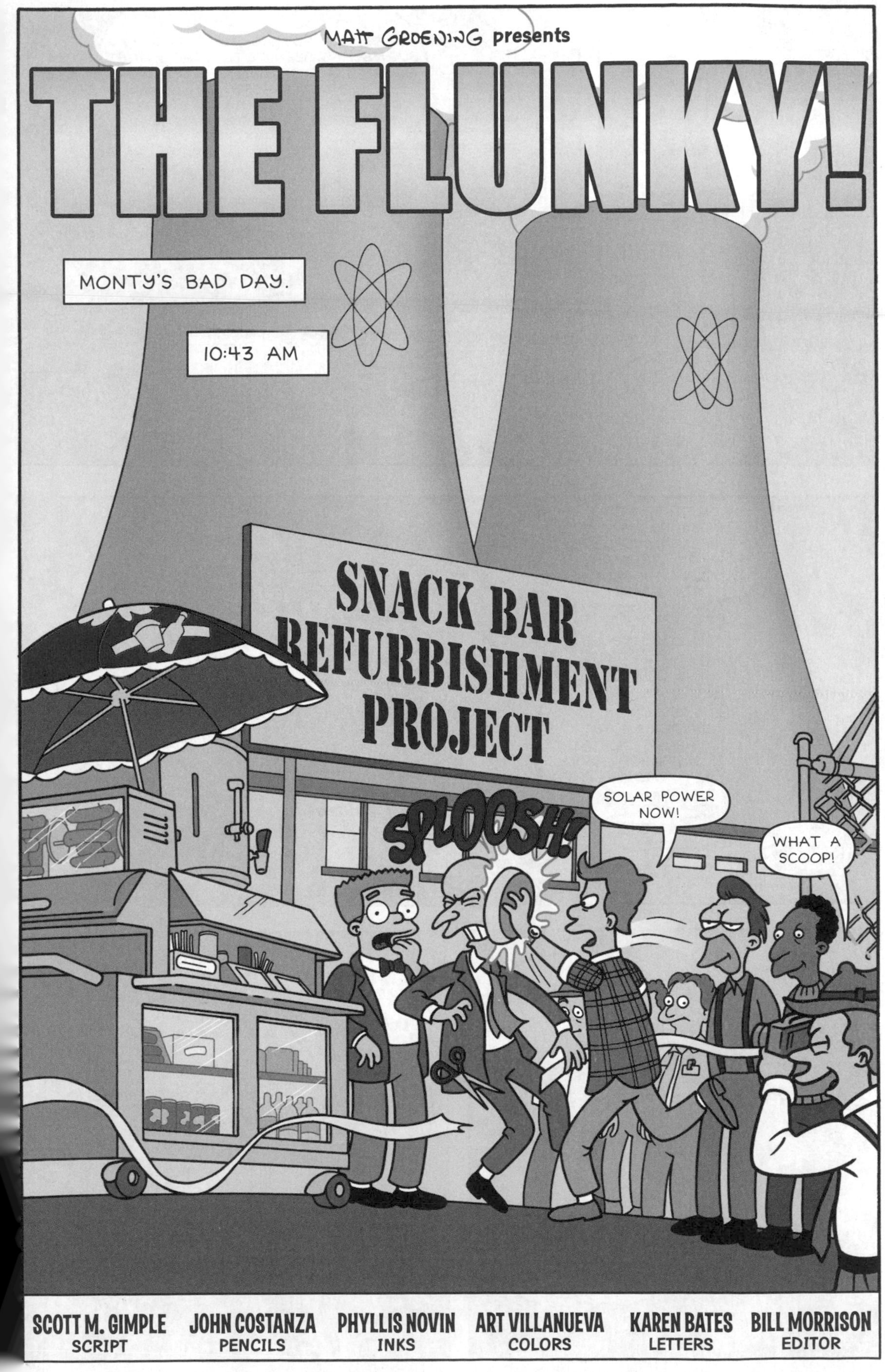
MATT GROENING presents
THE FLUNKY!
MONTY'S BAD DAY.
10:43 AM
SNACK BAR REFURBISHMENT PROJECT
SPLOOSH!
SOLAR POWER NOW!
WHAT A SCOOP!

SCOTT M. GIMPLE SCRIPT
JOHN COSTANZA PENCILS
PHYLLIS NOVIN INKS
ART VILLANUEVA COLORS
KAREN BATES LETTERS
BILL MORRISON EDITOR

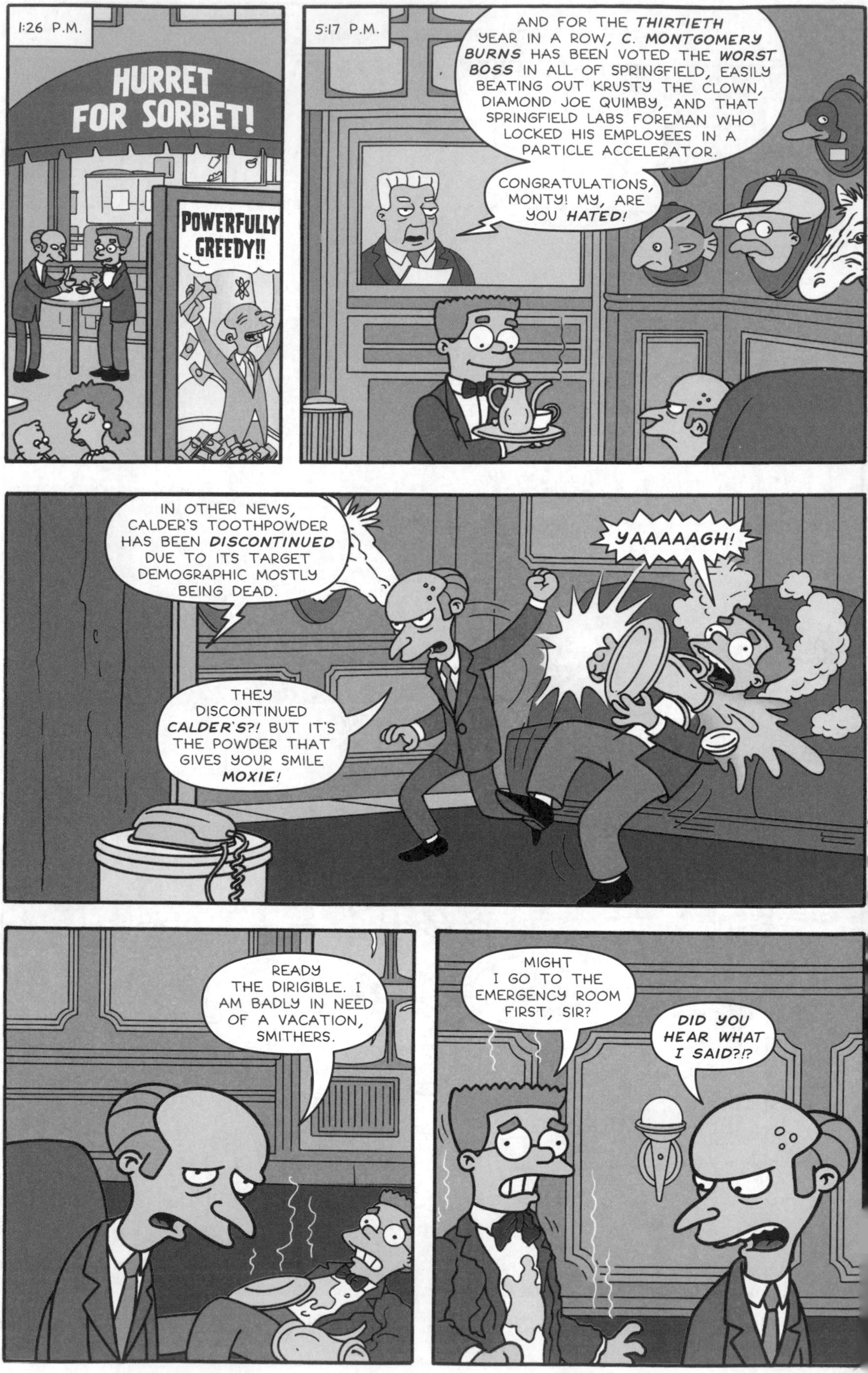
1:26 P.M.
HURRET FOR SORBET!
POWERFULLY GREEDY!!
5:17 P.M.
AND FOR THE THIRTIETH YEAR IN A ROW, C. MONTGOMERY BURNS HAS BEEN VOTED THE WORST BOSS IN ALL OF SPRINGFIELD, EASILY BEATING OUT KRUSTY THE CLOWN, DIAMOND JOE QUIMBY, AND THAT SPRINGFIELD LABS FOREMAN WHO LOCKED HIS EMPLOYEES IN A PARTICLE ACCELERATOR.
CONGRATULATIONS, MONTY! MY, ARE YOU HATED!
IN OTHER NEWS, CALDER'S TOOTHPOWDER HAS BEEN DISCONTINUED DUE TO ITS TARGET DEMOGRAPHIC MOSTLY BEING DEAD.
YAAAAAGH!
THEY DISCONTINUED CALDER'S?! BUT IT'S THE POWDER THAT GIVES YOUR SMILE MOXIE!
READY THE DIRIGIBLE. I AM BADLY IN NEED OF A VACATION, SMITHERS.
MIGHT I GO TO THE EMERGENCY ROOM FIRST, SIR?
DID YOU HEAR WHAT I SAID?!?

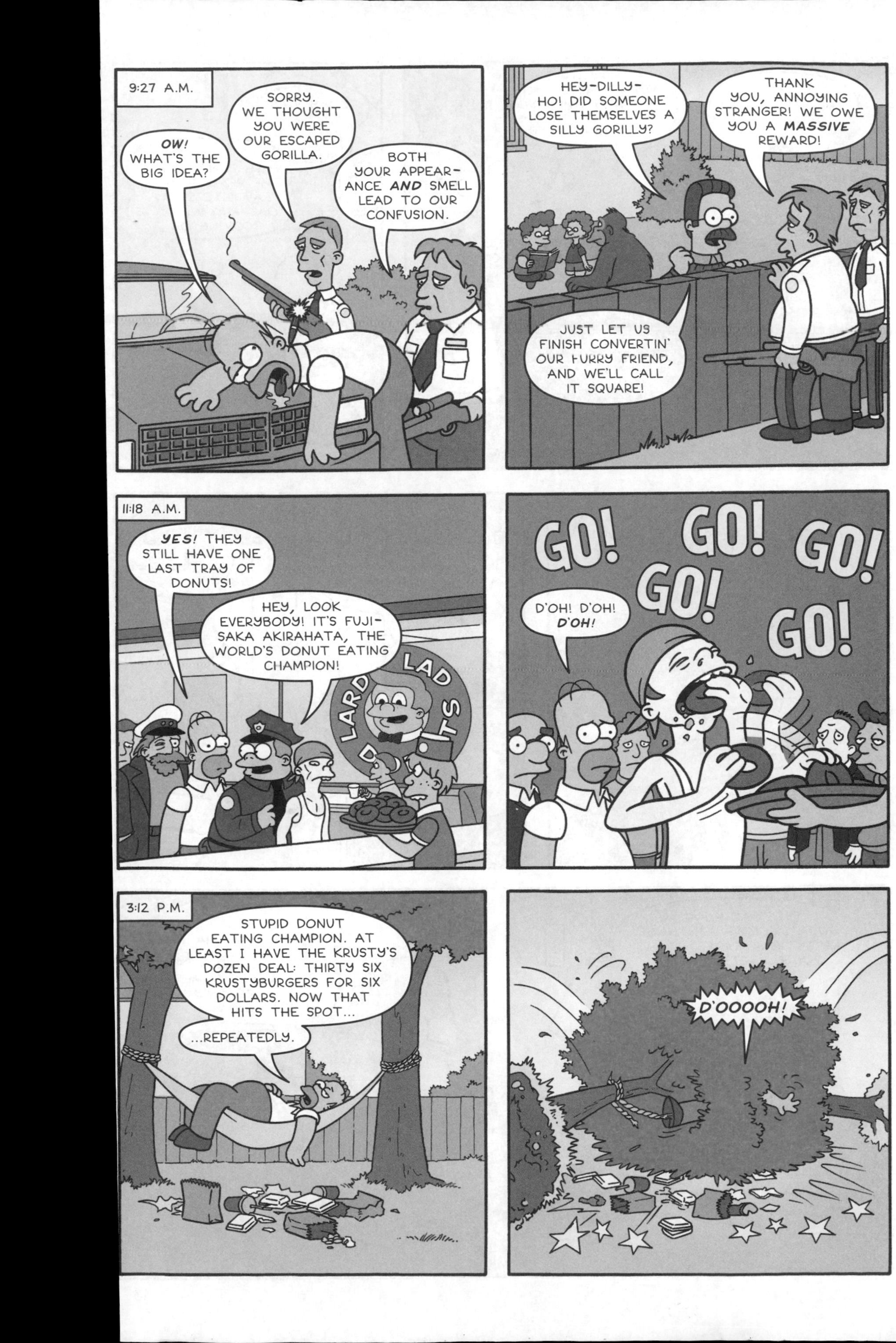
9:27 A.M.
OW! WHAT'S THE BIG IDEA?
SORRY. WE THOUGHT YOU WERE OUR ESCAPED GORILLA.
BOTH YOUR APPEARANCE AND SMELL LEAD TO OUR CONFUSION.
HEY-DILLY-HO! DID SOMEONE LOSE THEMSELVES A SILLY GORILLY?
THANK YOU, ANNOYING STRANGER! WE OWE YOU A MASSIVE REWARD!
JUST LET US FINISH CONVERTIN' OUR FURRY FRIEND, AND WE'LL CALL IT SQUARE!
11:18 A.M.
YES! THEY STILL HAVE ONE LAST TRAY OF DONUTS!
HEY, LOOK EVERYBODY! IT'S FUJISAKA AKIRAHATA, THE WORLD'S DONUT EATING CHAMPION!
LARD LAD
GO! GO! GO! GO! GO!
D'OH! D'OH! D'OH!
3:12 P.M.
STUPID DONUT EATING CHAMPION. AT LEAST I HAVE THE KRUSTY'S DOZEN DEAL: THIRTY SIX KRUSTYBURGERS FOR SIX DOLLARS. NOW THAT HITS THE SPOT...
...REPEATEDLY.
D'OOOOH!

TODAY WAS THE WORST DAY OF MY LIFE.

I THOUGHT THE WORST DAY OF YOUR LIFE WAS WHEN YOU THREW UP ON THE JAPANESE PRIME MINISTER.

TODAY WAS WORSE.

HERE'S A BEER WITH A NIPPLE AND THE REMOTE. YOUR FAVORITE SHOW, "OAF AND WIFEY" IS COMING ON.

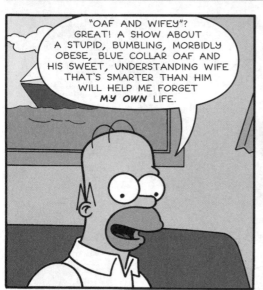

"OAF AND WIFEY"? GREAT! A SHOW ABOUT A STUPID, BUMBLING, MORBIDLY OBESE, BLUE COLLAR OAF AND HIS SWEET, UNDERSTANDING WIFE THAT'S SMARTER THAN HIM WILL HELP ME FORGET *MY OWN* LIFE.

"OAF AND WIFEY" WILL NOT BE SEEN TONIGHT SO THAT WE CAN BRING YOU FOX'S ALL REALITY SATURDAY!

D'OH!

CLICK!

FEEL BAD ABOUT *YOUR* LIFE? WATCH *THESE* ATTENTION-STARVED IDIOTS. *YOU'RE BETTER THAN THEM!*

HMMM...I *LIKE* PEOPLE I'M *BETTER* THAN.

MAYBE I'LL JUST *SAMPLE* SOME OF THIS *REALITY TELEVISION!*

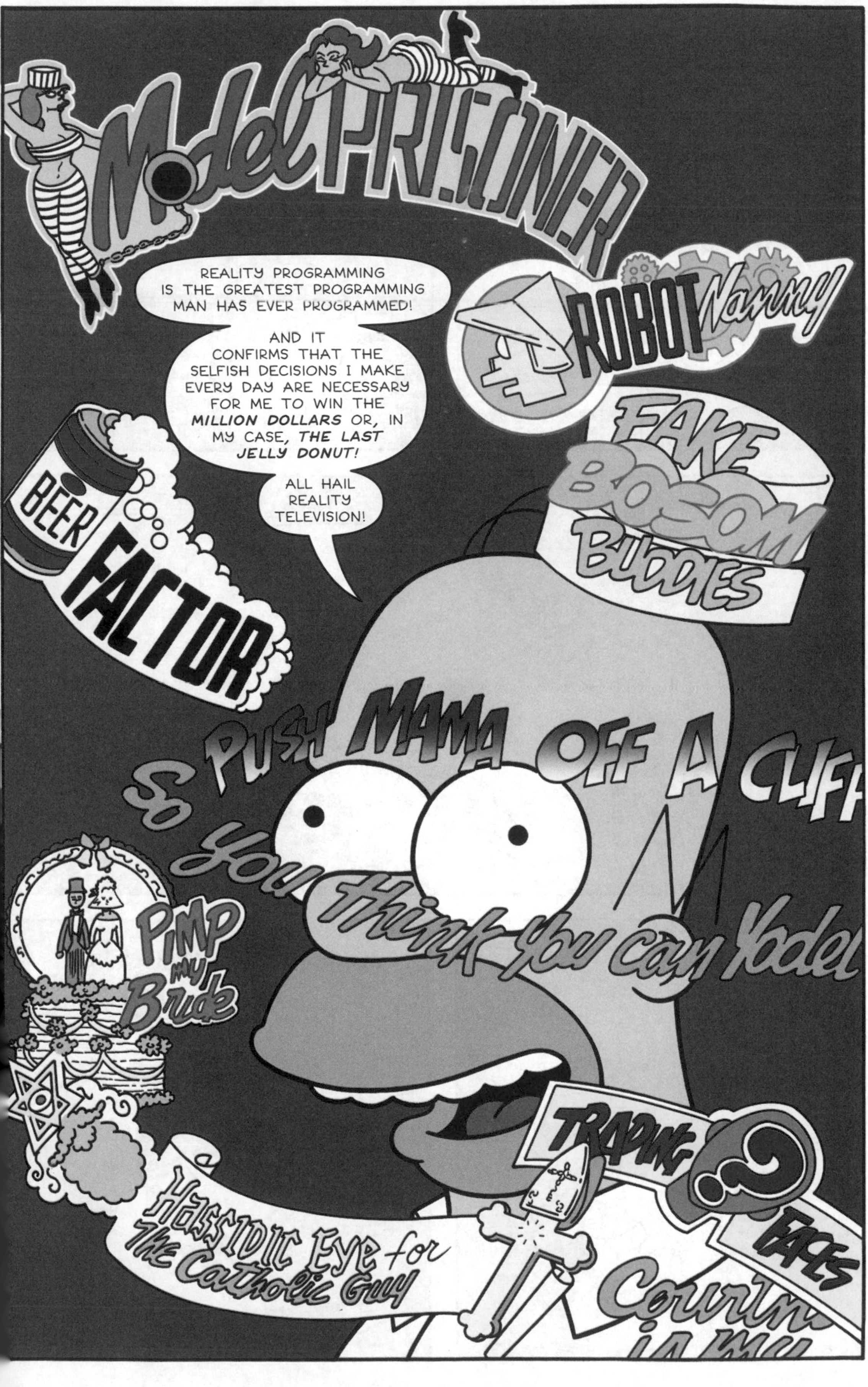

Model PRISONER
REALITY PROGRAMMING IS THE GREATEST PROGRAMMING MAN HAS EVER PROGRAMMED!
AND IT CONFIRMS THAT THE SELFISH DECISIONS I MAKE EVERY DAY ARE NECESSARY FOR ME TO WIN THE **MILLION DOLLARS** OR, IN MY CASE, **THE LAST JELLY DONUT!**
ALL HAIL REALITY TELEVISION!
ROBOT Nanny
FAKE BOSOM BUDDIES
BEER FACTOR
PUSH MAMA OFF A CLIFF
So you think you can Yodel
PIMP my Bride
TRADING FACES
HASSIDIC Eye for The Catholic Guy

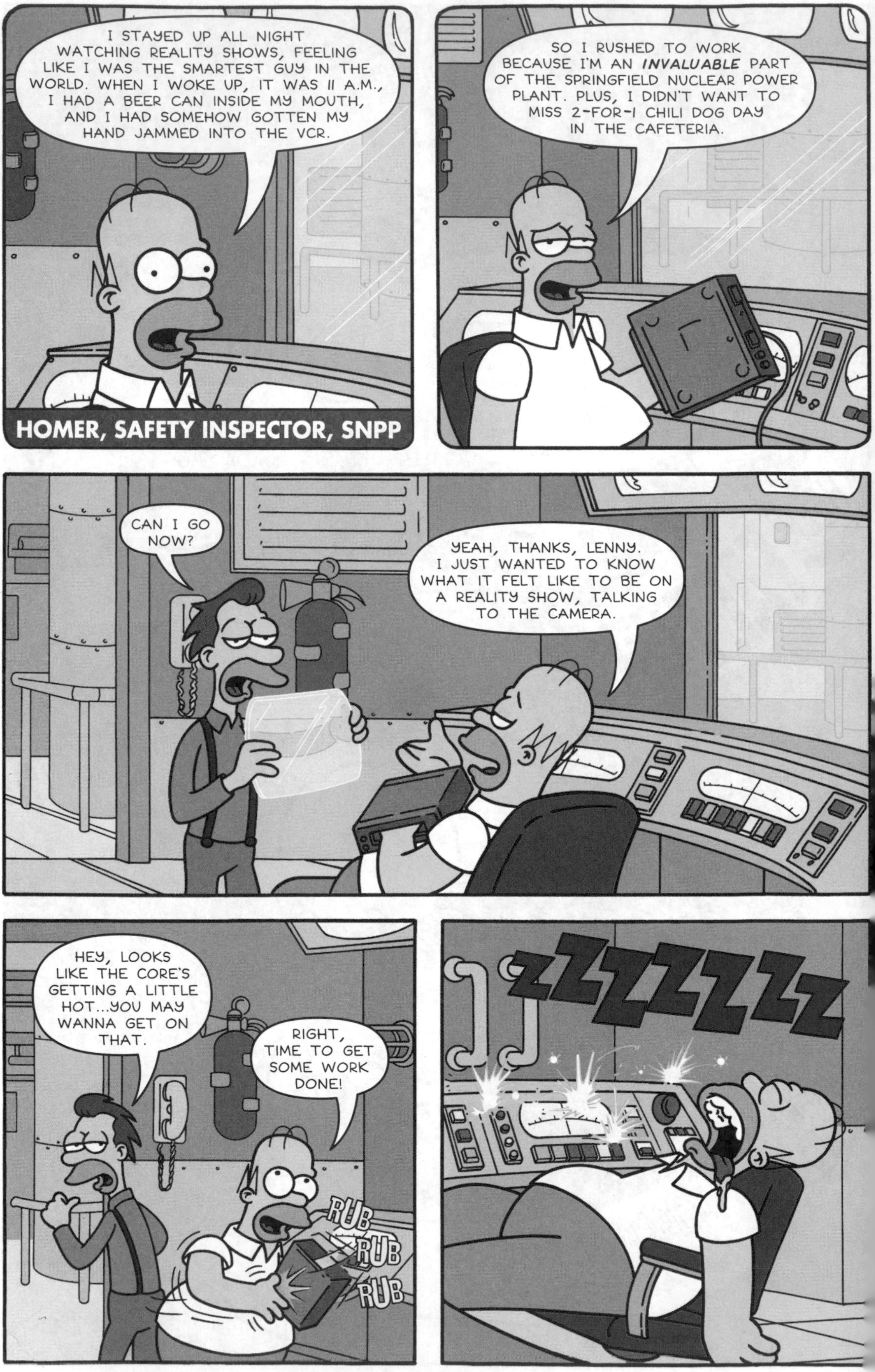
I STAYED UP ALL NIGHT WATCHING REALITY SHOWS, FEELING LIKE I WAS THE SMARTEST GUY IN THE WORLD. WHEN I WOKE UP, IT WAS 11 A.M., I HAD A BEER CAN INSIDE MY MOUTH, AND I HAD SOMEHOW GOTTEN MY HAND JAMMED INTO THE VCR.
HOMER, SAFETY INSPECTOR, SNPP
SO I RUSHED TO WORK BECAUSE I'M AN INVALUABLE PART OF THE SPRINGFIELD NUCLEAR POWER PLANT. PLUS, I DIDN'T WANT TO MISS 2-FOR-1 CHILI DOG DAY IN THE CAFETERIA.
CAN I GO NOW?
YEAH, THANKS, LENNY. I JUST WANTED TO KNOW WHAT IT FELT LIKE TO BE ON A REALITY SHOW, TALKING TO THE CAMERA.
HEY, LOOKS LIKE THE CORE'S GETTING A LITTLE HOT...YOU MAY WANNA GET ON THAT.
RIGHT, TIME TO GET SOME WORK DONE!
RUB
RUB
RUB
ZZZZZZZ

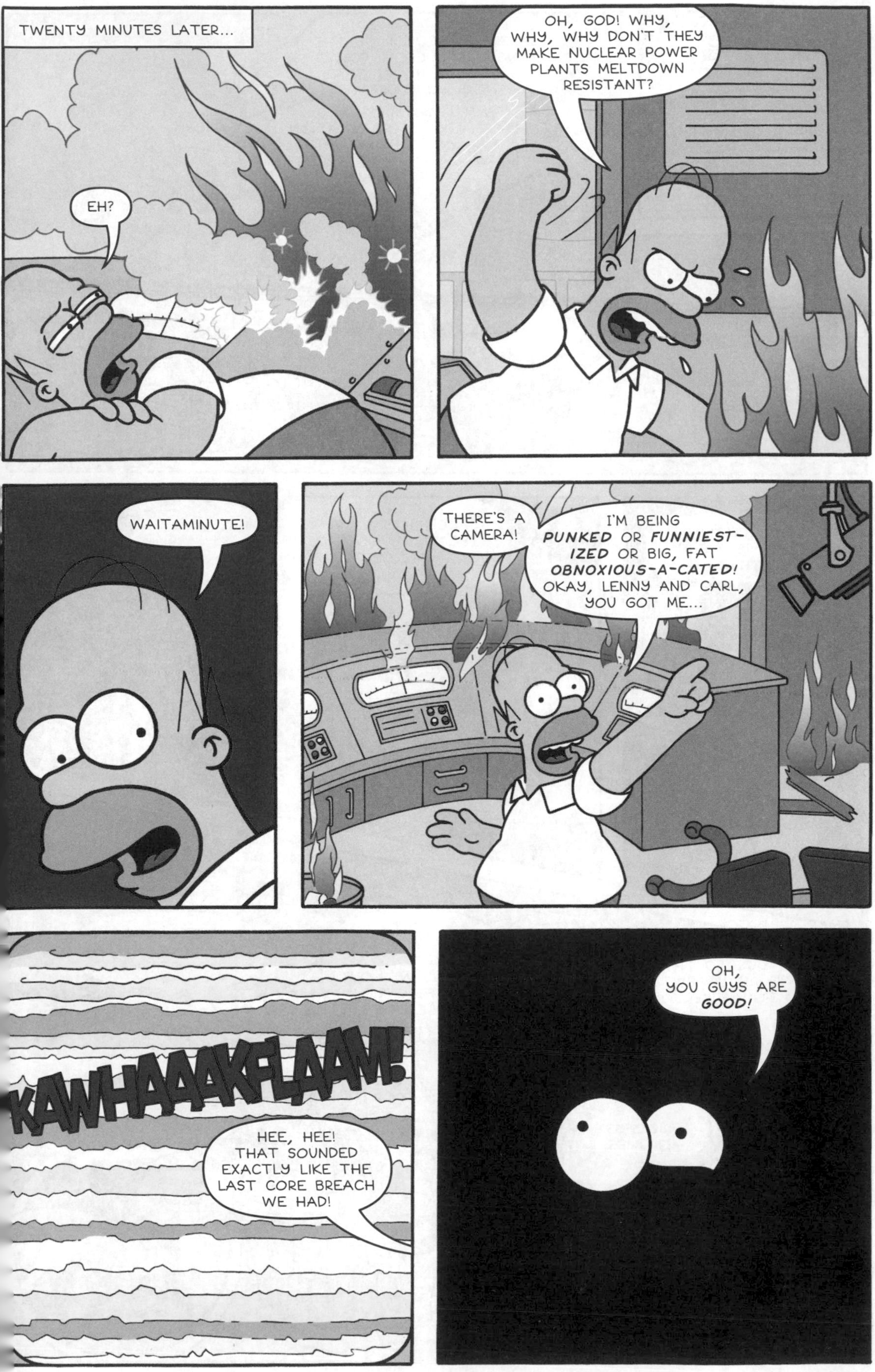
TWENTY MINUTES LATER...
EH?
OH, GOD! WHY, WHY, WHY DON'T THEY MAKE NUCLEAR POWER PLANTS MELTDOWN RESISTANT?
WAITAMINUTE!
THERE'S A CAMERA!
I'M BEING PUNKED OR FUNNIEST-IZED OR BIG, FAT OBNOXIOUS-A-CATED! OKAY, LENNY AND CARL, YOU GOT ME...
KAWHAAAKFLAAM!
HEE, HEE! THAT SOUNDED EXACTLY LIKE THE LAST CORE BREACH WE HAD!
OH, YOU GUYS ARE GOOD!

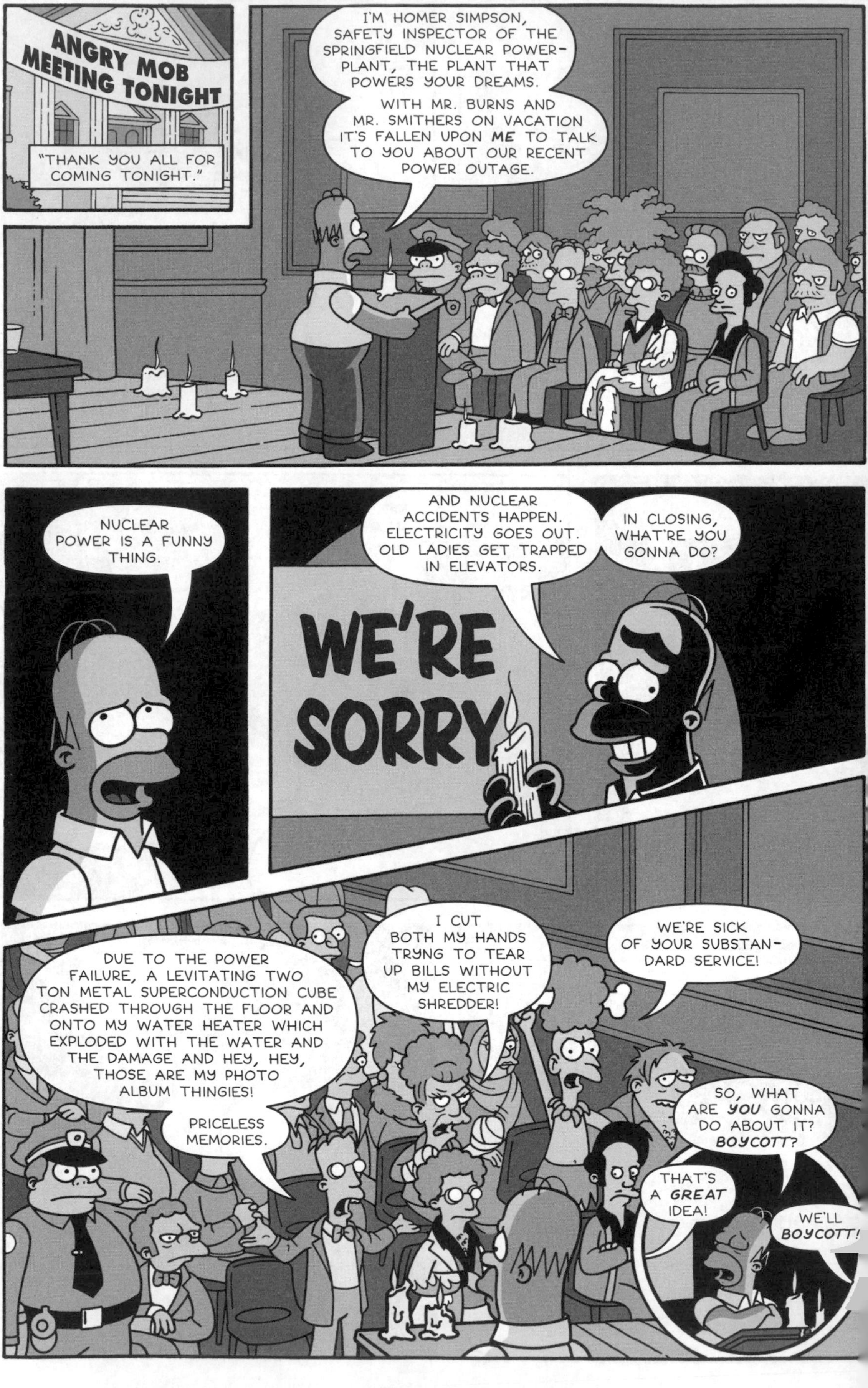
ANGRY MOB MEETING TONIGHT
"THANK YOU ALL FOR COMING TONIGHT."
I'M HOMER SIMPSON, SAFETY INSPECTOR OF THE SPRINGFIELD NUCLEAR POWER-PLANT, THE PLANT THAT POWERS YOUR DREAMS.
WITH MR. BURNS AND MR. SMITHERS ON VACATION IT'S FALLEN UPON **ME** TO TALK TO YOU ABOUT OUR RECENT POWER OUTAGE.
NUCLEAR POWER IS A FUNNY THING.
AND NUCLEAR ACCIDENTS HAPPEN. ELECTRICITY GOES OUT. OLD LADIES GET TRAPPED IN ELEVATORS.
IN CLOSING, WHAT'RE YOU GONNA DO?
WE'RE SORRY
DUE TO THE POWER FAILURE, A LEVITATING TWO TON METAL SUPERCONDUCTION CUBE CRASHED THROUGH THE FLOOR AND ONTO MY WATER HEATER WHICH EXPLODED WITH THE WATER AND THE DAMAGE AND HEY, HEY, THOSE ARE MY PHOTO ALBUM THINGIES!
PRICELESS MEMORIES.
I CUT BOTH MY HANDS TRYNG TO TEAR UP BILLS WITHOUT MY ELECTRIC SHREDDER!
WE'RE SICK OF YOUR SUBSTAN-DARD SERVICE!
SO, WHAT ARE ***YOU*** GONNA DO ABOUT IT? ***BOYCOTT***?
THAT'S A ***GREAT*** IDEA!
WE'LL ***BOYCOTT!***

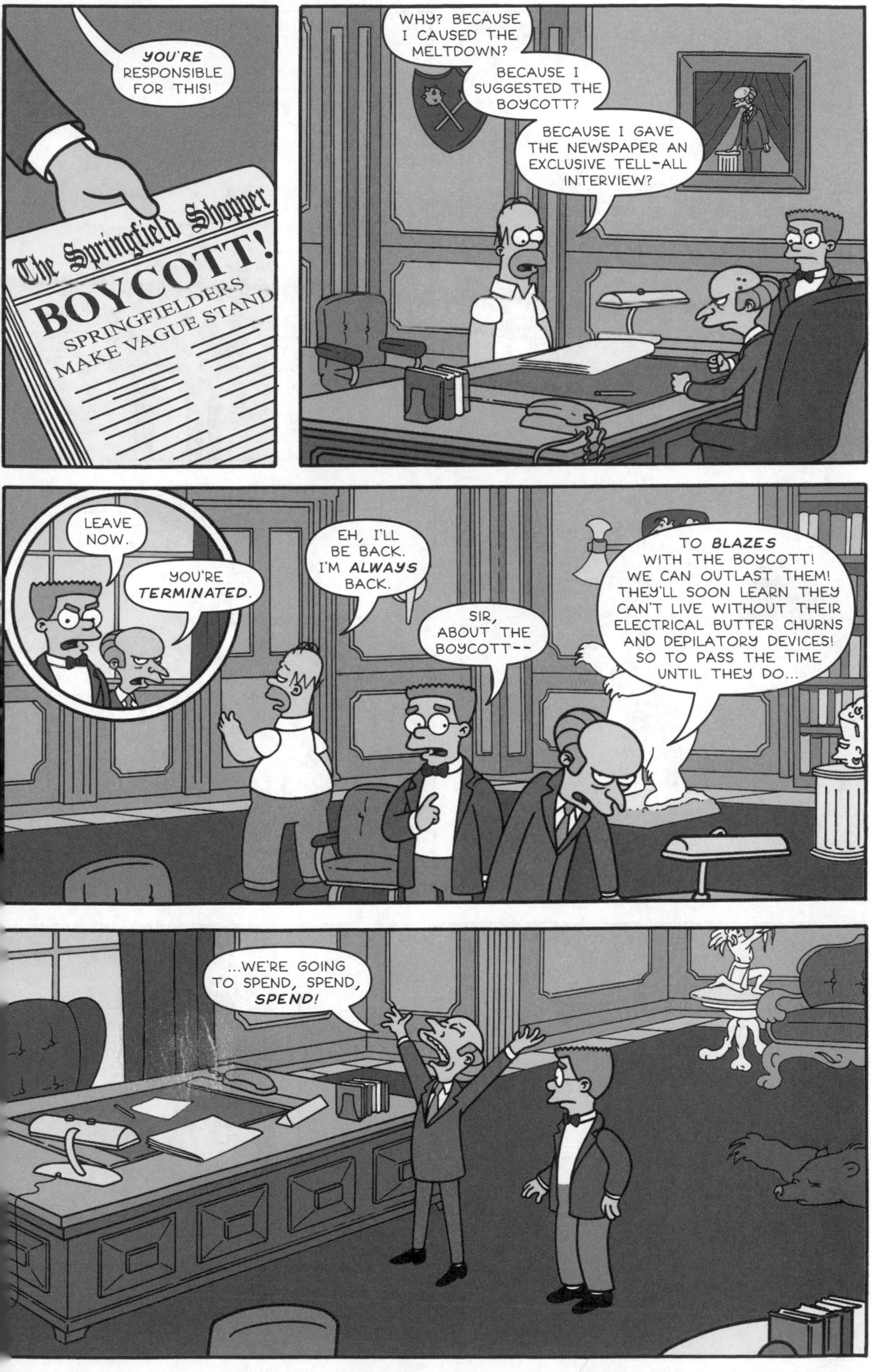
YOU'RE RESPONSIBLE FOR THIS!
The Springfield Shopper
BOYCOTT!
SPRINGFIELDERS MAKE VAGUE STAND
WHY? BECAUSE I CAUSED THE MELTDOWN?
BECAUSE I SUGGESTED THE BOYCOTT?
BECAUSE I GAVE THE NEWSPAPER AN EXCLUSIVE TELL-ALL INTERVIEW?
LEAVE NOW.
YOU'RE TERMINATED.
EH, I'LL BE BACK. I'M ALWAYS BACK.
SIR, ABOUT THE BOYCOTT--
TO BLAZES WITH THE BOYCOTT! WE CAN OUTLAST THEM! THEY'LL SOON LEARN THEY CAN'T LIVE WITHOUT THEIR ELECTRICAL BUTTER CHURNS AND DEPILATORY DEVICES! SO TO PASS THE TIME UNTIL THEY DO...
...WE'RE GOING TO SPEND, SPEND, SPEND!

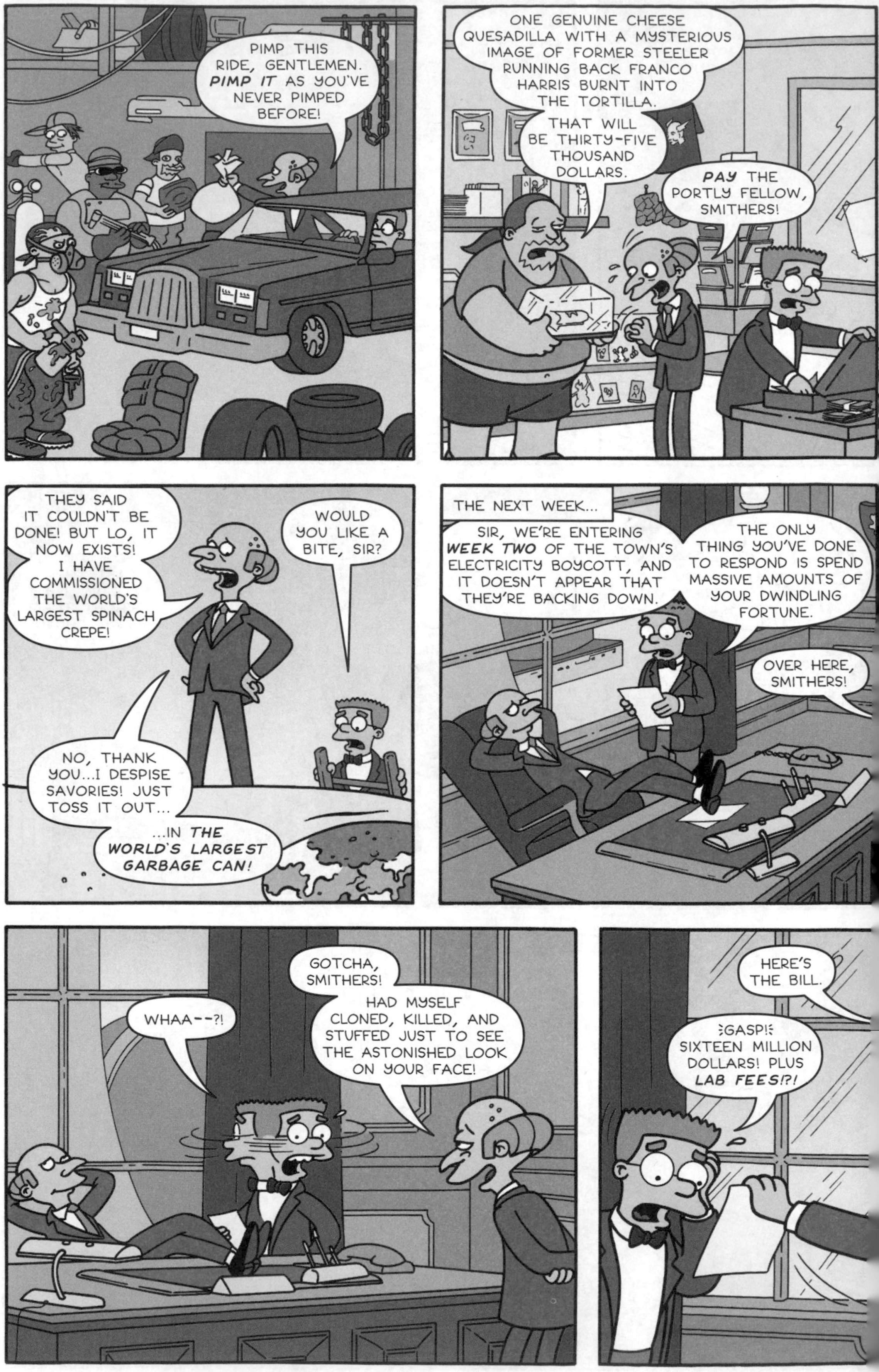
PIMP THIS RIDE, GENTLEMEN. PIMP IT AS YOU'VE NEVER PIMPED BEFORE!
ONE GENUINE CHEESE QUESADILLA WITH A MYSTERIOUS IMAGE OF FORMER STEELER RUNNING BACK FRANCO HARRIS BURNT INTO THE TORTILLA.
THAT WILL BE THIRTY-FIVE THOUSAND DOLLARS.
PAY THE PORTLY FELLOW, SMITHERS!
THEY SAID IT COULDN'T BE DONE! BUT LO, IT NOW EXISTS! I HAVE COMMISSIONED THE WORLD'S LARGEST SPINACH CREPE!
WOULD YOU LIKE A BITE, SIR?
NO, THANK YOU...I DESPISE SAVORIES! JUST TOSS IT OUT...
...IN THE WORLD'S LARGEST GARBAGE CAN!
THE NEXT WEEK...
SIR, WE'RE ENTERING WEEK TWO OF THE TOWN'S ELECTRICITY BOYCOTT, AND IT DOESN'T APPEAR THAT THEY'RE BACKING DOWN.
THE ONLY THING YOU'VE DONE TO RESPOND IS SPEND MASSIVE AMOUNTS OF YOUR DWINDLING FORTUNE.
OVER HERE, SMITHERS!
WHAA--?!
GOTCHA, SMITHERS!
HAD MYSELF CLONED, KILLED, AND STUFFED JUST TO SEE THE ASTONISHED LOOK ON YOUR FACE!
HERE'S THE BILL.
GASP! SIXTEEN MILLION DOLLARS! PLUS LAB FEES!?!

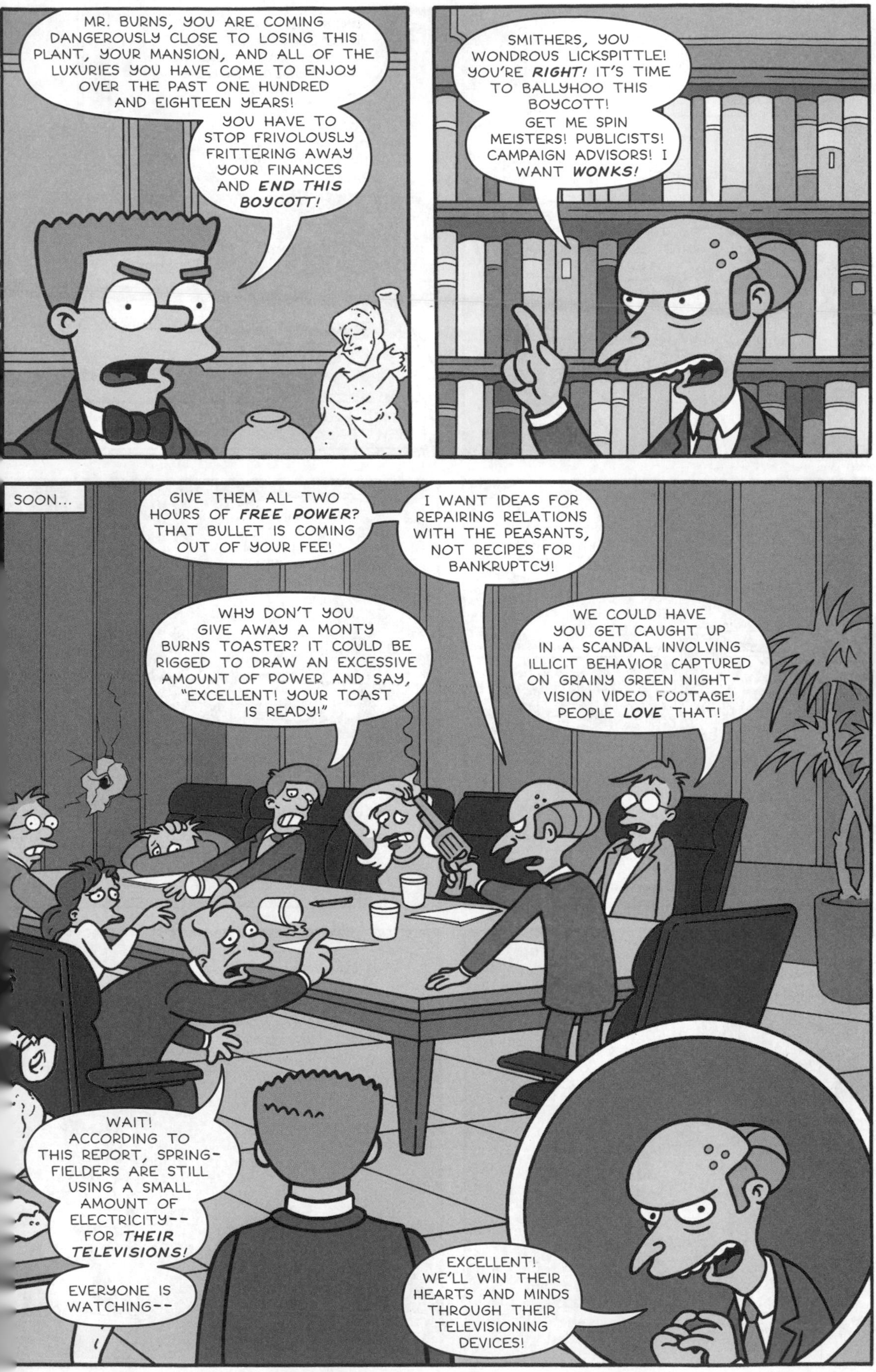
MR. BURNS, YOU ARE COMING DANGEROUSLY CLOSE TO LOSING THIS PLANT, YOUR MANSION, AND ALL OF THE LUXURIES YOU HAVE COME TO ENJOY OVER THE PAST ONE HUNDRED AND EIGHTEEN YEARS!
YOU HAVE TO STOP FRIVOLOUSLY FRITTERING AWAY YOUR FINANCES AND ***END THIS BOYCOTT***!
SMITHERS, YOU WONDROUS LICKSPITTLE! YOU'RE ***RIGHT***! IT'S TIME TO BALLYHOO THIS BOYCOTT!
GET ME SPIN MEISTERS! PUBLICISTS! CAMPAIGN ADVISORS! I WANT ***WONKS!***
SOON...
GIVE THEM ALL TWO HOURS OF ***FREE POWER***? THAT BULLET IS COMING OUT OF YOUR FEE!
I WANT IDEAS FOR REPAIRING RELATIONS WITH THE PEASANTS, NOT RECIPES FOR BANKRUPTCY!
WHY DON'T YOU GIVE AWAY A MONTY BURNS TOASTER? IT COULD BE RIGGED TO DRAW AN EXCESSIVE AMOUNT OF POWER AND SAY, "EXCELLENT! YOUR TOAST IS READY!"
WE COULD HAVE YOU GET CAUGHT UP IN A SCANDAL INVOLVING ILLICIT BEHAVIOR CAPTURED ON GRAINY GREEN NIGHT-VISION VIDEO FOOTAGE! PEOPLE ***LOVE*** THAT!
WAIT! ACCORDING TO THIS REPORT, SPRING-FIELDERS ARE STILL USING A SMALL AMOUNT OF ELECTRICITY-- FOR ***THEIR TELEVISIONS!***
EVERYONE IS WATCHING--
EXCELLENT! WE'LL WIN THEIR HEARTS AND MINDS THROUGH THEIR TELEVISIONING DEVICES!

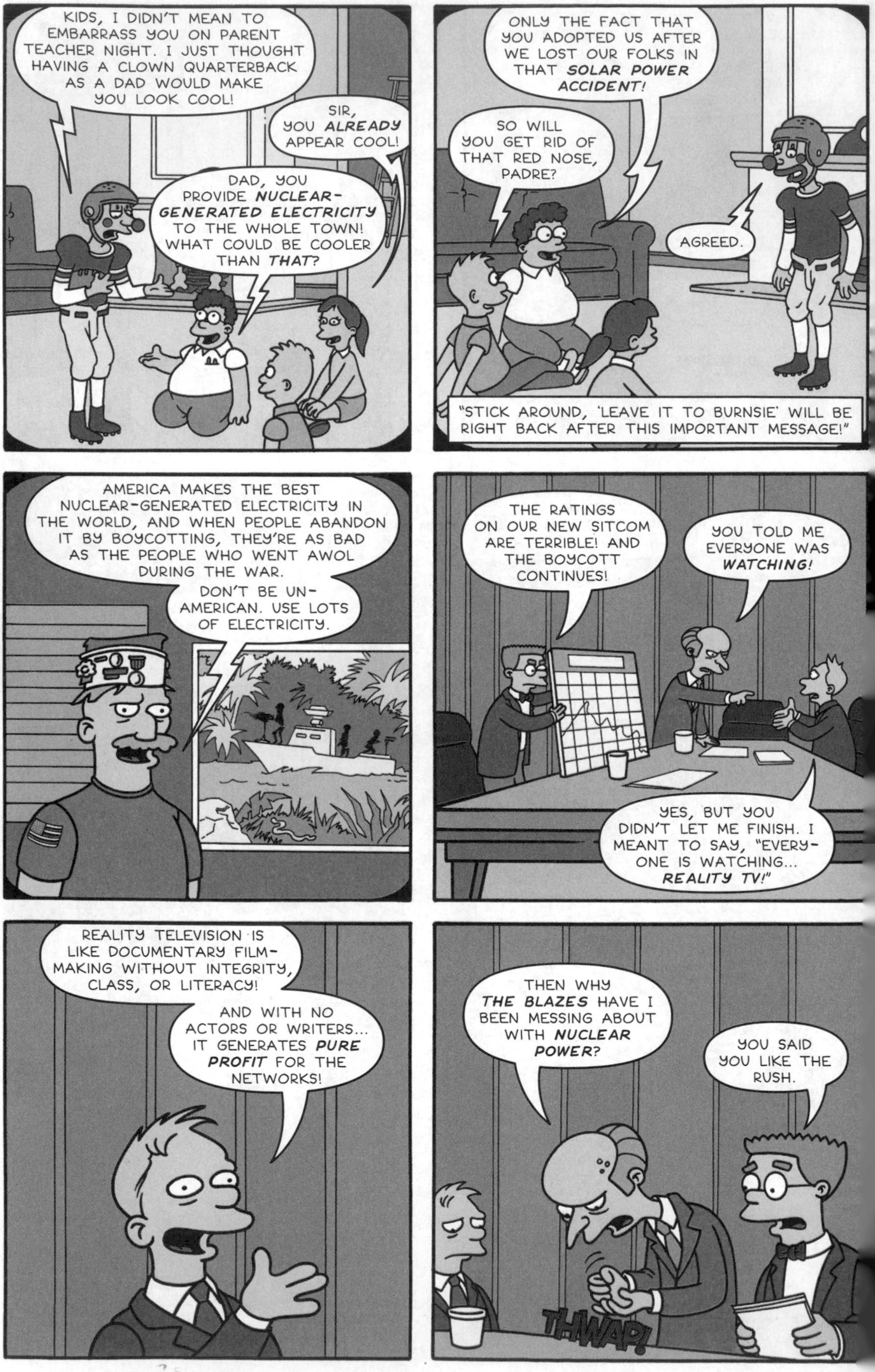
KIDS, I DIDN'T MEAN TO EMBARRASS YOU ON PARENT TEACHER NIGHT. I JUST THOUGHT HAVING A CLOWN QUARTERBACK AS A DAD WOULD MAKE YOU LOOK COOL!
SIR, YOU ALREADY APPEAR COOL!
DAD, YOU PROVIDE NUCLEAR-GENERATED ELECTRICITY TO THE WHOLE TOWN! WHAT COULD BE COOLER THAN THAT?
ONLY THE FACT THAT YOU ADOPTED US AFTER WE LOST OUR FOLKS IN THAT SOLAR POWER ACCIDENT!
SO WILL YOU GET RID OF THAT RED NOSE, PADRE?
AGREED.
"STICK AROUND, 'LEAVE IT TO BURNSIE' WILL BE RIGHT BACK AFTER THIS IMPORTANT MESSAGE!"
AMERICA MAKES THE BEST NUCLEAR-GENERATED ELECTRICITY IN THE WORLD, AND WHEN PEOPLE ABANDON IT BY BOYCOTTING, THEY'RE AS BAD AS THE PEOPLE WHO WENT AWOL DURING THE WAR.
DON'T BE UN-AMERICAN. USE LOTS OF ELECTRICITY.
THE RATINGS ON OUR NEW SITCOM ARE TERRIBLE! AND THE BOYCOTT CONTINUES!
YOU TOLD ME EVERYONE WAS WATCHING!
YES, BUT YOU DIDN'T LET ME FINISH. I MEANT TO SAY, "EVERYONE IS WATCHING... REALITY TV!"
REALITY TELEVISION IS LIKE DOCUMENTARY FILM-MAKING WITHOUT INTEGRITY, CLASS, OR LITERACY!
AND WITH NO ACTORS OR WRITERS... IT GENERATES PURE PROFIT FOR THE NETWORKS!
THEN WHY THE BLAZES HAVE I BEEN MESSING ABOUT WITH NUCLEAR POWER?
YOU SAID YOU LIKE THE RUSH.
THWAP!

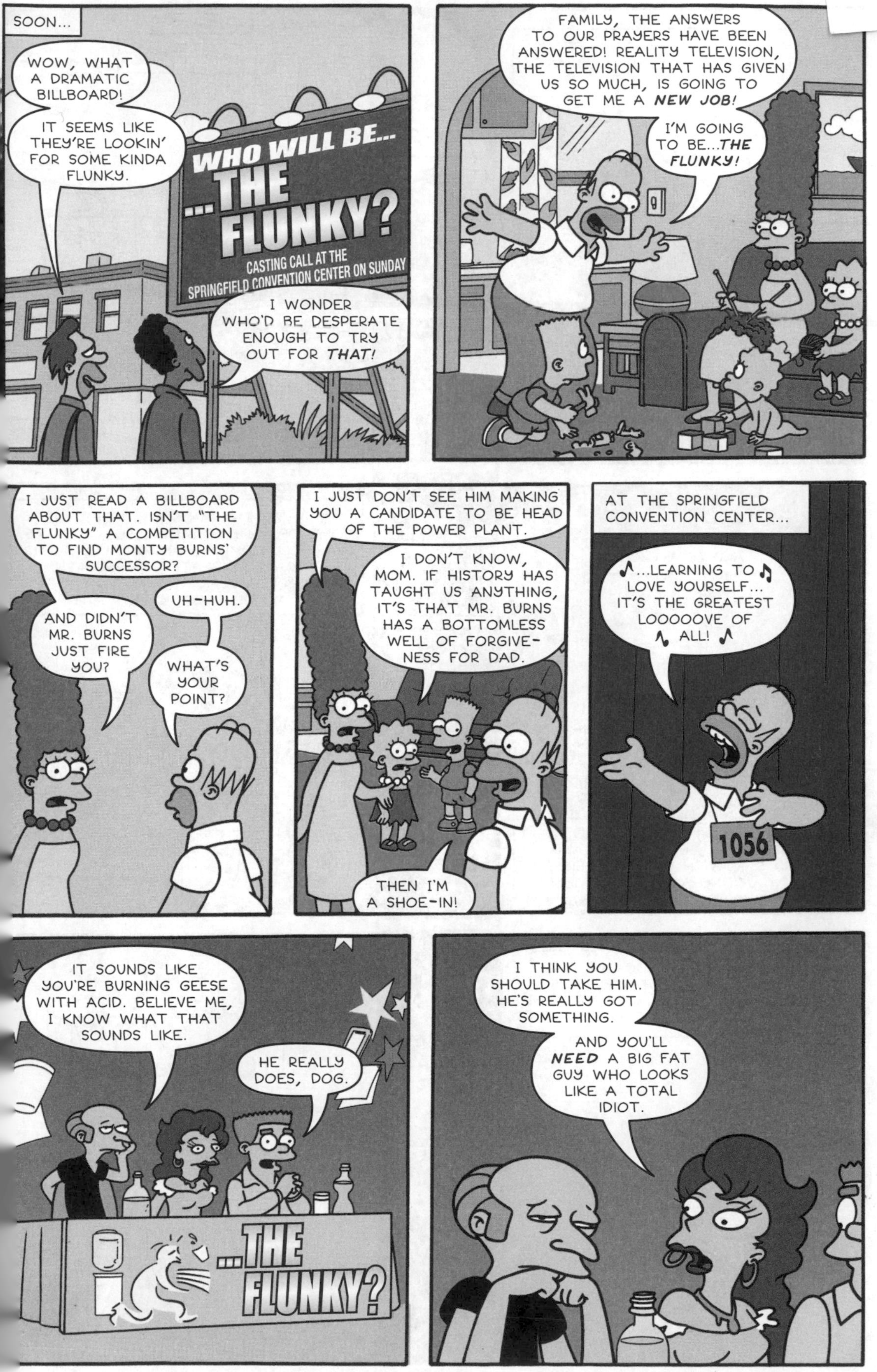
SOON...
WOW, WHAT A DRAMATIC BILLBOARD!
IT SEEMS LIKE THEY'RE LOOKIN' FOR SOME KINDA FLUNKY.
WHO WILL BE... ...THE FLUNKY?
CASTING CALL AT THE SPRINGFIELD CONVENTION CENTER ON SUNDAY
I WONDER WHO'D BE DESPERATE ENOUGH TO TRY OUT FOR THAT!
FAMILY, THE ANSWERS TO OUR PRAYERS HAVE BEEN ANSWERED! REALITY TELEVISION, THE TELEVISION THAT HAS GIVEN US SO MUCH, IS GOING TO GET ME A NEW JOB!
I'M GOING TO BE...THE FLUNKY!
I JUST READ A BILLBOARD ABOUT THAT. ISN'T "THE FLUNKY" A COMPETITION TO FIND MONTY BURNS' SUCCESSOR?
UH-HUH.
AND DIDN'T MR. BURNS JUST FIRE YOU?
WHAT'S YOUR POINT?
I JUST DON'T SEE HIM MAKING YOU A CANDIDATE TO BE HEAD OF THE POWER PLANT.
I DON'T KNOW, MOM. IF HISTORY HAS TAUGHT US ANYTHING, IT'S THAT MR. BURNS HAS A BOTTOMLESS WELL OF FORGIVE-NESS FOR DAD.
THEN I'M A SHOE-IN!
AT THE SPRINGFIELD CONVENTION CENTER...
♪ ...LEARNING TO ♫ LOVE YOURSELF... IT'S THE GREATEST LOOOOOVE OF ♪ ALL! ♪
1056
IT SOUNDS LIKE YOU'RE BURNING GEESE WITH ACID. BELIEVE ME, I KNOW WHAT THAT SOUNDS LIKE.
HE REALLY DOES, DOG.
...THE FLUNKY?
I THINK YOU SHOULD TAKE HIM. HE'S REALLY GOT SOMETHING.
AND YOU'LL NEED A BIG FAT GUY WHO LOOKS LIKE A TOTAL IDIOT.

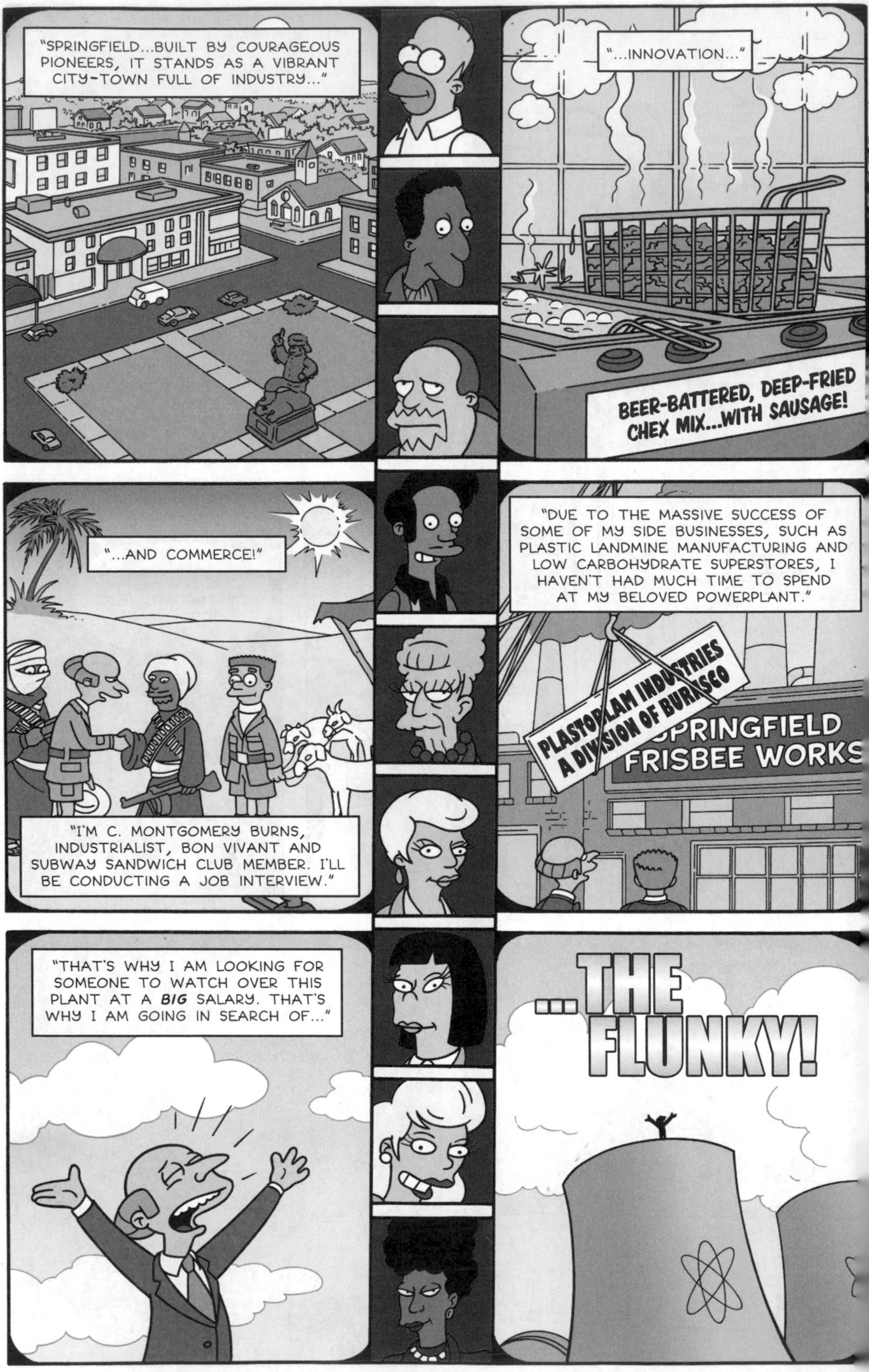
"SPRINGFIELD...BUILT BY COURAGEOUS PIONEERS, IT STANDS AS A VIBRANT CITY-TOWN FULL OF INDUSTRY..."
"...INNOVATION..."
BEER-BATTERED, DEEP-FRIED CHEX MIX...WITH SAUSAGE!
"...AND COMMERCE!"
"I'M C. MONTGOMERY BURNS, INDUSTRIALIST, BON VIVANT AND SUBWAY SANDWICH CLUB MEMBER. I'LL BE CONDUCTING A JOB INTERVIEW."
"DUE TO THE MASSIVE SUCCESS OF SOME OF MY SIDE BUSINESSES, SUCH AS PLASTIC LANDMINE MANUFACTURING AND LOW CARBOHYDRATE SUPERSTORES, I HAVEN'T HAD MUCH TIME TO SPEND AT MY BELOVED POWERPLANT."
PLASTOBLAM INDUSTRIES A DIVISION OF BURNSCO
SPRINGFIELD FRISBEE WORKS
"THAT'S WHY I AM LOOKING FOR SOMEONE TO WATCH OVER THIS PLANT AT A *BIG* SALARY. THAT'S WHY I AM GOING IN SEARCH OF..."
...THE FLUNKY!

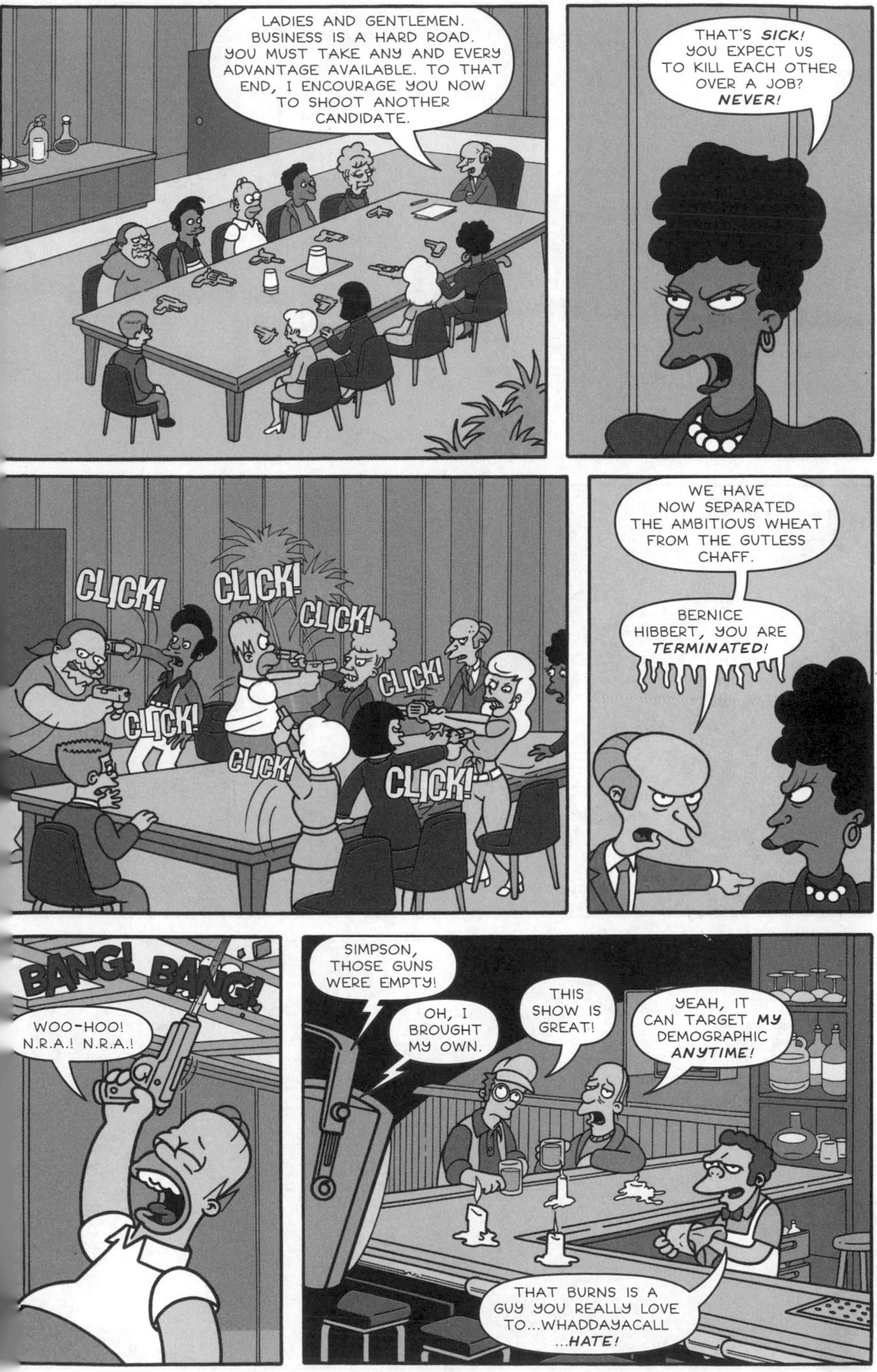

LADIES AND GENTLEMEN. BUSINESS IS A HARD ROAD. YOU MUST TAKE ANY AND EVERY ADVANTAGE AVAILABLE. TO THAT END, I ENCOURAGE YOU NOW TO SHOOT ANOTHER CANDIDATE.
THAT'S SICK! YOU EXPECT US TO KILL EACH OTHER OVER A JOB? NEVER!
CLICK!
CLICK!
CLICK!
CLICK!
CLICK!
CLICK!
CLICK!
WE HAVE NOW SEPARATED THE AMBITIOUS WHEAT FROM THE GUTLESS CHAFF.
BERNICE HIBBERT, YOU ARE TERMINATED!
BANG! BANG!
WOO-HOO! N.R.A.! N.R.A.!
SIMPSON, THOSE GUNS WERE EMPTY!
OH, I BROUGHT MY OWN.
THIS SHOW IS GREAT!
YEAH, IT CAN TARGET MY DEMOGRAPHIC ANYTIME!
THAT BURNS IS A GUY YOU REALLY LOVE TO...WHADDAYACALL ...HATE!

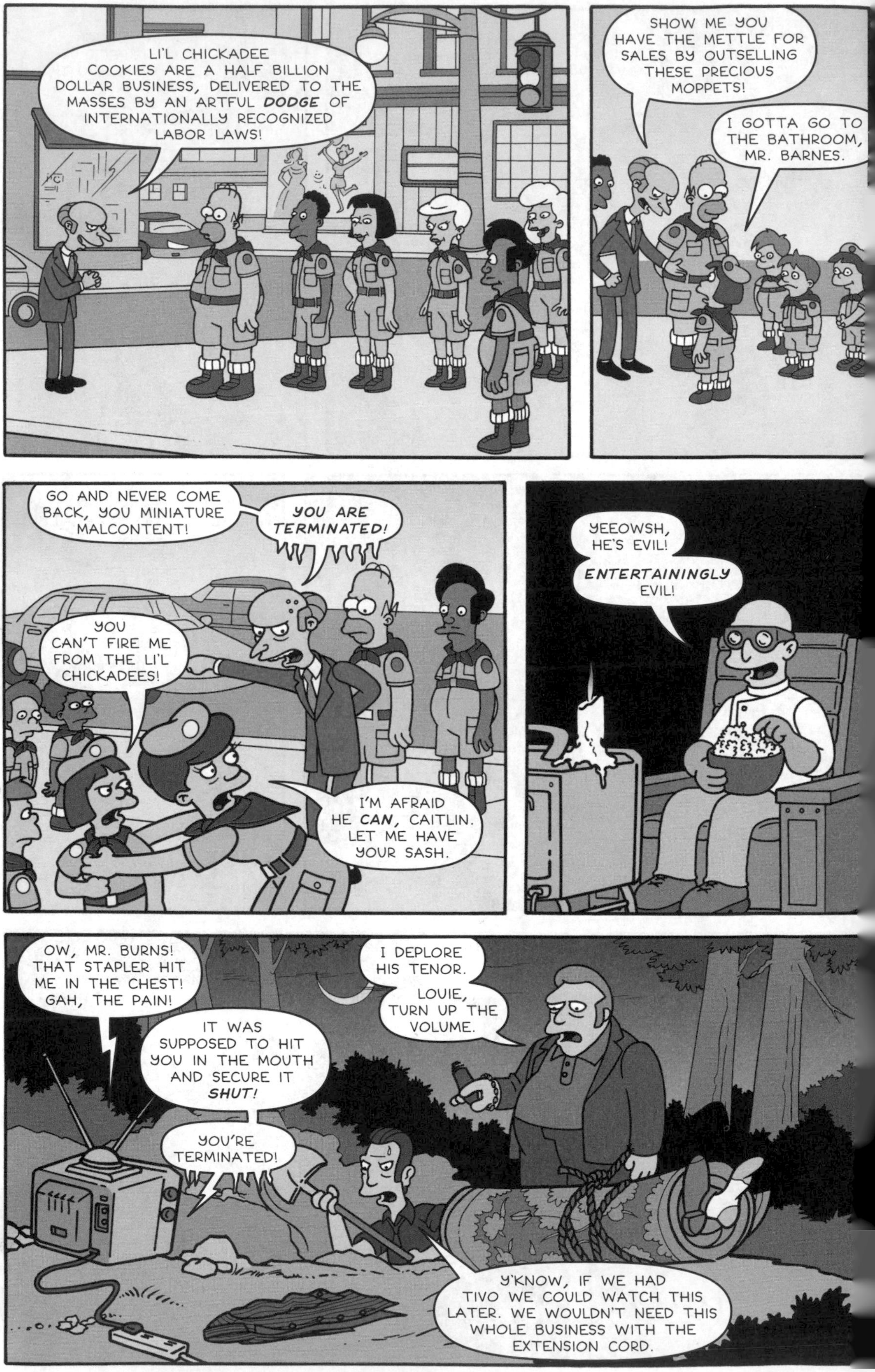
LI'L CHICKADEE COOKIES ARE A HALF BILLION DOLLAR BUSINESS, DELIVERED TO THE MASSES BY AN ARTFUL DODGE OF INTERNATIONALLY RECOGNIZED LABOR LAWS!
SHOW ME YOU HAVE THE METTLE FOR SALES BY OUTSELLING THESE PRECIOUS MOPPETS!
I GOTTA GO TO THE BATHROOM, MR. BARNES.
GO AND NEVER COME BACK, YOU MINIATURE MALCONTENT!
YOU ARE TERMINATED!
YOU CAN'T FIRE ME FROM THE LI'L CHICKADEES!
I'M AFRAID HE CAN, CAITLIN. LET ME HAVE YOUR SASH.
YEEOWSH, HE'S EVIL!
ENTERTAININGLY EVIL!
OW, MR. BURNS! THAT STAPLER HIT ME IN THE CHEST! GAH, THE PAIN!
IT WAS SUPPOSED TO HIT YOU IN THE MOUTH AND SECURE IT SHUT!
YOU'RE TERMINATED!
I DEPLORE HIS TENOR.
LOUIE, TURN UP THE VOLUME.
Y'KNOW, IF WE HAD TIVO WE COULD WATCH THIS LATER. WE WOULDN'T NEED THIS WHOLE BUSINESS WITH THE EXTENSION CORD.

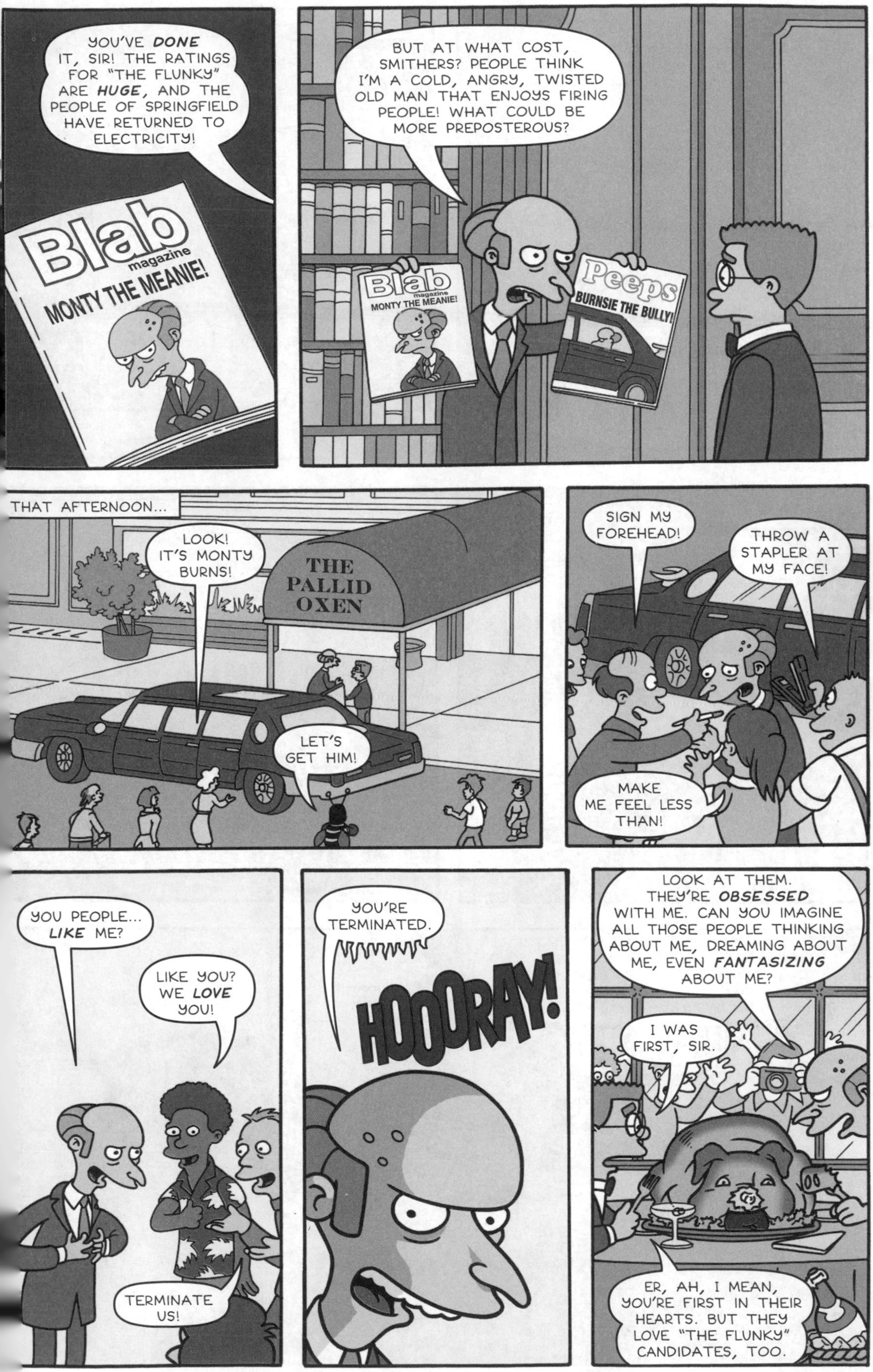
YOU'VE DONE IT, SIR! THE RATINGS FOR "THE FLUNKY" ARE HUGE, AND THE PEOPLE OF SPRINGFIELD HAVE RETURNED TO ELECTRICITY!
Blab magazine
MONTY THE MEANIE!
BUT AT WHAT COST, SMITHERS? PEOPLE THINK I'M A COLD, ANGRY, TWISTED OLD MAN THAT ENJOYS FIRING PEOPLE! WHAT COULD BE MORE PREPOSTEROUS?
Blab magazine
MONTY THE MEANIE!
Peeps
BURNSIE THE BULLY!
THAT AFTERNOON...
LOOK! IT'S MONTY BURNS!
THE PALLID OXEN
LET'S GET HIM!
SIGN MY FOREHEAD!
THROW A STAPLER AT MY FACE!
MAKE ME FEEL LESS THAN!
YOU PEOPLE... LIKE ME?
LIKE YOU? WE LOVE YOU!
TERMINATE US!
YOU'RE TERMINATED.
HOOORAY!
LOOK AT THEM. THEY'RE OBSESSED WITH ME. CAN YOU IMAGINE ALL THOSE PEOPLE THINKING ABOUT ME, DREAMING ABOUT ME, EVEN FANTASIZING ABOUT ME?
I WAS FIRST, SIR.
ER, AH, I MEAN, YOU'RE FIRST IN THEIR HEARTS. BUT THEY LOVE "THE FLUNKY" CANDIDATES, TOO.

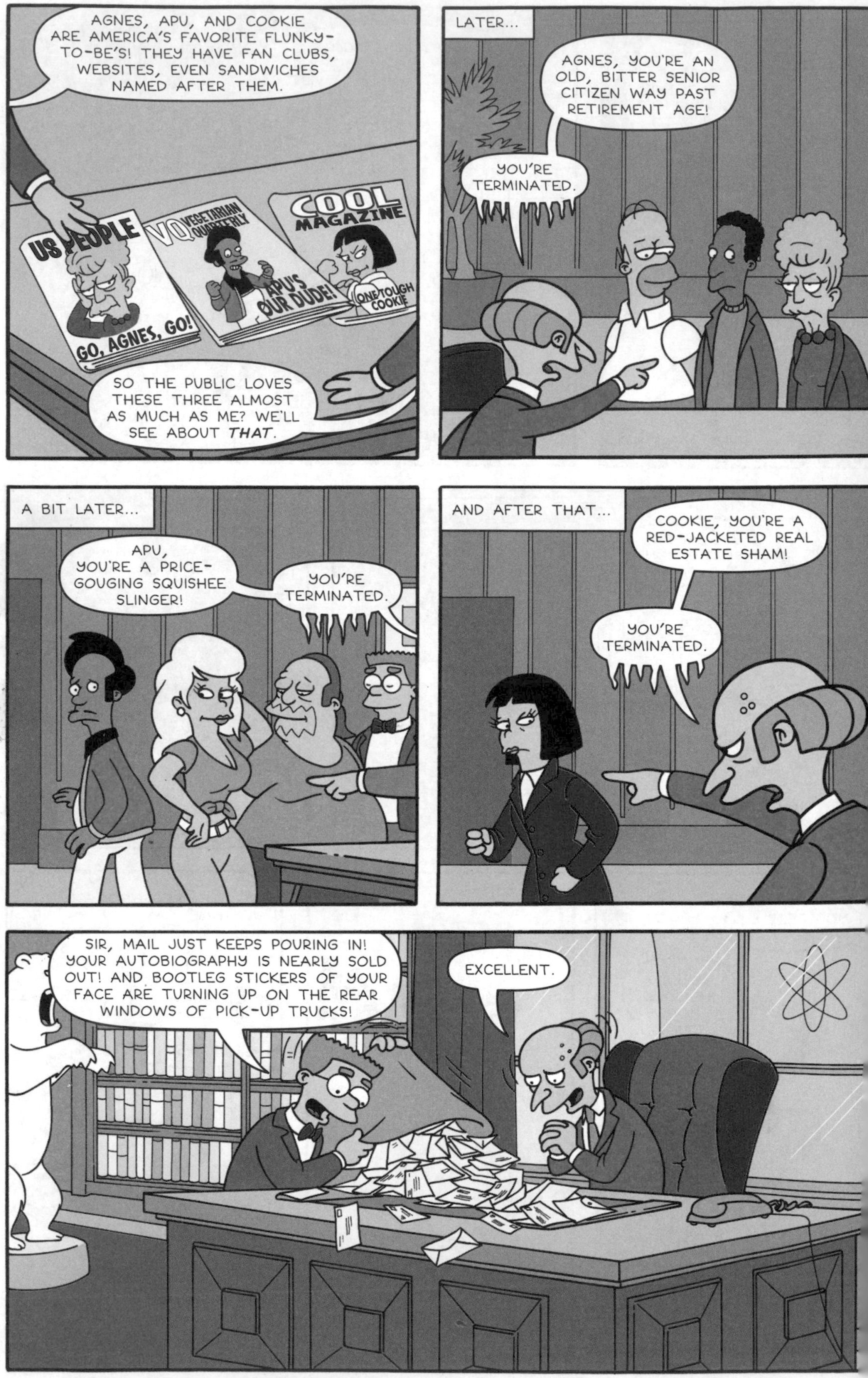
AGNES, APU, AND COOKIE ARE AMERICA'S FAVORITE FLUNKY-TO-BE'S! THEY HAVE FAN CLUBS, WEBSITES, EVEN SANDWICHES NAMED AFTER THEM.
US PEOPLE
GO, AGNES, GO!
VQ VEGETARIAN QUARTERLY
APU'S OUR DUDE!
COOL MAGAZINE
ONE TOUGH COOKIE
SO THE PUBLIC LOVES THESE THREE ALMOST AS MUCH AS ME? WE'LL SEE ABOUT *THAT*.
LATER...
AGNES, YOU'RE AN OLD, BITTER SENIOR CITIZEN WAY PAST RETIREMENT AGE!
YOU'RE TERMINATED.
A BIT LATER...
APU, YOU'RE A PRICE-GOUGING SQUISHEE SLINGER!
YOU'RE TERMINATED.
AND AFTER THAT...
COOKIE, YOU'RE A RED-JACKETED REAL ESTATE SHAM!
YOU'RE TERMINATED.
SIR, MAIL JUST KEEPS POURING IN! YOUR AUTOBIOGRAPHY IS NEARLY SOLD OUT! AND BOOTLEG STICKERS OF YOUR FACE ARE TURNING UP ON THE REAR WINDOWS OF PICK-UP TRUCKS!
EXCELLENT.

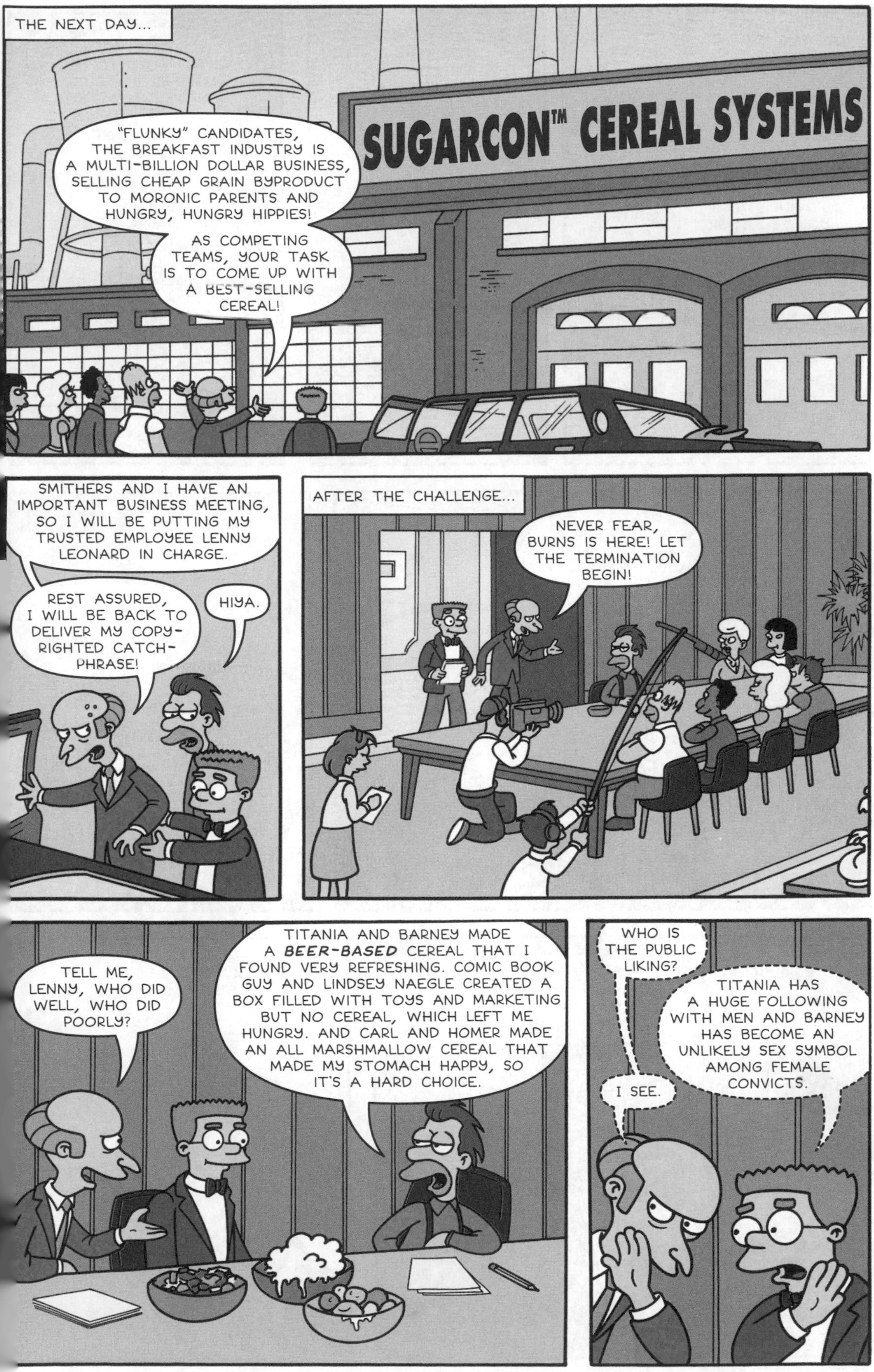
THE NEXT DAY...
SUGARCON™ CEREAL SYSTEMS
"FLUNKY" CANDIDATES, THE BREAKFAST INDUSTRY IS A MULTI-BILLION DOLLAR BUSINESS, SELLING CHEAP GRAIN BYPRODUCT TO MORONIC PARENTS AND HUNGRY, HUNGRY HIPPIES!
AS COMPETING TEAMS, YOUR TASK IS TO COME UP WITH A BEST-SELLING CEREAL!
SMITHERS AND I HAVE AN IMPORTANT BUSINESS MEETING, SO I WILL BE PUTTING MY TRUSTED EMPLOYEE LENNY LEONARD IN CHARGE.
REST ASSURED, I WILL BE BACK TO DELIVER MY COPY-RIGHTED CATCH-PHRASE!
HIYA.
AFTER THE CHALLENGE...
NEVER FEAR, BURNS IS HERE! LET THE TERMINATION BEGIN!
TELL ME, LENNY, WHO DID WELL, WHO DID POORLY?
TITANIA AND BARNEY MADE A ***BEER-BASED*** CEREAL THAT I FOUND VERY REFRESHING. COMIC BOOK GUY AND LINDSEY NAEGLE CREATED A BOX FILLED WITH TOYS AND MARKETING BUT NO CEREAL, WHICH LEFT ME HUNGRY. AND CARL AND HOMER MADE AN ALL MARSHMALLOW CEREAL THAT MADE MY STOMACH HAPPY, SO IT'S A HARD CHOICE.
WHO IS THE PUBLIC LIKING?
TITANIA HAS A HUGE FOLLOWING WITH MEN AND BARNEY HAS BECOME AN UNLIKELY SEX SYMBOL AMONG FEMALE CONVICTS.
I SEE.

TITANIA, YOUR *BATHING SUIT* IS SMARTER THAN YOU!

YOU'RE TERMINATED!

BARNEY, YOU ONLY EXCEL AT RELEASING CARBON DIOXIDE!

YOU'RE TERMINATED!

LINDSEY NAEGLE, I SUGGEST YOU GO OUT AND MARKET YOURSELF...FOR A NEW JOB.

YOU'RE TERMINATED!

AND, AS FOR THE PORTLY MAN NERD...YOU'RE TERMINATED BUT WILL RECEIVE A FULL BOX OF BURNSBARS!

REMEMBER, WHEN YOU NEED FUEL TO GO, TRY A *BURNSBAR*, THE ENERGY BAR THAT TELLS YOUR HUNGER, "YOU'RE TERMINATED!"

BURNSBAR

IT WILL DISPLAY NICELY NEXT TO MY UNOPENED CASE OF SAN DIEGO CHICKEN BUBBLE GUM!

BURNSB

WELL THAT'S THAT. I BELIEVE I HAVE A COMMERCIAL SHOOT SCHEDULED FOR THE NEW BURNSCARD, THE CARD THAT CHARGES TWICE THE INTEREST, BUT HAS *MY FACE* ON IT!

SIR, YOU'VE JUST WHITTLED THE CANDIDATE POOL DOWN TO THE FINAL TWO! EITHER CARL CARLSON OR HOMER SIMPSON WILL BE...

...THE FLUNKY!

SUPER BEER CRISP

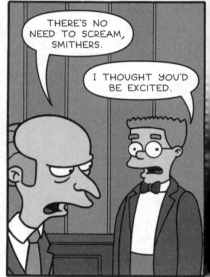

THERE'S NO NEED TO SCREAM, SMITHERS.

I THOUGHT YOU'D BE EXCITED.

ABOUT WHAT?

THE CLIMAX OF YOUR TELEVISION SHOW, SIR. YOU NEED TO WORK UP A LITTLE ENTHUSIASM IF YOU'RE GOING TO HIT THE TALK SHOW CIRCUIT AND PLUG THE FINALE.

TALK SHOWS?

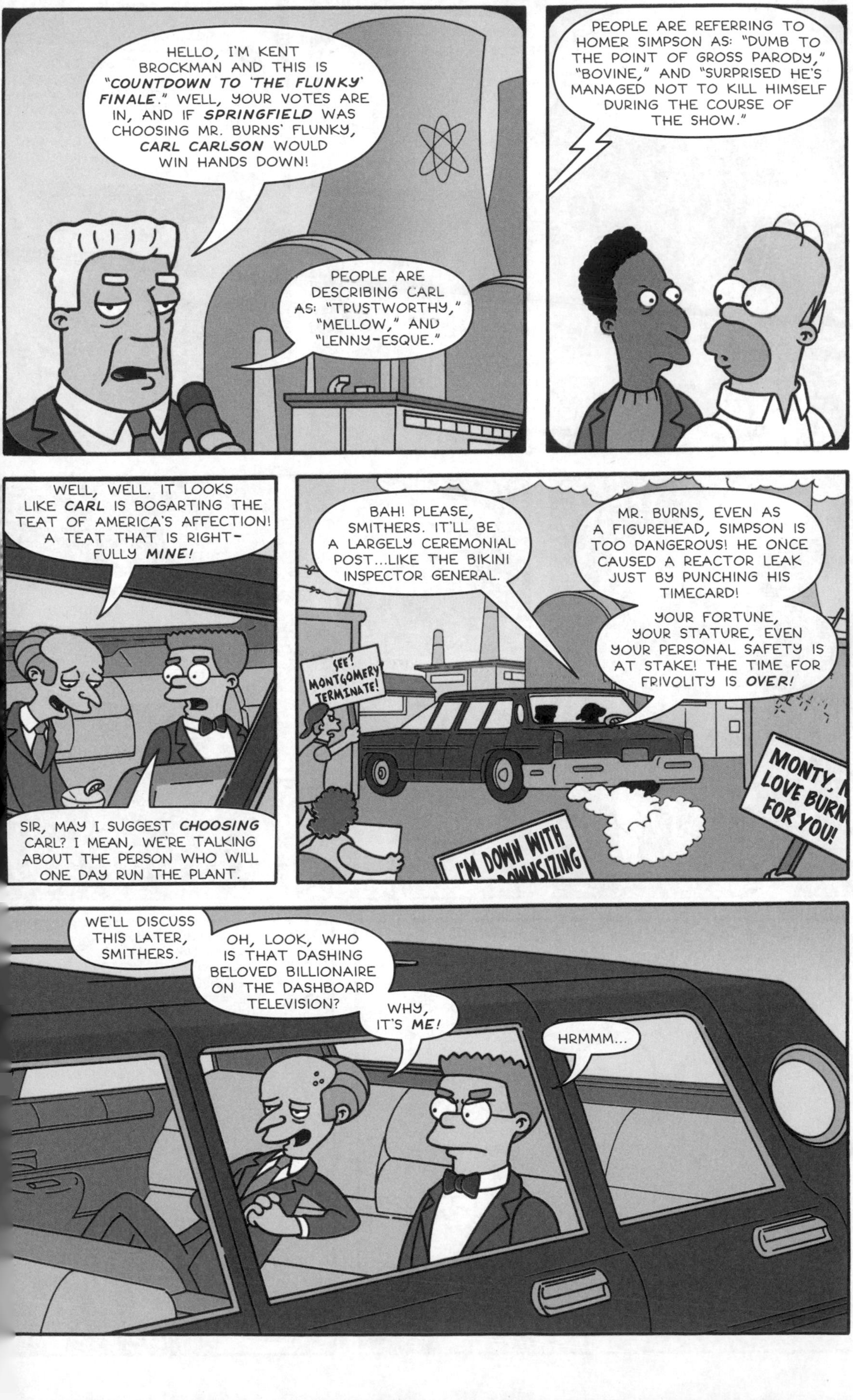
HELLO, I'M KENT BROCKMAN AND THIS IS "COUNTDOWN TO 'THE FLUNKY' FINALE." WELL, YOUR VOTES ARE IN, AND IF SPRINGFIELD WAS CHOOSING MR. BURNS' FLUNKY, CARL CARLSON WOULD WIN HANDS DOWN!
PEOPLE ARE DESCRIBING CARL AS: "TRUSTWORTHY," "MELLOW," AND "LENNY-ESQUE."
PEOPLE ARE REFERRING TO HOMER SIMPSON AS: "DUMB TO THE POINT OF GROSS PARODY," "BOVINE," AND "SURPRISED HE'S MANAGED NOT TO KILL HIMSELF DURING THE COURSE OF THE SHOW."
WELL, WELL. IT LOOKS LIKE CARL IS BOGARTING THE TEAT OF AMERICA'S AFFECTION! A TEAT THAT IS RIGHT-FULLY MINE!
SIR, MAY I SUGGEST CHOOSING CARL? I MEAN, WE'RE TALKING ABOUT THE PERSON WHO WILL ONE DAY RUN THE PLANT.
BAH! PLEASE, SMITHERS. IT'LL BE A LARGELY CEREMONIAL POST...LIKE THE BIKINI INSPECTOR GENERAL.
MR. BURNS, EVEN AS A FIGUREHEAD, SIMPSON IS TOO DANGEROUS! HE ONCE CAUSED A REACTOR LEAK JUST BY PUNCHING HIS TIMECARD!
YOUR FORTUNE, YOUR STATURE, EVEN YOUR PERSONAL SAFETY IS AT STAKE! THE TIME FOR FRIVOLITY IS OVER!
SEE? MONTGOMERY TERMINATE!
I'M DOWN WITH
LOVE BURN
FOR YOU!
WE'LL DISCUSS THIS LATER, SMITHERS.
OH, LOOK, WHO IS THAT DASHING BELOVED BILLIONAIRE ON THE DASHBOARD TELEVISION?
WHY, IT'S ME!
HRMMM...

AT THE FINALE...

...CARL'S TASK WAS TO ORGANIZE THE BIG SPRINGFIELD POLICE CELEBRITY CHARITY SOFTBALL GAME. HE DID A GOOD JOB.

THE BEER WAS REALLY COLD, THERE WAS BRATWURST, KNOCKWURST, SAUERKRAUT, IRISH COFFEE, GUMMY WORMS, AND PLENTY OF SAWDUST.

BANG UP JOB, CARL.

DID HE, SAY...RECRUIT ANY CELEBRITIES?

I, UH, DON'T REMEMBER. I PASSED OUT IN THE FOURTH INNING.

I GOT THAT GUY FROM THE SHOW WITH THE COPS AND ONE FROM THE SHOW WITH THE LAWYERS AND ONE FROM THE SHOW WITH THE DOCTORS AND MR. B OVER THERE, WHO TOLD EVERYONE THE KEG WAS TERMINATED.

IT WAS MY PLEASURE.

KRUSTO, HOW DID HOMER DO?

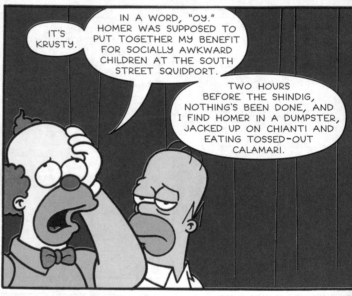

IT'S KRUSTY.

IN A WORD, "OY." HOMER WAS SUPPOSED TO PUT TOGETHER MY BENEFIT FOR SOCIALLY AWKWARD CHILDREN AT THE SOUTH STREET SQUIDPORT.

TWO HOURS BEFORE THE SHINDIG, NOTHING'S BEEN DONE, AND I FIND HOMER IN A DUMPSTER, JACKED UP ON CHIANTI AND EATING TOSSED-OUT CALAMARI.

MY SKIN IS LIKE ICE AND MY BLOOD IS ON FIRE.

HE TOSSED THE BENEFIT TOGETHER IN TWO HOURS AND THEN HE THREW UP ON LINDSEY LOHAN.

GENTLEMEN. THESE DESCRIPTIONS OF HOW THE TASKS WERE COMPLETED HAVE EQUIPPED ME WITH THE KNOWLEDGE I NEED TO MAKE MY FINAL DECISION.

AS TO WHO IS GOING TO RUN MY POWER PLANT...

CARL...

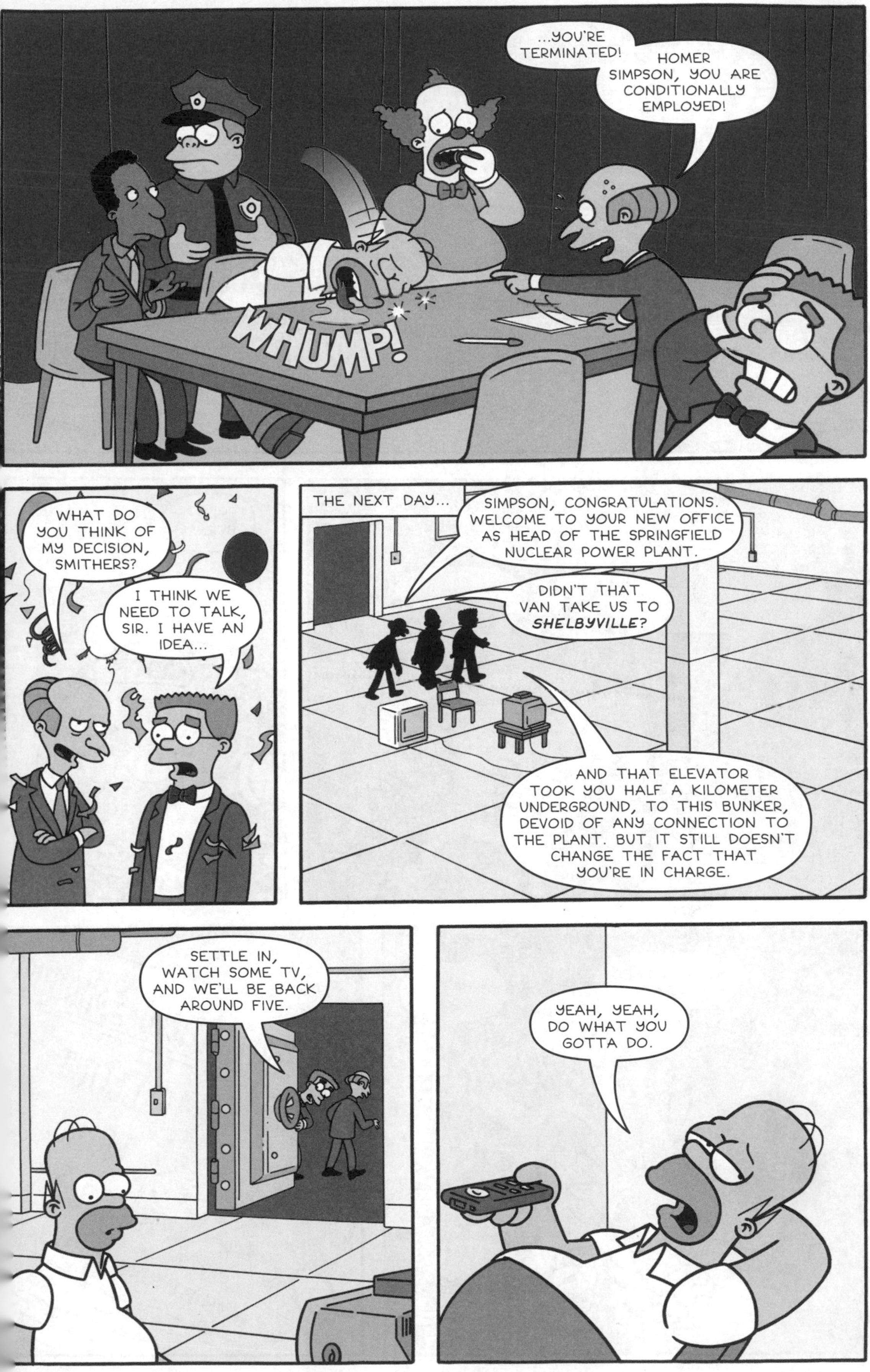
...YOU'RE TERMINATED!
HOMER SIMPSON, YOU ARE CONDITIONALLY EMPLOYED!
WHUMP!
WHAT DO YOU THINK OF MY DECISION, SMITHERS?
I THINK WE NEED TO TALK, SIR. I HAVE AN IDEA...
THE NEXT DAY...
SIMPSON, CONGRATULATIONS. WELCOME TO YOUR NEW OFFICE AS HEAD OF THE SPRINGFIELD NUCLEAR POWER PLANT.
DIDN'T THAT VAN TAKE US TO SHELBYVILLE?
AND THAT ELEVATOR TOOK YOU HALF A KILOMETER UNDERGROUND, TO THIS BUNKER, DEVOID OF ANY CONNECTION TO THE PLANT. BUT IT STILL DOESN'T CHANGE THE FACT THAT YOU'RE IN CHARGE.
SETTLE IN, WATCH SOME TV, AND WE'LL BE BACK AROUND FIVE.
YEAH, YEAH, DO WHAT YOU GOTTA DO.

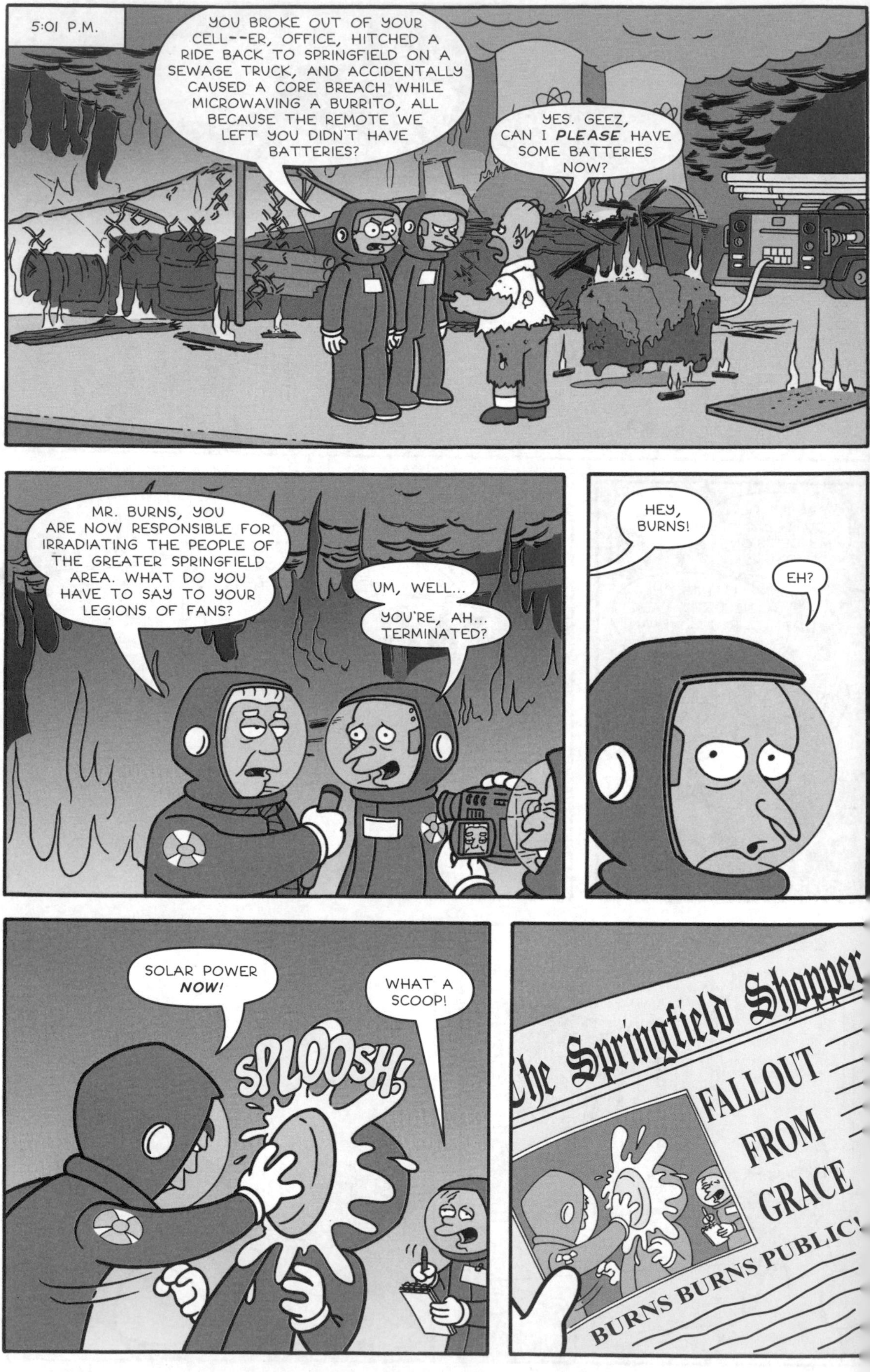
5:01 P.M.
YOU BROKE OUT OF YOUR CELL--ER, OFFICE, HITCHED A RIDE BACK TO SPRINGFIELD ON A SEWAGE TRUCK, AND ACCIDENTALLY CAUSED A CORE BREACH WHILE MICROWAVING A BURRITO, ALL BECAUSE THE REMOTE WE LEFT YOU DIDN'T HAVE BATTERIES?
YES. GEEZ, CAN I ***PLEASE*** HAVE SOME BATTERIES NOW?
MR. BURNS, YOU ARE NOW RESPONSIBLE FOR IRRADIATING THE PEOPLE OF THE GREATER SPRINGFIELD AREA. WHAT DO YOU HAVE TO SAY TO YOUR LEGIONS OF FANS?
UM, WELL...
YOU'RE, AH... TERMINATED?
HEY, BURNS!
EH?
SOLAR POWER ***NOW!***
SPLOOSH!
WHAT A SCOOP!
The Springfield Shopper
FALLOUT FROM GRACE
BURNS BURNS PUBLIC!

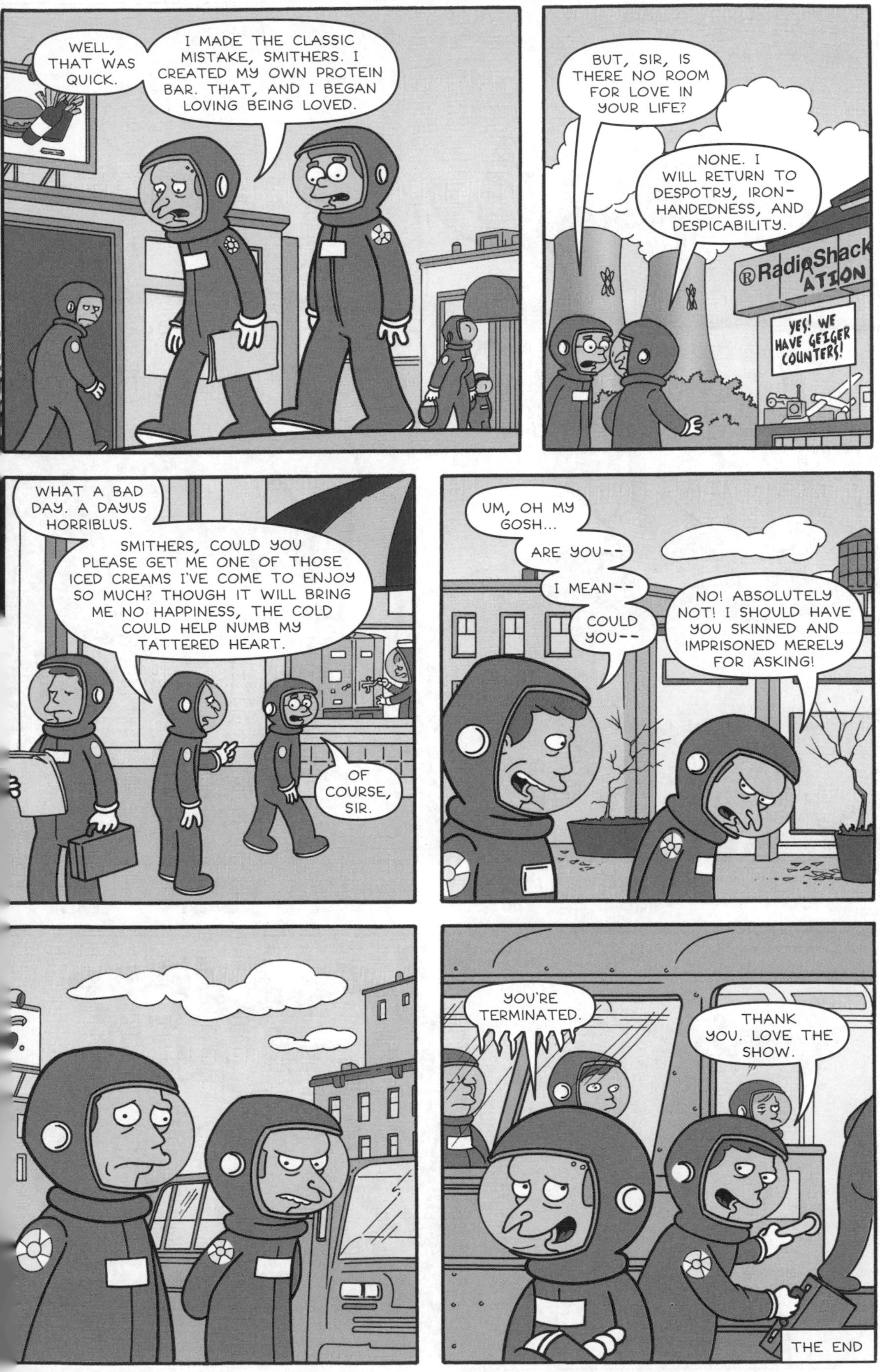
WELL, THAT WAS QUICK.
I MADE THE CLASSIC MISTAKE, SMITHERS. I CREATED MY OWN PROTEIN BAR. THAT, AND I BEGAN LOVING BEING LOVED.
BUT, SIR, IS THERE NO ROOM FOR LOVE IN YOUR LIFE?
NONE. I WILL RETURN TO DESPOTRY, IRON-HANDEDNESS, AND DESPICABILITY.
RadioShack
ATION
YES! WE HAVE GEIGER COUNTERS!
WHAT A BAD DAY. A DAYUS HORRIBLUS.
SMITHERS, COULD YOU PLEASE GET ME ONE OF THOSE ICED CREAMS I'VE COME TO ENJOY SO MUCH? THOUGH IT WILL BRING ME NO HAPPINESS, THE COLD COULD HELP NUMB MY TATTERED HEART.
OF COURSE, SIR.
UM, OH MY GOSH...
ARE YOU--
I MEAN--
COULD YOU--
NO! ABSOLUTELY NOT! I SHOULD HAVE YOU SKINNED AND IMPRISONED MERELY FOR ASKING!
YOU'RE TERMINATED.
THANK YOU. LOVE THE SHOW.
THE END

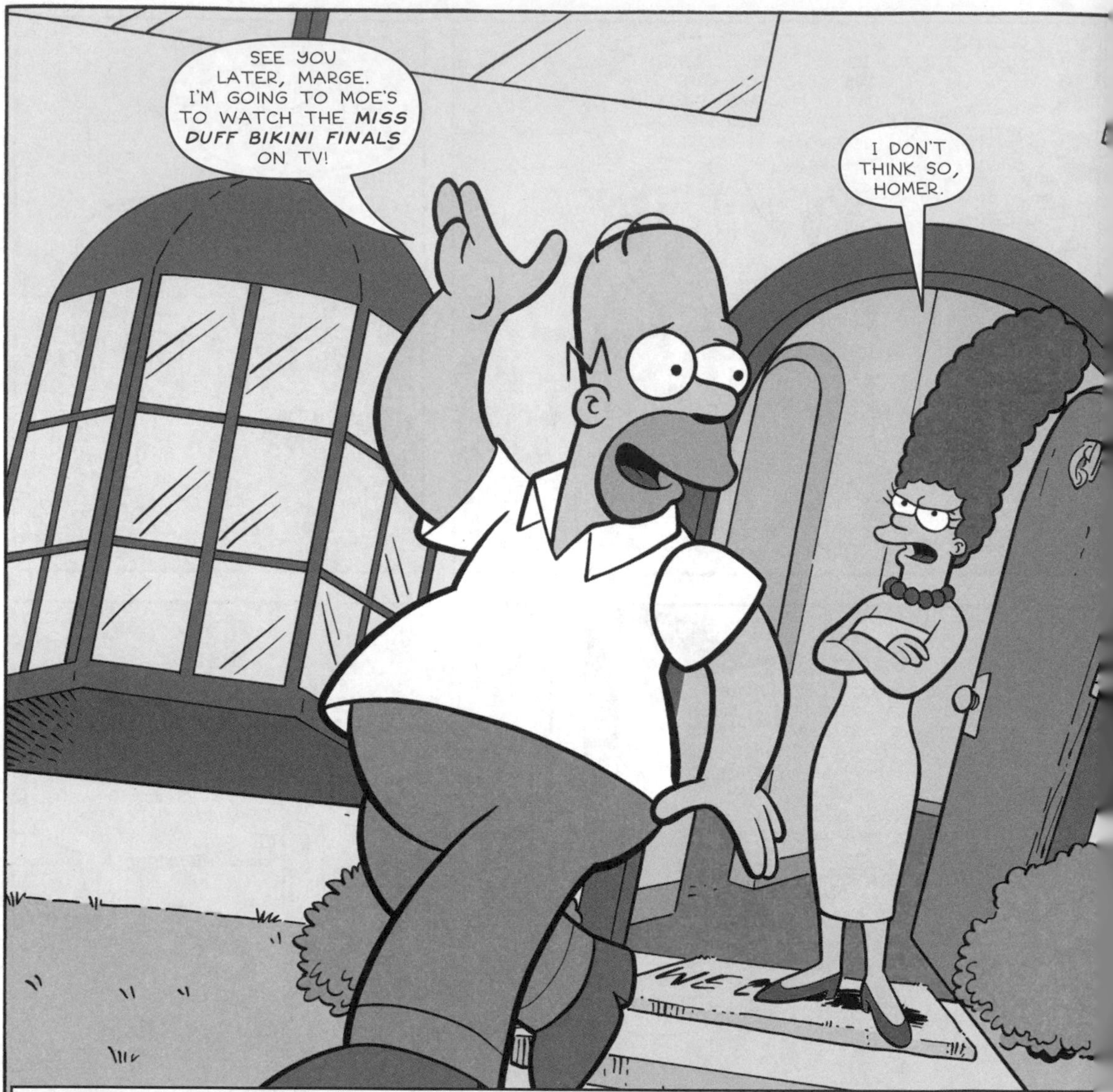

SEE YOU LATER, MARGE. I'M GOING TO MOE'S TO WATCH THE MISS DUFF BIKINI FINALS ON TV!
I DON'T THINK SO, HOMER.

JAMES W. BATES SCRIPT · **JOHN DELANEY** PENCILS · **ANDREW PEPOY** INKS · **ART VILLANUEVA** COLORS · **KAREN BATES** LETTERS · **BILL MORRISON** EDITOR

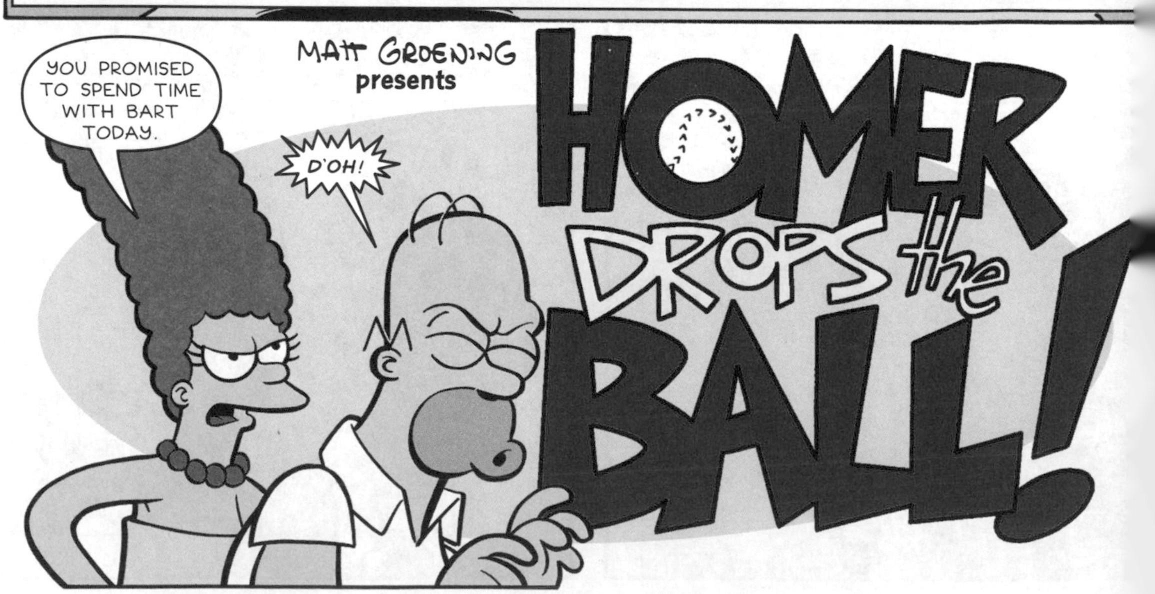

YOU PROMISED TO SPEND TIME WITH BART TODAY.
MATT GROENING presents
D'OH!
HOMER DROPS the BALL!

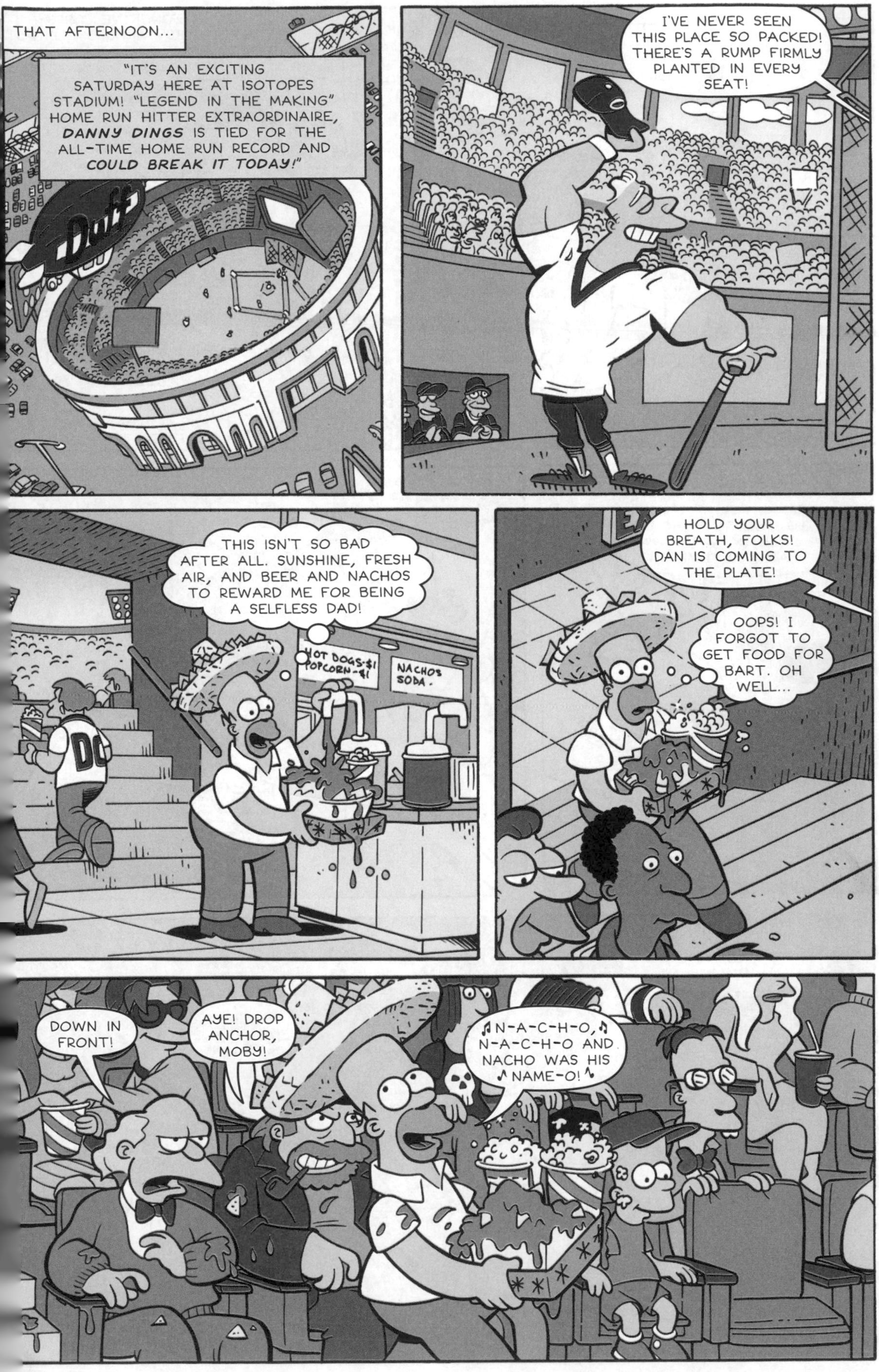
THAT AFTERNOON...
"IT'S AN EXCITING SATURDAY HERE AT ISOTOPES STADIUM! "LEGEND IN THE MAKING" HOME RUN HITTER EXTRAORDINAIRE, DANNY DINGS IS TIED FOR THE ALL-TIME HOME RUN RECORD AND COULD BREAK IT TODAY!"
Duff
I'VE NEVER SEEN THIS PLACE SO PACKED! THERE'S A RUMP FIRMLY PLANTED IN EVERY SEAT!
THIS ISN'T SO BAD AFTER ALL. SUNSHINE, FRESH AIR, AND BEER AND NACHOS TO REWARD ME FOR BEING A SELFLESS DAD!
HOT DOGS-$1 POPCORN-$1
NACHOS SODA
HOLD YOUR BREATH, FOLKS! DAN IS COMING TO THE PLATE!
OOPS! I FORGOT TO GET FOOD FOR BART. OH WELL...
DOWN IN FRONT!
AYE! DROP ANCHOR, MOBY!
♪ N-A-C-H-O, ♪ N-A-C-H-O AND NACHO WAS HIS ♪ NAME-O! ♪

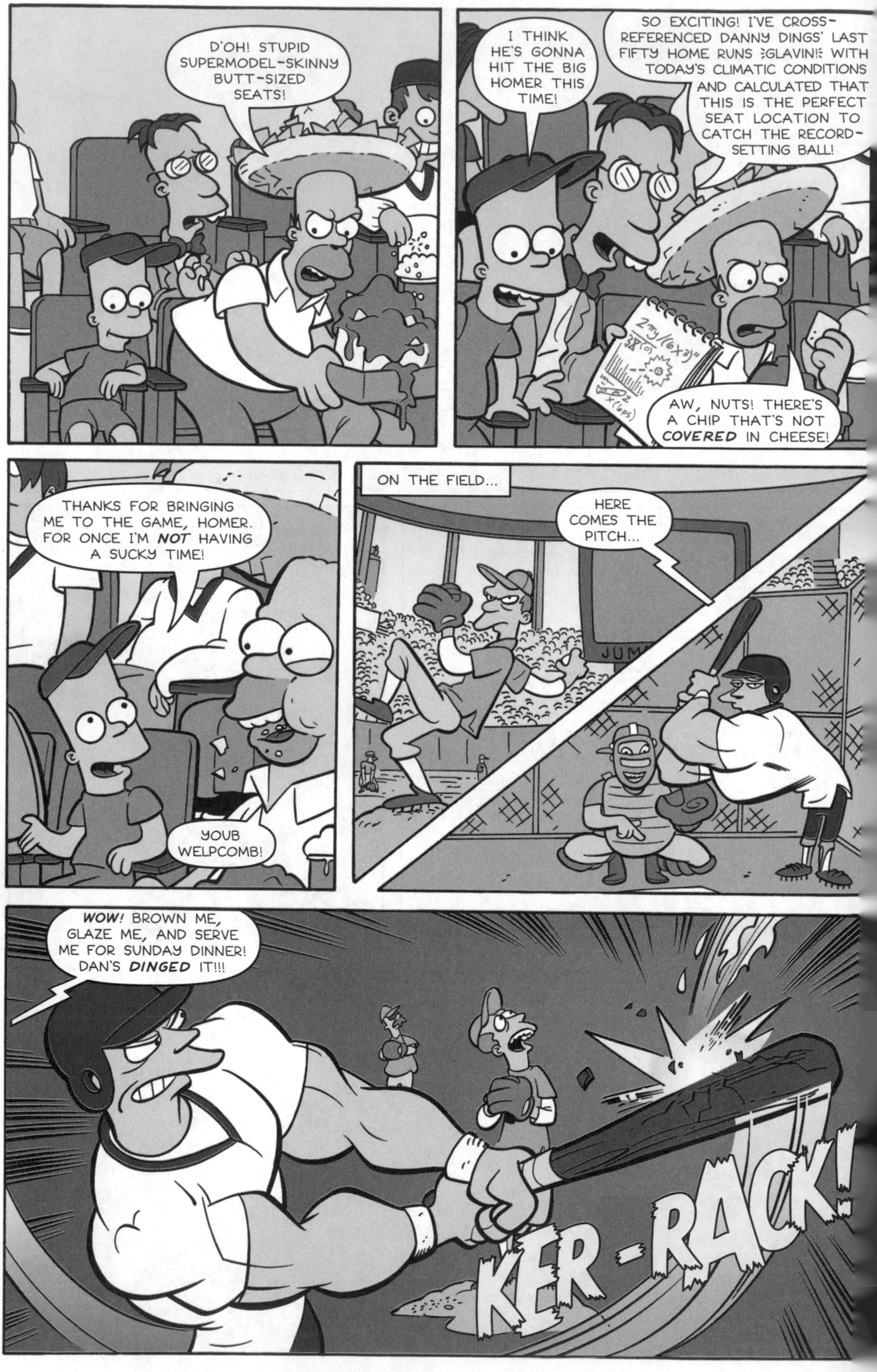

D'OH! STUPID SUPERMODEL-SKINNY BUTT-SIZED SEATS!
I THINK HE'S GONNA HIT THE BIG HOMER THIS TIME!
SO EXCITING! I'VE CROSS-REFERENCED DANNY DINGS' LAST FIFTY HOME RUNS :GLAVIN!: WITH TODAY'S CLIMATIC CONDITIONS AND CALCULATED THAT THIS IS THE PERFECT SEAT LOCATION TO CATCH THE RECORD-SETTING BALL!
AW, NUTS! THERE'S A CHIP THAT'S NOT COVERED IN CHEESE!
THANKS FOR BRINGING ME TO THE GAME, HOMER. FOR ONCE I'M NOT HAVING A SUCKY TIME!
YOUB WELPCOMB!
ON THE FIELD...
HERE COMES THE PITCH...
WOW! BROWN ME, GLAZE ME, AND SERVE ME FOR SUNDAY DINNER! DAN'S DINGED IT!!!
KER-RACK!

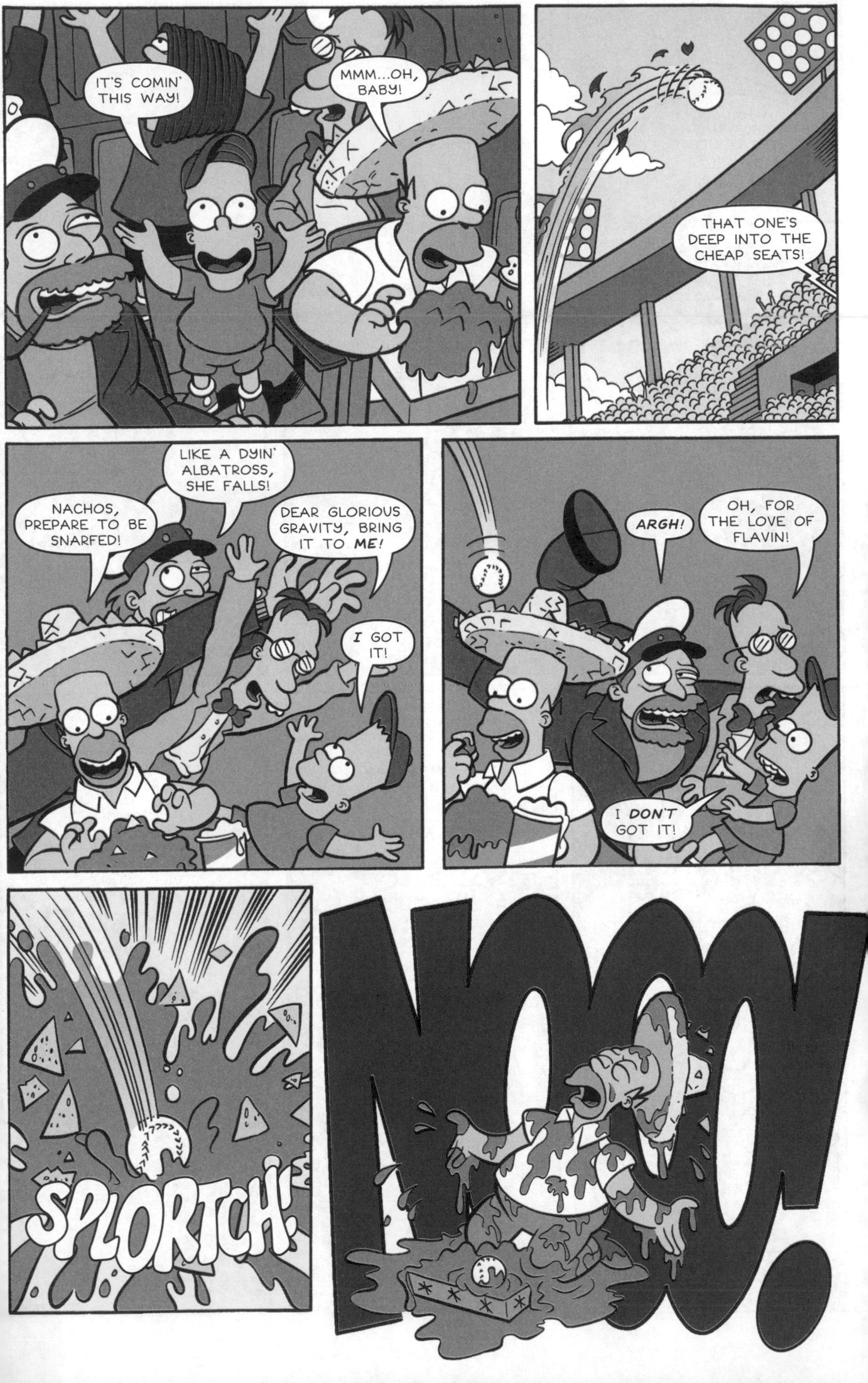
IT'S COMIN' THIS WAY!
MMM...OH, BABY!
THAT ONE'S DEEP INTO THE CHEAP SEATS!
LIKE A DYIN' ALBATROSS, SHE FALLS!
NACHOS, PREPARE TO BE SNARFED!
DEAR GLORIOUS GRAVITY, BRING IT TO ME!
I GOT IT!
ARGH!
OH, FOR THE LOVE OF FLAVIN!
I DON'T GOT IT!
SPLORTCH!
NOOO!

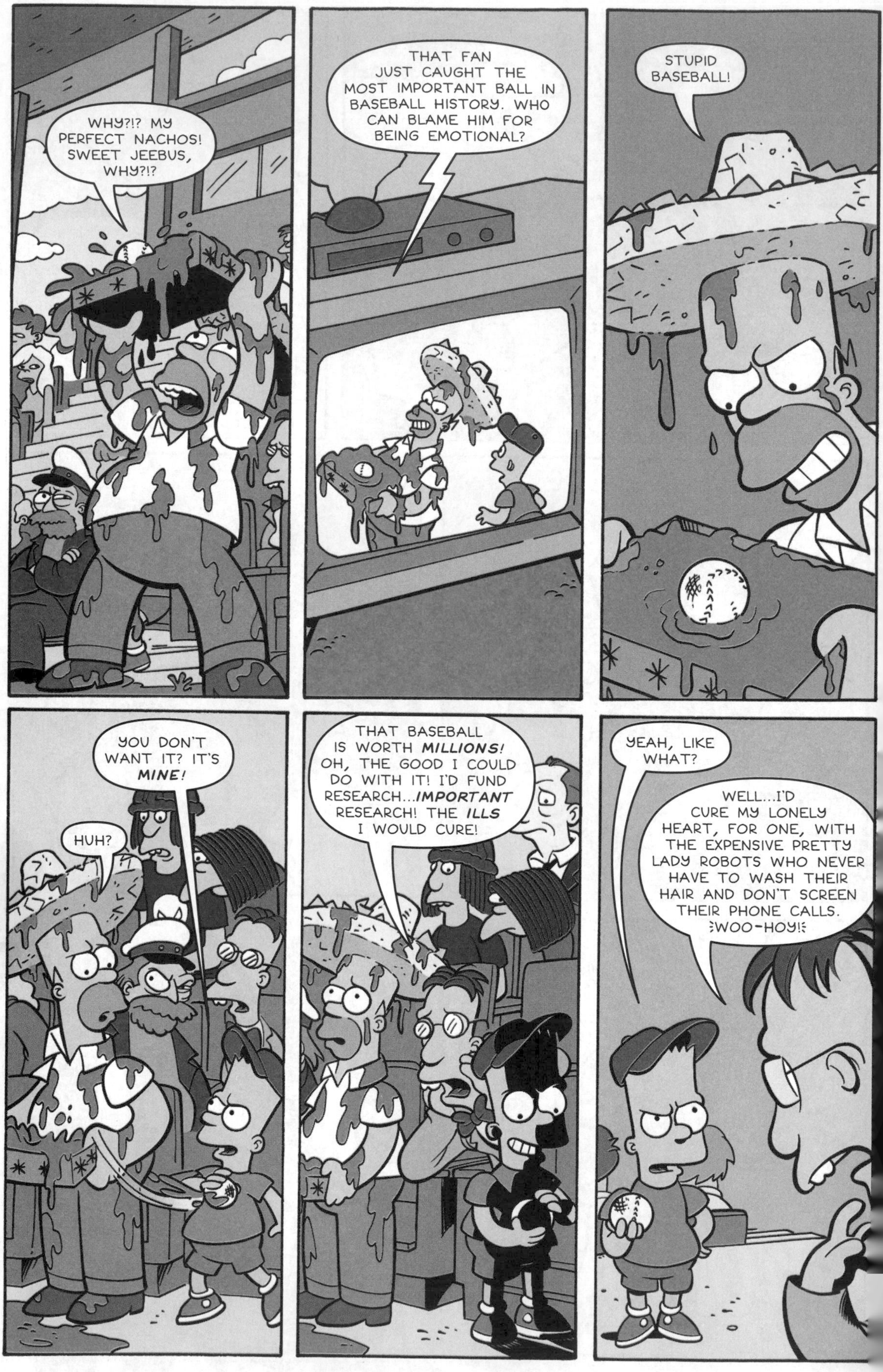
WHY?!? MY PERFECT NACHOS! SWEET JEEBUS, WHY?!?
THAT FAN JUST CAUGHT THE MOST IMPORTANT BALL IN BASEBALL HISTORY. WHO CAN BLAME HIM FOR BEING EMOTIONAL?
STUPID BASEBALL!
YOU DON'T WANT IT? IT'S MINE!
HUH?
THAT BASEBALL IS WORTH MILLIONS! OH, THE GOOD I COULD DO WITH IT! I'D FUND RESEARCH...IMPORTANT RESEARCH! THE ILLS I WOULD CURE!
YEAH, LIKE WHAT?
WELL...I'D CURE MY LONELY HEART, FOR ONE, WITH THE EXPENSIVE PRETTY LADY ROBOTS WHO NEVER HAVE TO WASH THEIR HAIR AND DON'T SCREEN THEIR PHONE CALLS. WOO-HOY!

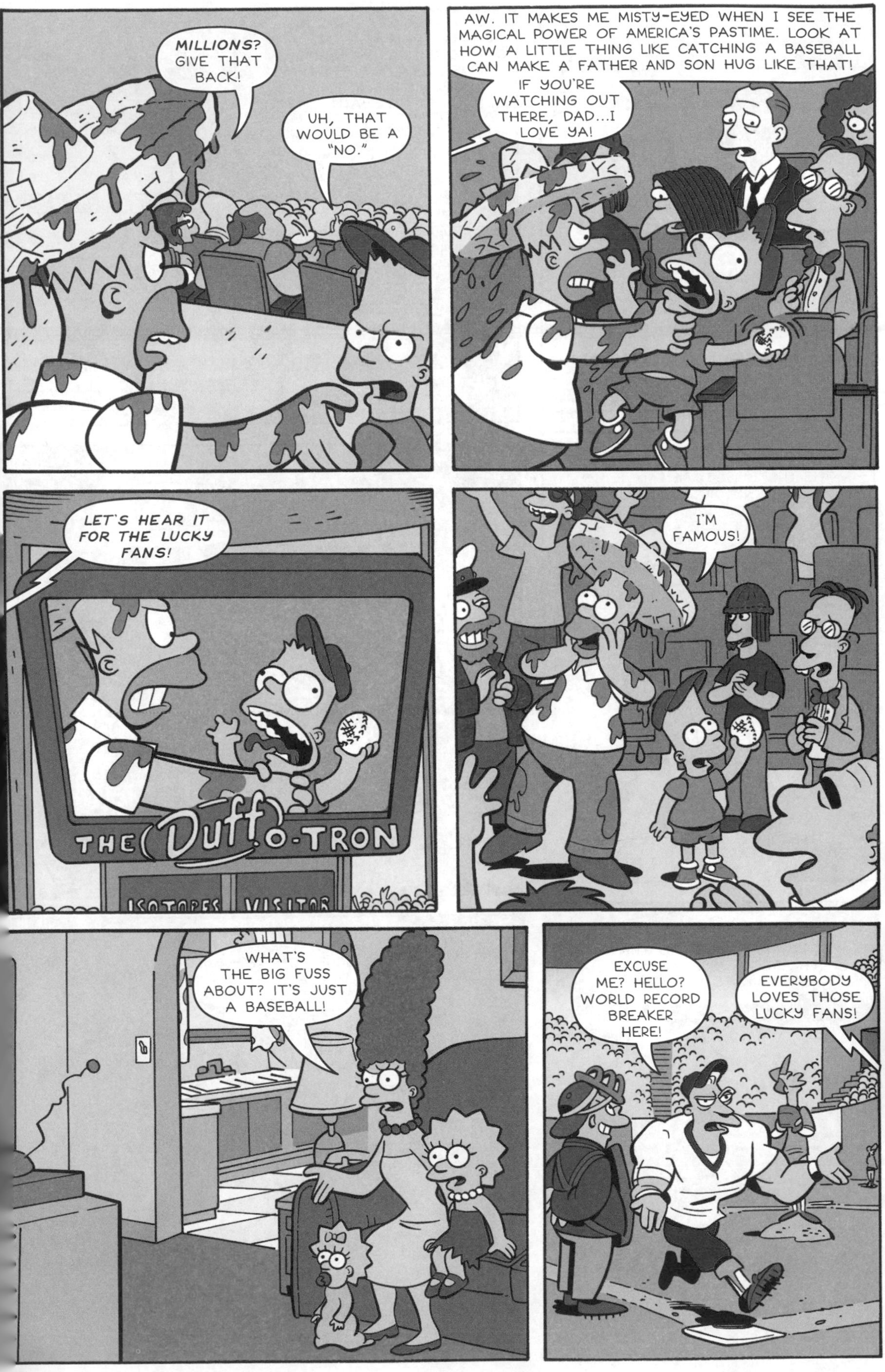
MILLIONS? GIVE THAT BACK!
UH, THAT WOULD BE A "NO."
AW. IT MAKES ME MISTY-EYED WHEN I SEE THE MAGICAL POWER OF AMERICA'S PASTIME. LOOK AT HOW A LITTLE THING LIKE CATCHING A BASEBALL CAN MAKE A FATHER AND SON HUG LIKE THAT!
IF YOU'RE WATCHING OUT THERE, DAD...I LOVE YA!
LET'S HEAR IT FOR THE LUCKY FANS!
THE Duff O-TRON
ISOTOPES
VISITOR
I'M FAMOUS!
WHAT'S THE BIG FUSS ABOUT? IT'S JUST A BASEBALL!
EXCUSE ME? HELLO? WORLD RECORD BREAKER HERE!
EVERYBODY LOVES THOSE LUCKY FANS!

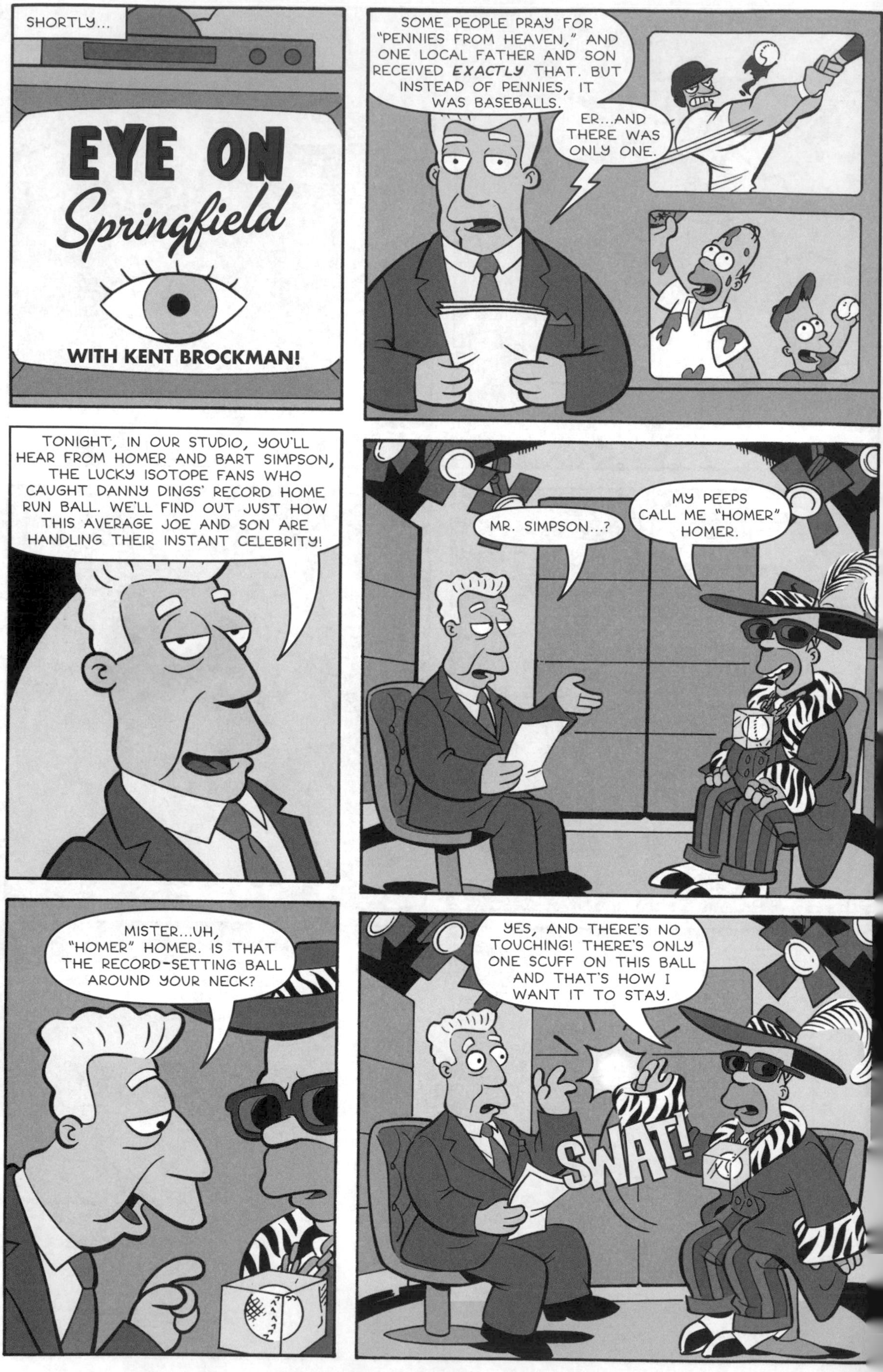
SHORTLY...
EYE ON Springfield
WITH KENT BROCKMAN!
SOME PEOPLE PRAY FOR "PENNIES FROM HEAVEN," AND ONE LOCAL FATHER AND SON RECEIVED EXACTLY THAT. BUT INSTEAD OF PENNIES, IT WAS BASEBALLS.
ER...AND THERE WAS ONLY ONE.
TONIGHT, IN OUR STUDIO, YOU'LL HEAR FROM HOMER AND BART SIMPSON, THE LUCKY ISOTOPE FANS WHO CAUGHT DANNY DINGS' RECORD HOME RUN BALL. WE'LL FIND OUT JUST HOW THIS AVERAGE JOE AND SON ARE HANDLING THEIR INSTANT CELEBRITY!
MR. SIMPSON...?
MY PEEPS CALL ME "HOMER" HOMER.
MISTER...UH, "HOMER" HOMER. IS THAT THE RECORD-SETTING BALL AROUND YOUR NECK?
YES, AND THERE'S NO TOUCHING! THERE'S ONLY ONE SCUFF ON THIS BALL AND THAT'S HOW I WANT IT TO STAY.
SWAT!

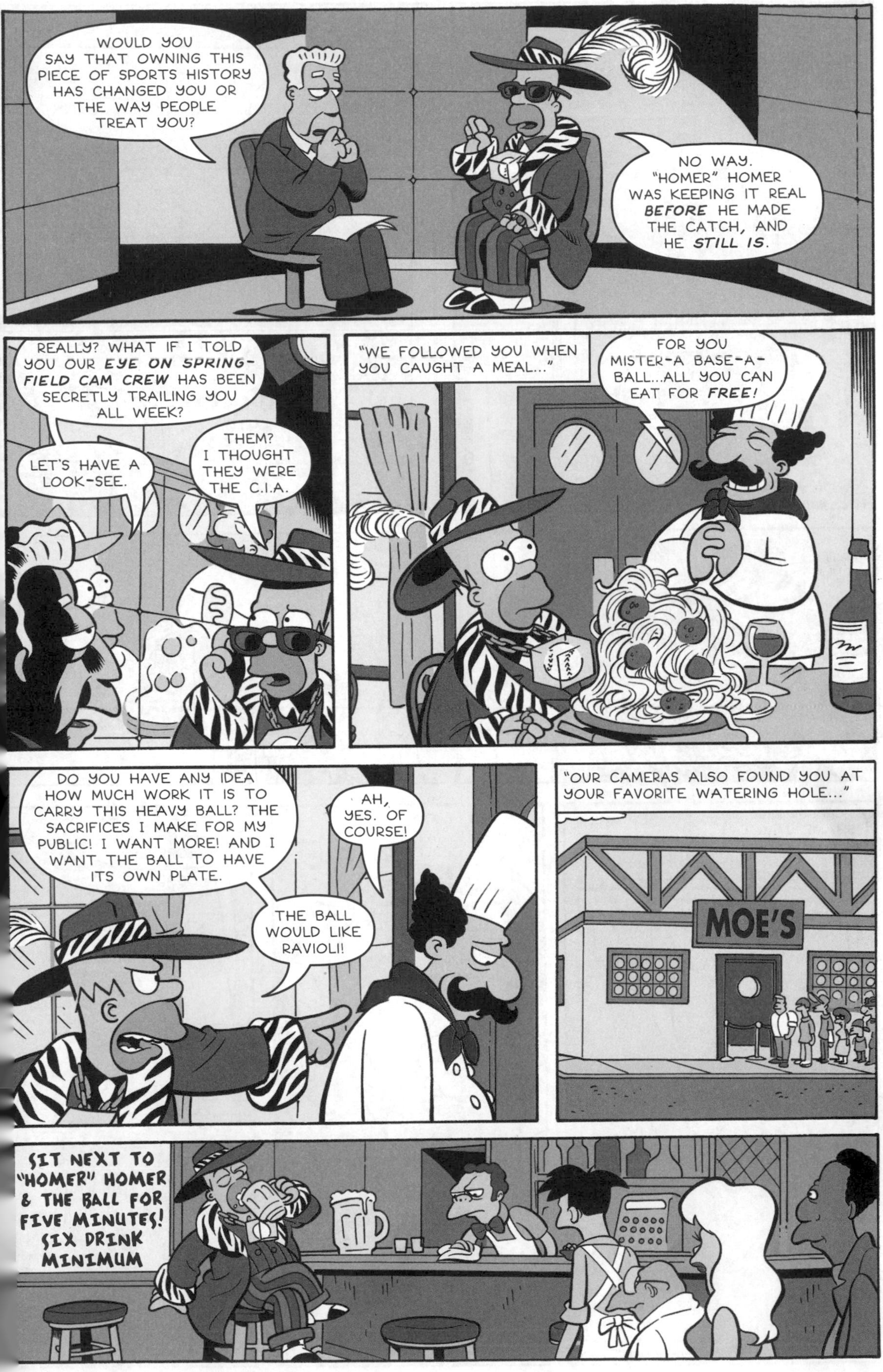
WOULD YOU SAY THAT OWNING THIS PIECE OF SPORTS HISTORY HAS CHANGED YOU OR THE WAY PEOPLE TREAT YOU?
NO WAY. "HOMER" HOMER WAS KEEPING IT REAL BEFORE HE MADE THE CATCH, AND HE STILL IS.
REALLY? WHAT IF I TOLD YOU OUR EYE ON SPRINGFIELD CAM CREW HAS BEEN SECRETLY TRAILING YOU ALL WEEK?
THEM? I THOUGHT THEY WERE THE C.I.A.
LET'S HAVE A LOOK-SEE.
"WE FOLLOWED YOU WHEN YOU CAUGHT A MEAL..."
FOR YOU MISTER-A BASE-A-BALL...ALL YOU CAN EAT FOR FREE!
DO YOU HAVE ANY IDEA HOW MUCH WORK IT IS TO CARRY THIS HEAVY BALL? THE SACRIFICES I MAKE FOR MY PUBLIC! I WANT MORE! AND I WANT THE BALL TO HAVE ITS OWN PLATE.
AH, YES. OF COURSE!
THE BALL WOULD LIKE RAVIOLI!
"OUR CAMERAS ALSO FOUND YOU AT YOUR FAVORITE WATERING HOLE..."
MOE'S
SIT NEXT TO "HOMER" HOMER & THE BALL FOR FIVE MINUTES! SIX DRINK MINIMUM

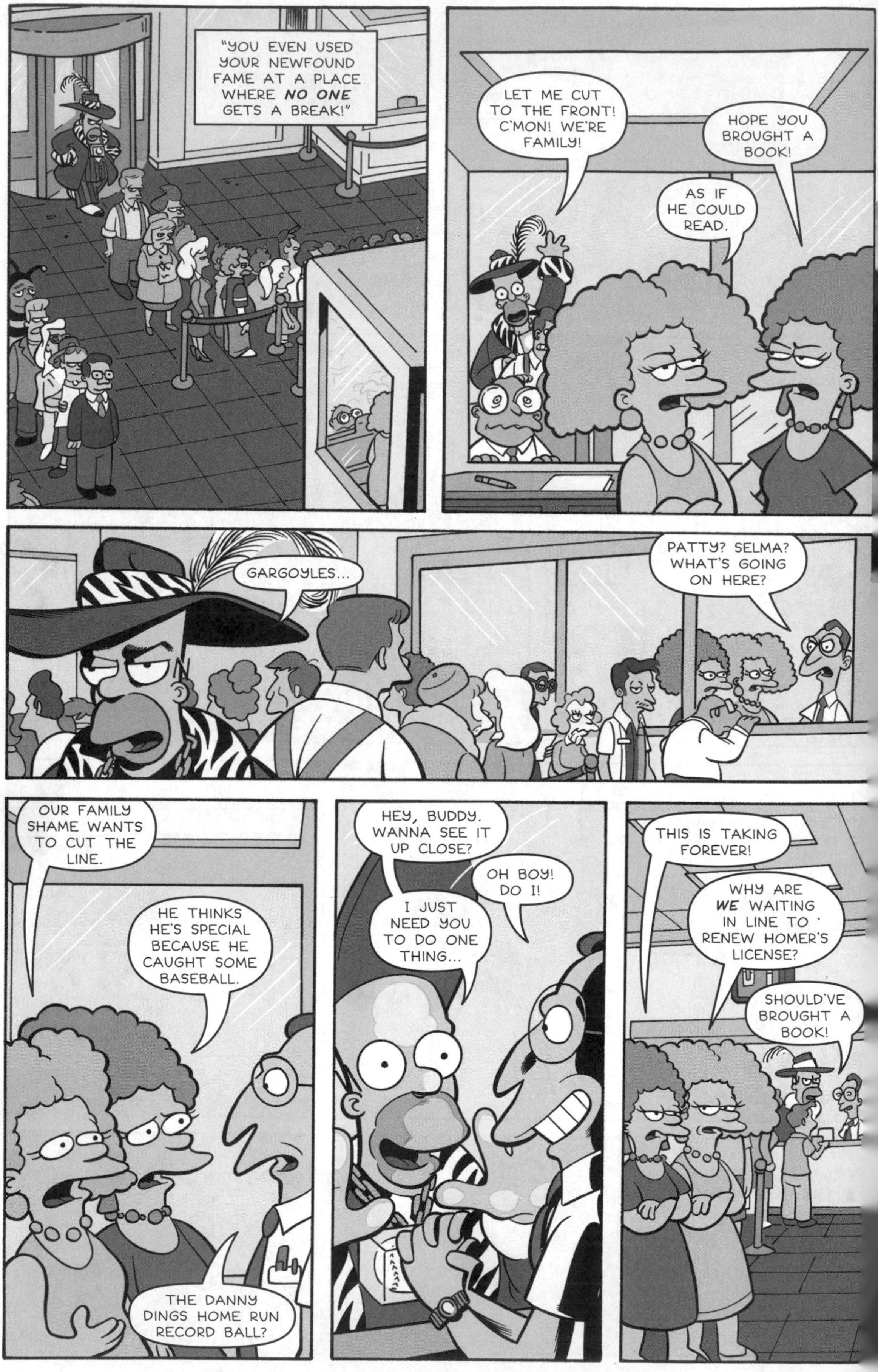
"YOU EVEN USED YOUR NEWFOUND FAME AT A PLACE WHERE *NO ONE* GETS A BREAK!"
LET ME CUT TO THE FRONT! C'MON! WE'RE FAMILY!
HOPE YOU BROUGHT A BOOK!
AS IF HE COULD READ.
GARGOYLES...
PATTY? SELMA? WHAT'S GOING ON HERE?
OUR FAMILY SHAME WANTS TO CUT THE LINE.
HE THINKS HE'S SPECIAL BECAUSE HE CAUGHT SOME BASEBALL.
THE DANNY DINGS HOME RUN RECORD BALL?
HEY, BUDDY. WANNA SEE IT UP CLOSE?
OH BOY! DO I!
I JUST NEED YOU TO DO ONE THING...
THIS IS TAKING FOREVER!
WHY ARE *WE* WAITING IN LINE TO RENEW HOMER'S LICENSE?
SHOULD'VE BROUGHT A BOOK!

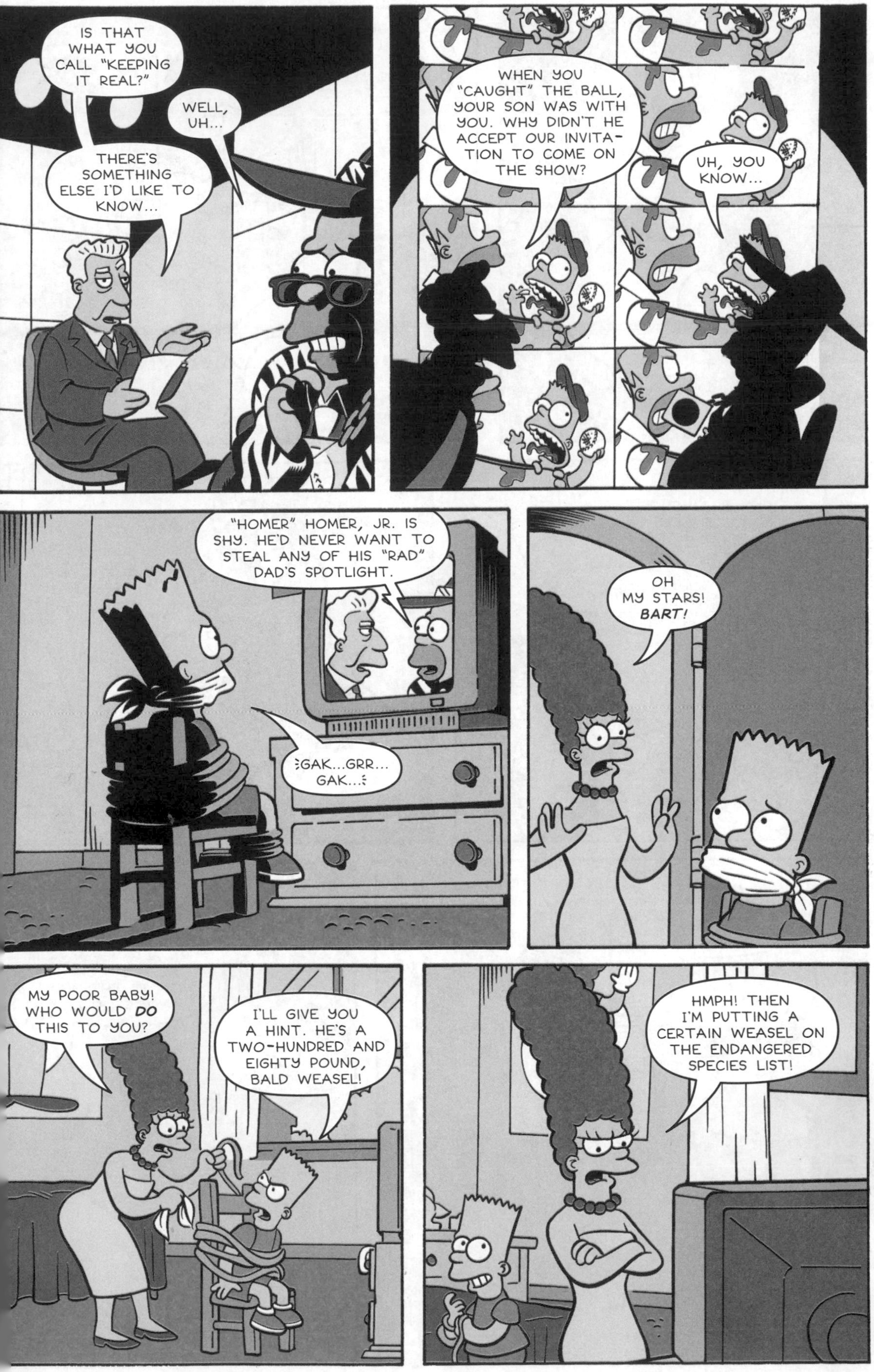
IS THAT WHAT YOU CALL "KEEPING IT REAL?"
WELL, UH...
THERE'S SOMETHING ELSE I'D LIKE TO KNOW...
WHEN YOU "CAUGHT" THE BALL, YOUR SON WAS WITH YOU. WHY DIDN'T HE ACCEPT OUR INVITATION TO COME ON THE SHOW?
UH, YOU KNOW...
"HOMER" HOMER, JR. IS SHY. HE'D NEVER WANT TO STEAL ANY OF HIS "RAD" DAD'S SPOTLIGHT.
GAK...GRR... GAK...
OH MY STARS! BART!
MY POOR BABY! WHO WOULD DO THIS TO YOU?
I'LL GIVE YOU A HINT. HE'S A TWO-HUNDRED AND EIGHTY POUND, BALD WEASEL!
HMPH! THEN I'M PUTTING A CERTAIN WEASEL ON THE ENDANGERED SPECIES LIST!

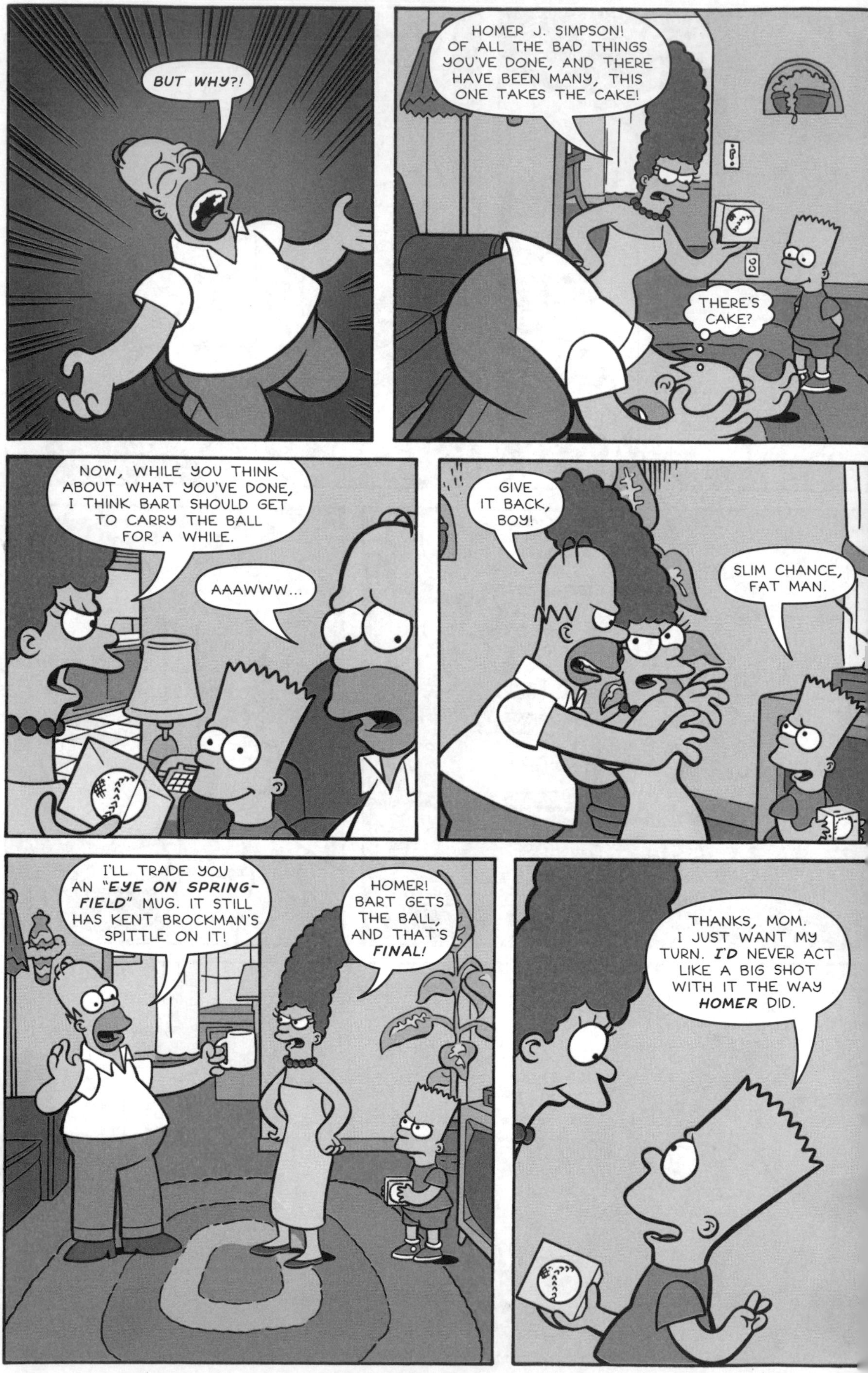
BUT WHY?!
HOMER J. SIMPSON! OF ALL THE BAD THINGS YOU'VE DONE, AND THERE HAVE BEEN MANY, THIS ONE TAKES THE CAKE!
THERE'S CAKE?
NOW, WHILE YOU THINK ABOUT WHAT YOU'VE DONE, I THINK BART SHOULD GET TO CARRY THE BALL FOR A WHILE.
AAAWWW...
GIVE IT BACK, BOY!
SLIM CHANCE, FAT MAN.
I'LL TRADE YOU AN "EYE ON SPRING-FIELD" MUG. IT STILL HAS KENT BROCKMAN'S SPITTLE ON IT!
HOMER! BART GETS THE BALL, AND THAT'S FINAL!
THANKS, MOM. I JUST WANT MY TURN. I'D NEVER ACT LIKE A BIG SHOT WITH IT THE WAY HOMER DID.

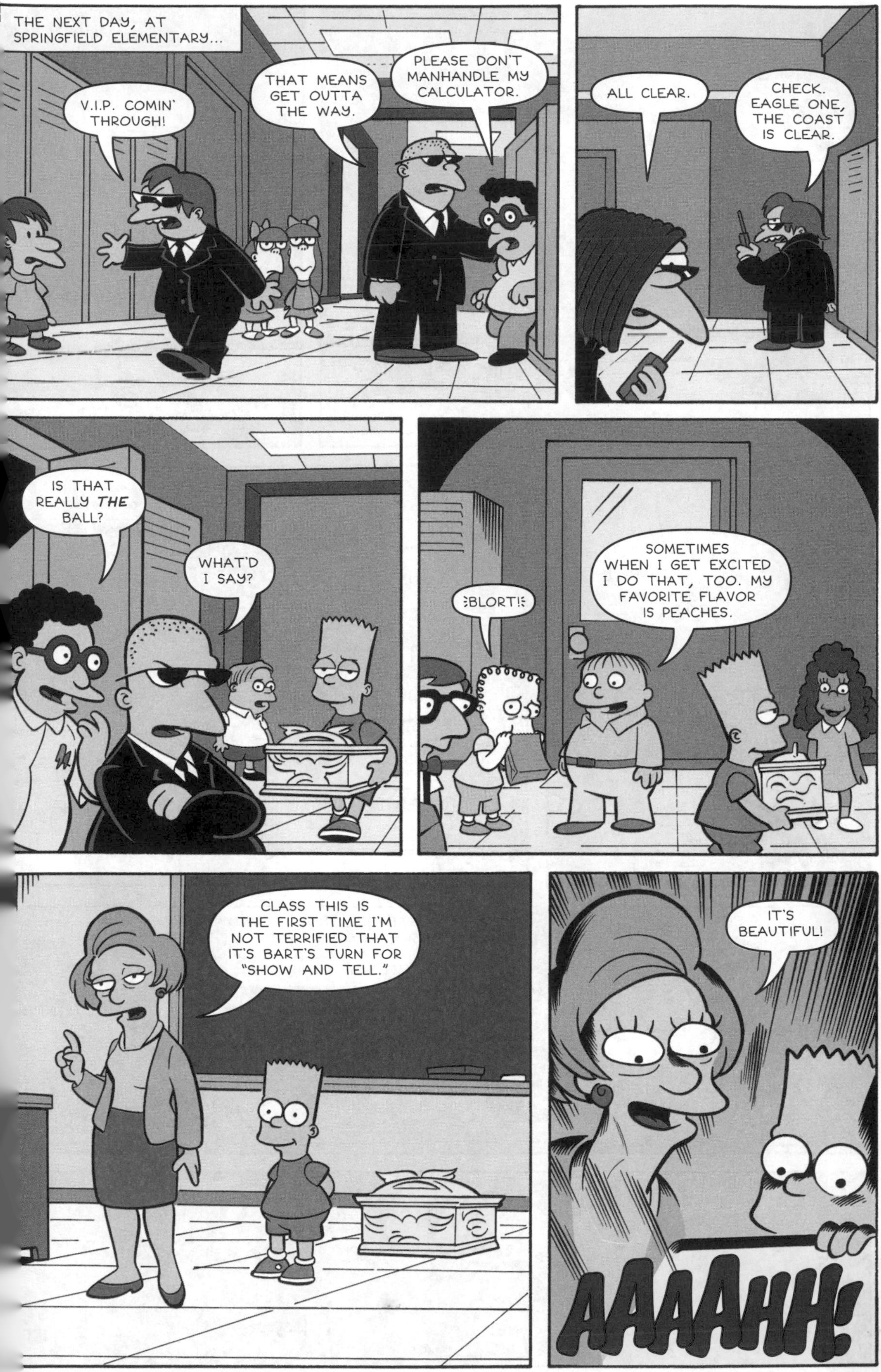
THE NEXT DAY, AT SPRINGFIELD ELEMENTARY...
V.I.P. COMIN' THROUGH!
THAT MEANS GET OUTTA THE WAY.
PLEASE DON'T MANHANDLE MY CALCULATOR.
ALL CLEAR.
CHECK. EAGLE ONE, THE COAST IS CLEAR.
IS THAT REALLY *THE* BALL?
WHAT'D I SAY?
BLORT!
SOMETIMES WHEN I GET EXCITED I DO THAT, TOO. MY FAVORITE FLAVOR IS PEACHES.
CLASS THIS IS THE FIRST TIME I'M NOT TERRIFIED THAT IT'S BART'S TURN FOR "SHOW AND TELL."
IT'S BEAUTIFUL!
AAAAHH!

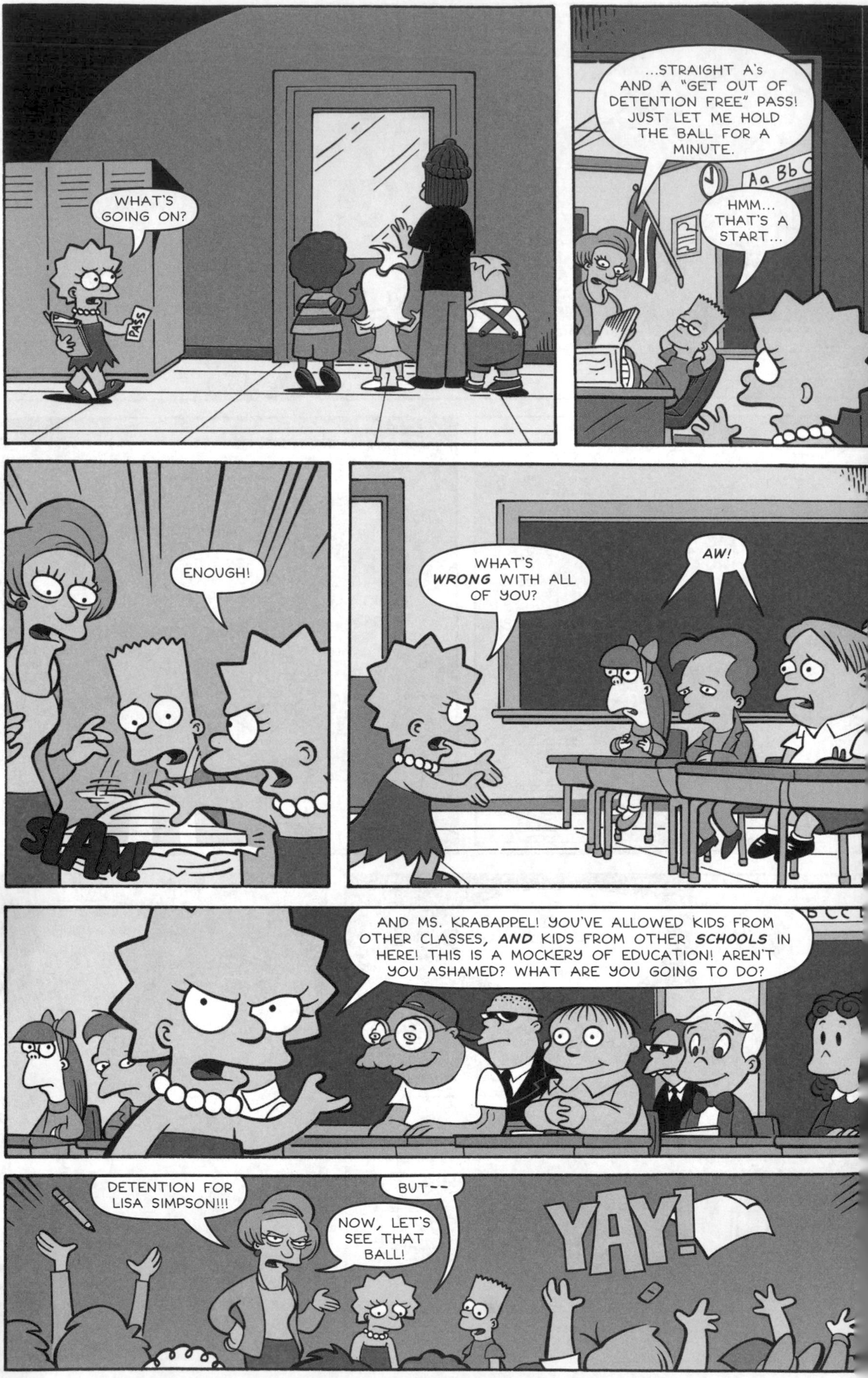
WHAT'S GOING ON?
...STRAIGHT A's AND A "GET OUT OF DETENTION FREE" PASS! JUST LET ME HOLD THE BALL FOR A MINUTE.
HMM... THAT'S A START...
PASS
Aa Bb C
ENOUGH!
SLAM!
WHAT'S WRONG WITH ALL OF YOU?
AW!
AND MS. KRABAPPEL! YOU'VE ALLOWED KIDS FROM OTHER CLASSES, AND KIDS FROM OTHER SCHOOLS IN HERE! THIS IS A MOCKERY OF EDUCATION! AREN'T YOU ASHAMED? WHAT ARE YOU GOING TO DO?
DETENTION FOR LISA SIMPSON!!!
BUT--
NOW, LET'S SEE THAT BALL!
YAY!

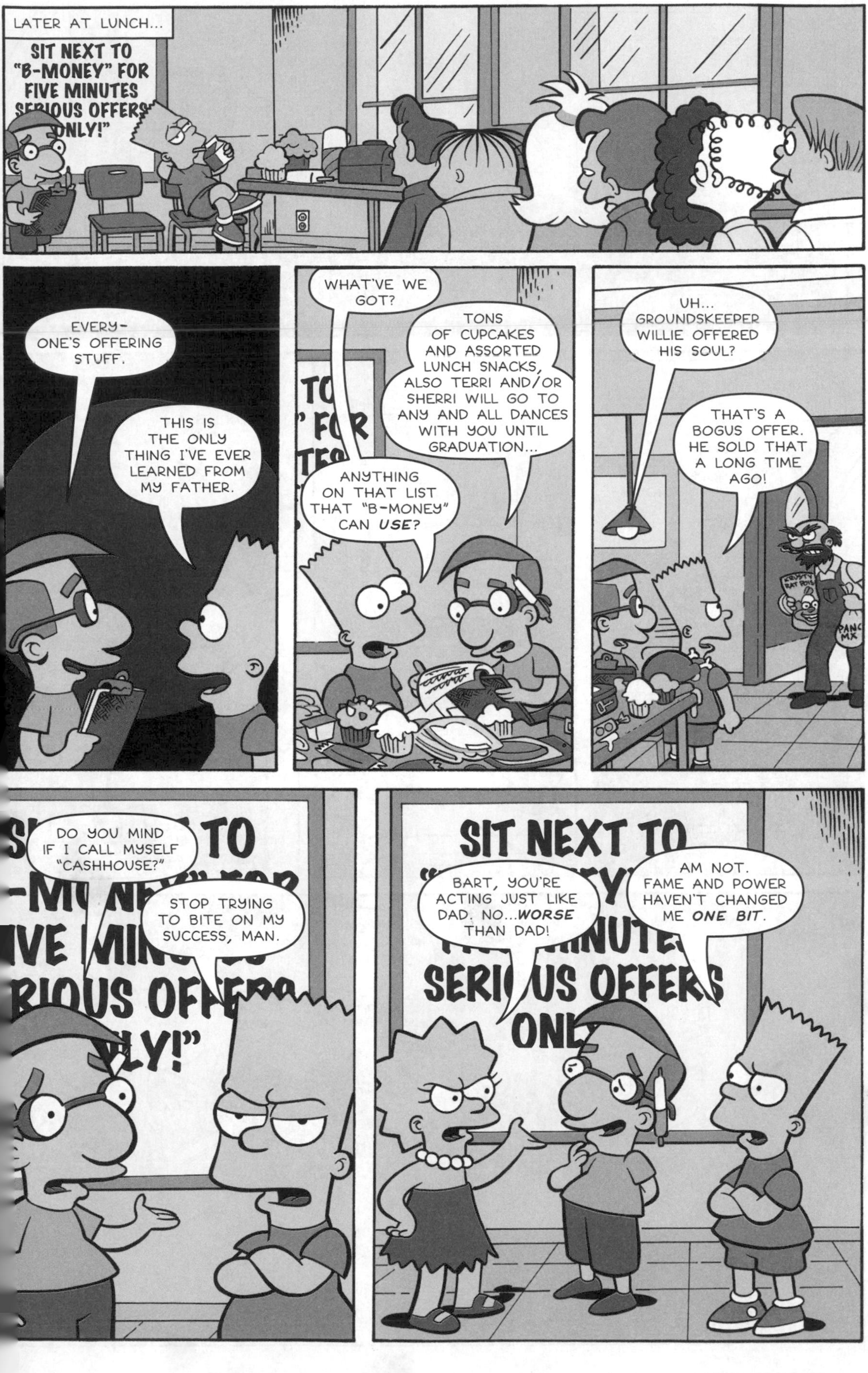
LATER AT LUNCH...
SIT NEXT TO “B-MONEY” FOR FIVE MINUTES
EVERY-ONE'S OFFERING STUFF.
THIS IS THE ONLY THING I'VE EVER LEARNED FROM MY FATHER.
WHAT'VE WE GOT?
TONS OF CUPCAKES AND ASSORTED LUNCH SNACKS, ALSO TERRI AND/OR SHERRI WILL GO TO ANY AND ALL DANCES WITH YOU UNTIL GRADUATION...
ANYTHING ON THAT LIST THAT “B-MONEY” CAN *USE*?
UH... GROUNDSKEEPER WILLIE OFFERED HIS SOUL?
THAT'S A BOGUS OFFER. HE SOLD THAT A LONG TIME AGO!
DO YOU MIND IF I CALL MYSELF “CASHHOUSE?”
STOP TRYING TO BITE ON MY SUCCESS, MAN.
SIT NEXT TO
BART, YOU'RE ACTING JUST LIKE DAD. NO...*WORSE* THAN DAD!
AM NOT. FAME AND POWER HAVEN'T CHANGED ME *ONE BIT*.

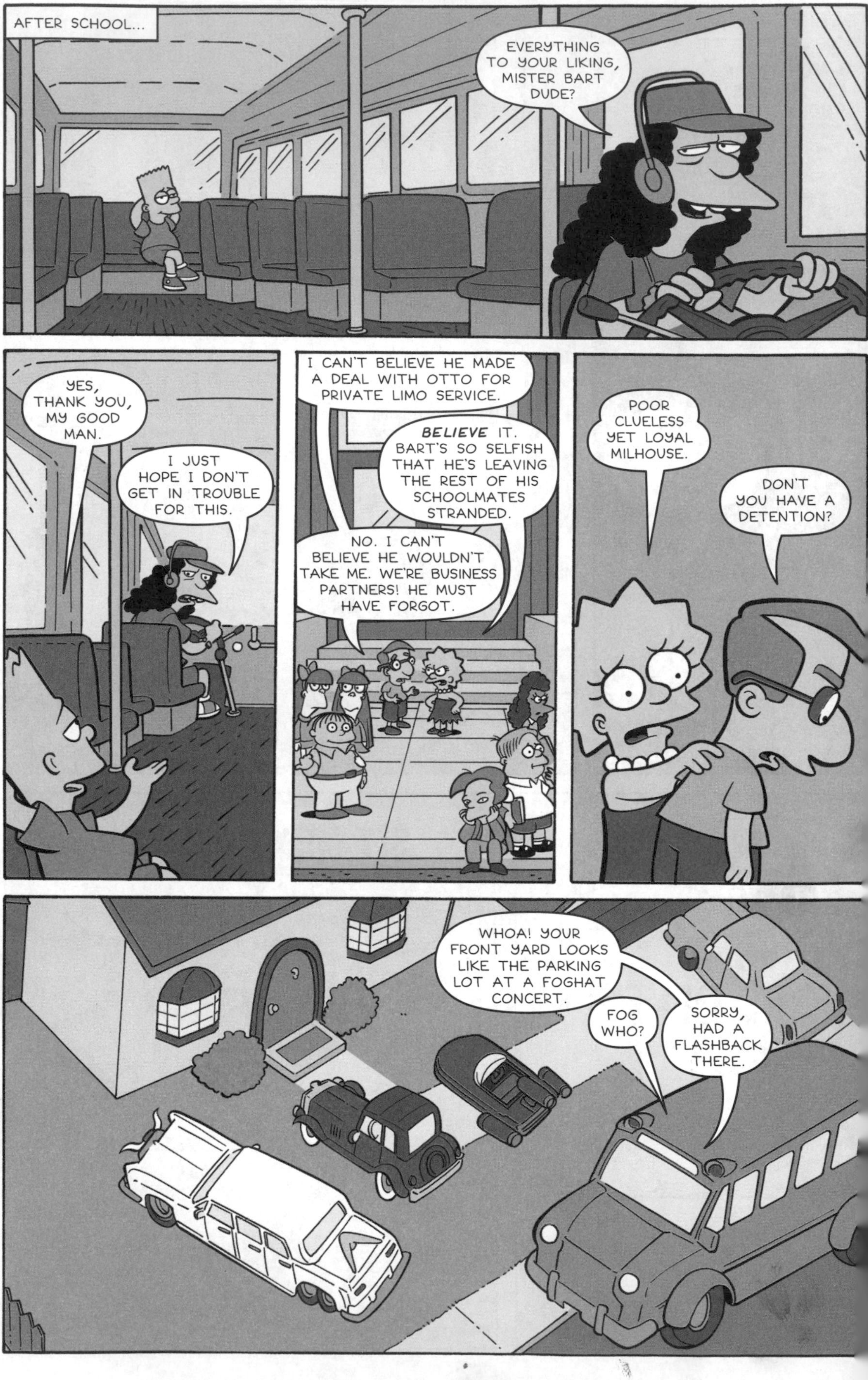
AFTER SCHOOL...
EVERYTHING TO YOUR LIKING, MISTER BART DUDE?
YES, THANK YOU, MY GOOD MAN.
I JUST HOPE I DON'T GET IN TROUBLE FOR THIS.
I CAN'T BELIEVE HE MADE A DEAL WITH OTTO FOR PRIVATE LIMO SERVICE.
BELIEVE IT. BART'S SO SELFISH THAT HE'S LEAVING THE REST OF HIS SCHOOLMATES STRANDED.
NO. I CAN'T BELIEVE HE WOULDN'T TAKE ME. WE'RE BUSINESS PARTNERS! HE MUST HAVE FORGOT.
POOR CLUELESS YET LOYAL MILHOUSE.
DON'T YOU HAVE A DETENTION?
WHOA! YOUR FRONT YARD LOOKS LIKE THE PARKING LOT AT A FOGHAT CONCERT.
FOG WHO?
SORRY, HAD A FLASHBACK THERE.

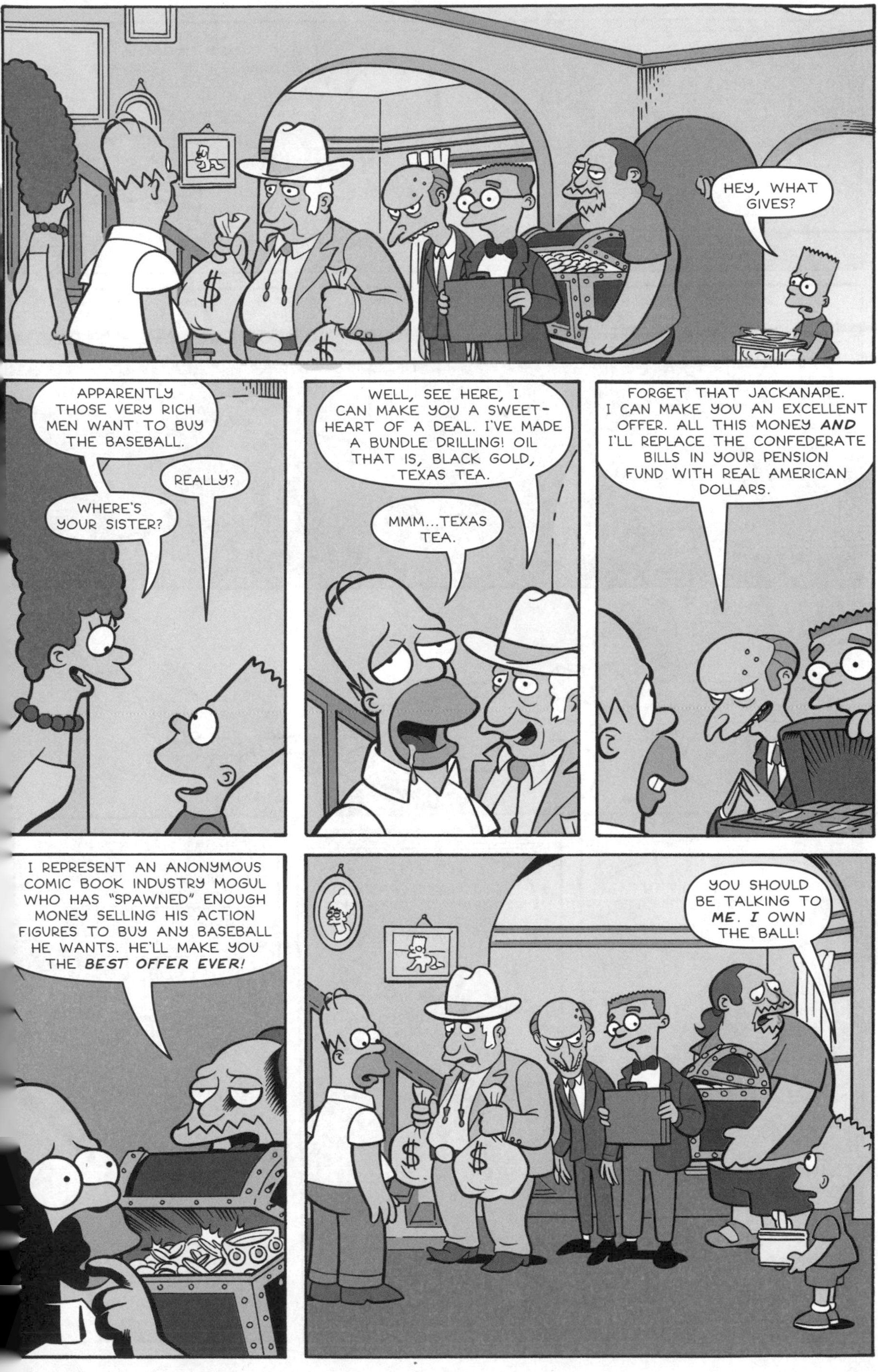
HEY, WHAT GIVES?
APPARENTLY THOSE VERY RICH MEN WANT TO BUY THE BASEBALL.
REALLY?
WHERE'S YOUR SISTER?
WELL, SEE HERE, I CAN MAKE YOU A SWEET-HEART OF A DEAL. I'VE MADE A BUNDLE DRILLING! OIL THAT IS, BLACK GOLD, TEXAS TEA.
MMM...TEXAS TEA.
FORGET THAT JACKANAPE. I CAN MAKE YOU AN EXCELLENT OFFER. ALL THIS MONEY ***AND*** I'LL REPLACE THE CONFEDERATE BILLS IN YOUR PENSION FUND WITH REAL AMERICAN DOLLARS.
I REPRESENT AN ANONYMOUS COMIC BOOK INDUSTRY MOGUL WHO HAS "SPAWNED" ENOUGH MONEY SELLING HIS ACTION FIGURES TO BUY ANY BASEBALL HE WANTS. HE'LL MAKE YOU THE ***BEST OFFER EVER!***
YOU SHOULD BE TALKING TO ***ME***. ***I*** OWN THE BALL!

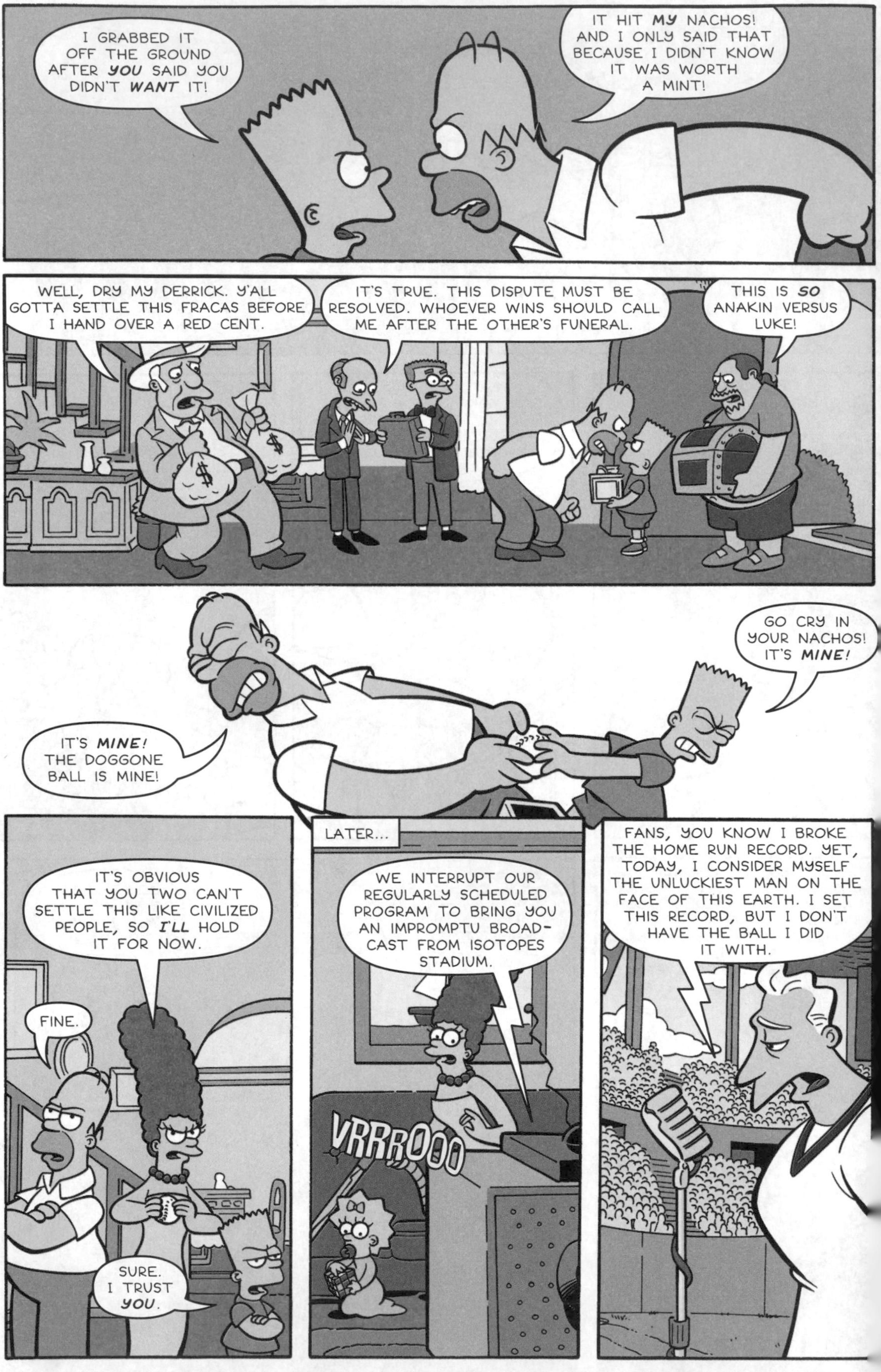
I GRABBED IT OFF THE GROUND AFTER YOU SAID YOU DIDN'T WANT IT!
IT HIT MY NACHOS! AND I ONLY SAID THAT BECAUSE I DIDN'T KNOW IT WAS WORTH A MINT!
WELL, DRY MY DERRICK. Y'ALL GOTTA SETTLE THIS FRACAS BEFORE I HAND OVER A RED CENT.
IT'S TRUE. THIS DISPUTE MUST BE RESOLVED. WHOEVER WINS SHOULD CALL ME AFTER THE OTHER'S FUNERAL.
THIS IS SO ANAKIN VERSUS LUKE!
IT'S MINE! THE DOGGONE BALL IS MINE!
GO CRY IN YOUR NACHOS! IT'S MINE!
IT'S OBVIOUS THAT YOU TWO CAN'T SETTLE THIS LIKE CIVILIZED PEOPLE, SO I'LL HOLD IT FOR NOW.
FINE.
SURE. I TRUST YOU.
LATER...
WE INTERRUPT OUR REGULARLY SCHEDULED PROGRAM TO BRING YOU AN IMPROMPTU BROAD-CAST FROM ISOTOPES STADIUM.
VRRROOO
FANS, YOU KNOW I BROKE THE HOME RUN RECORD. YET, TODAY, I CONSIDER MYSELF THE UNLUCKIEST MAN ON THE FACE OF THIS EARTH. I SET THIS RECORD, BUT I DON'T HAVE THE BALL I DID IT WITH.

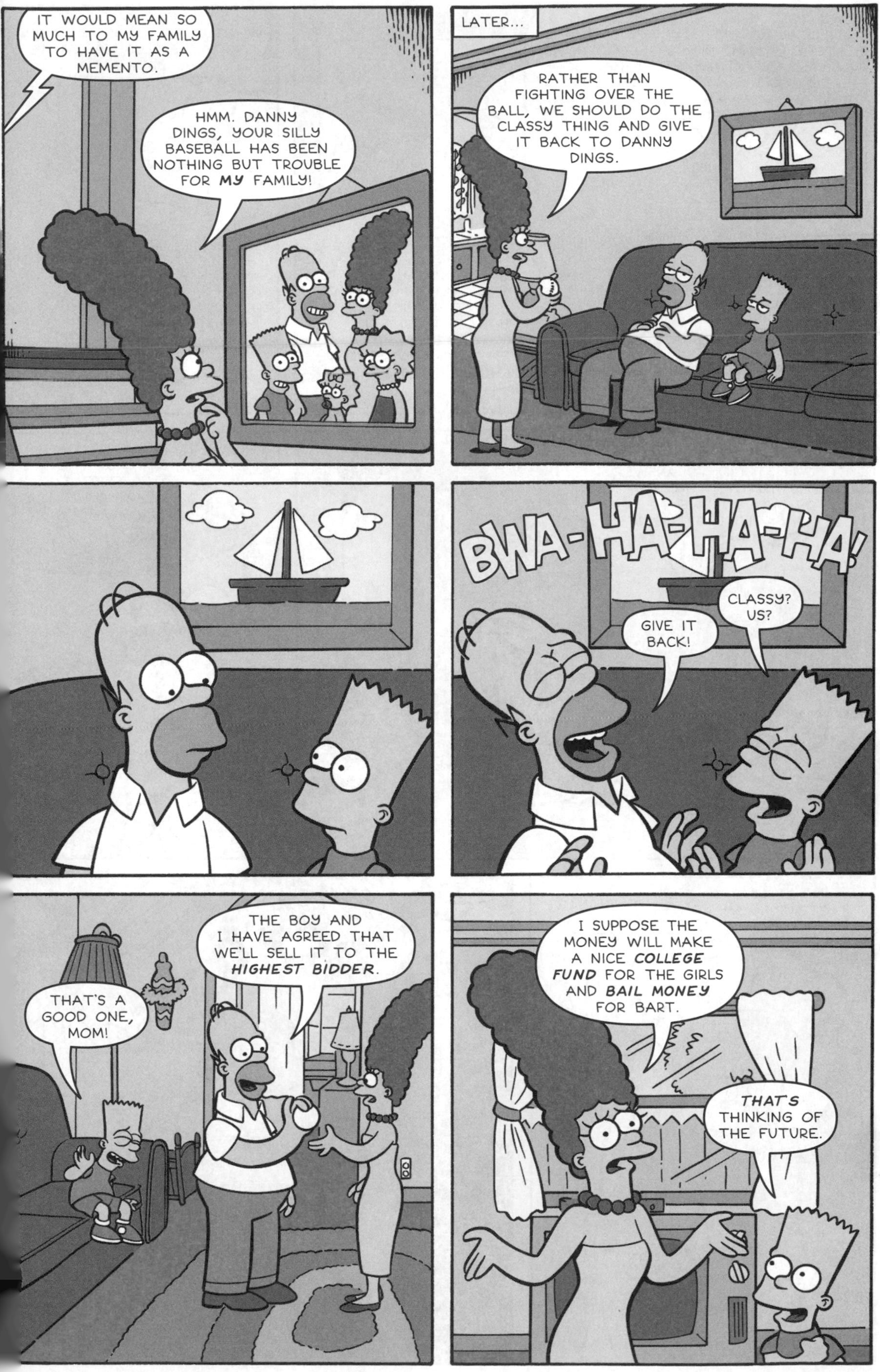
IT WOULD MEAN SO MUCH TO MY FAMILY TO HAVE IT AS A MEMENTO.
HMM. DANNY DINGS, YOUR SILLY BASEBALL HAS BEEN NOTHING BUT TROUBLE FOR MY FAMILY!
LATER...
RATHER THAN FIGHTING OVER THE BALL, WE SHOULD DO THE CLASSY THING AND GIVE IT BACK TO DANNY DINGS.
BWA-HA-HA-HA!
GIVE IT BACK!
CLASSY? US?
THAT'S A GOOD ONE, MOM!
THE BOY AND I HAVE AGREED THAT WE'LL SELL IT TO THE HIGHEST BIDDER.
I SUPPOSE THE MONEY WILL MAKE A NICE COLLEGE FUND FOR THE GIRLS AND BAIL MONEY FOR BART.
THAT'S THINKING OF THE FUTURE.

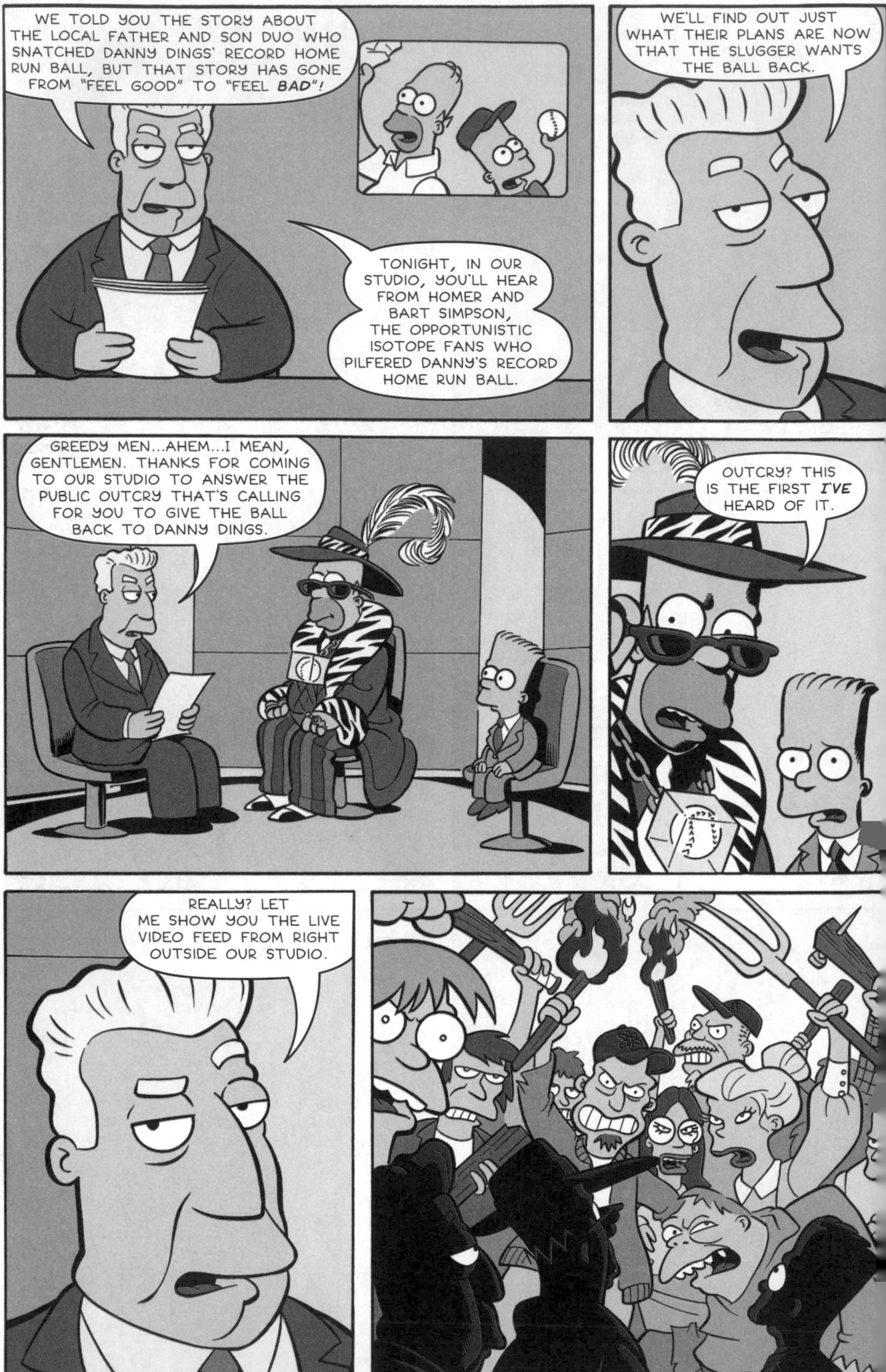
WE TOLD YOU THE STORY ABOUT THE LOCAL FATHER AND SON DUO WHO SNATCHED DANNY DINGS' RECORD HOME RUN BALL, BUT THAT STORY HAS GONE FROM "FEEL GOOD" TO "FEEL *BAD*"!
TONIGHT, IN OUR STUDIO, YOU'LL HEAR FROM HOMER AND BART SIMPSON, THE OPPORTUNISTIC ISOTOPE FANS WHO PILFERED DANNY'S RECORD HOME RUN BALL.
WE'LL FIND OUT JUST WHAT THEIR PLANS ARE NOW THAT THE SLUGGER WANTS THE BALL BACK.
GREEDY MEN...AHEM...I MEAN, GENTLEMEN. THANKS FOR COMING TO OUR STUDIO TO ANSWER THE PUBLIC OUTCRY THAT'S CALLING FOR YOU TO GIVE THE BALL BACK TO DANNY DINGS.
OUTCRY? THIS IS THE FIRST *I'VE* HEARD OF IT.
REALLY? LET ME SHOW YOU THE LIVE VIDEO FEED FROM RIGHT OUTSIDE OUR STUDIO.

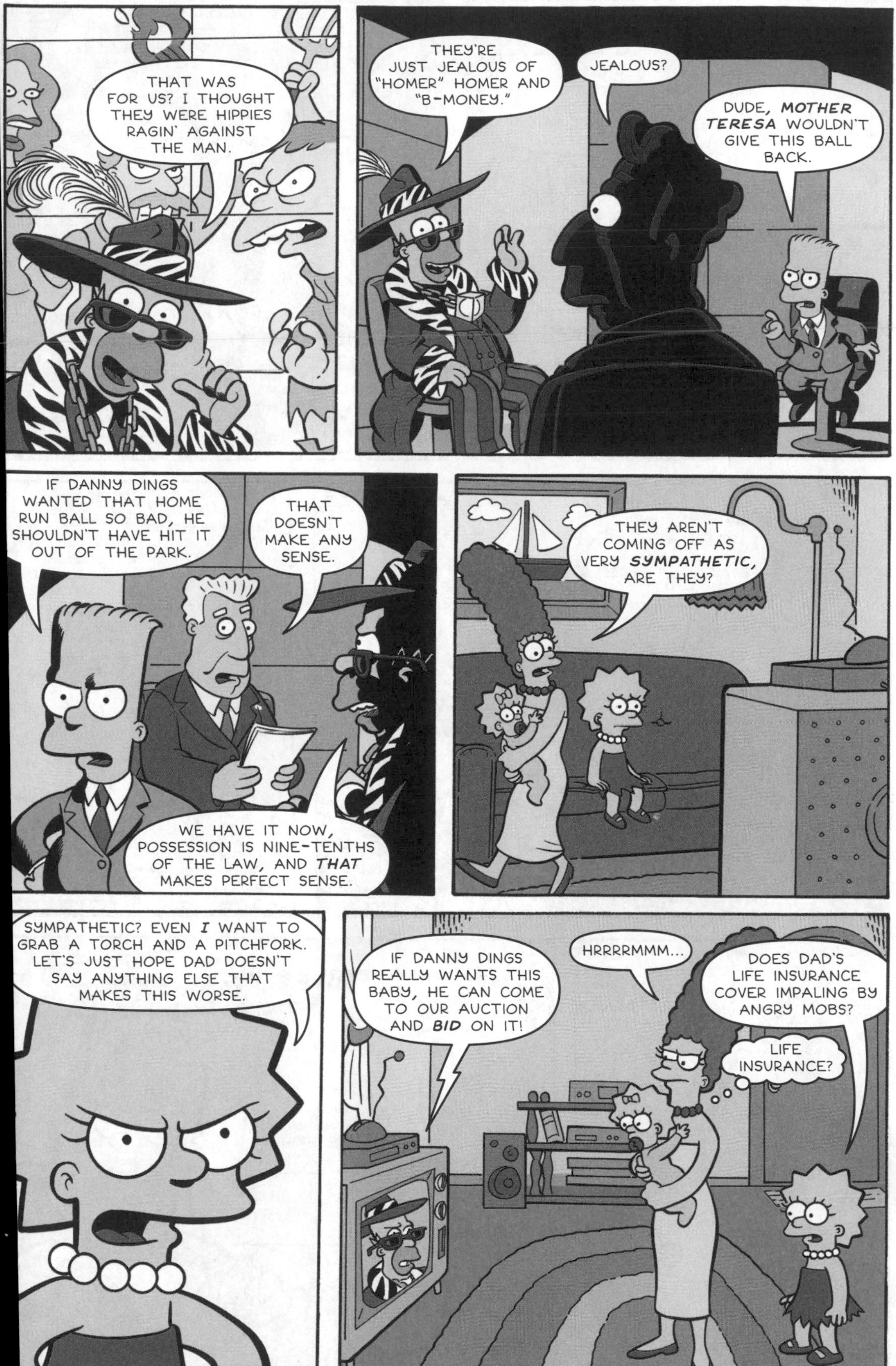
THAT WAS FOR US? I THOUGHT THEY WERE HIPPIES RAGIN' AGAINST THE MAN.
THEY'RE JUST JEALOUS OF "HOMER" HOMER AND "B-MONEY."
JEALOUS?
DUDE, *MOTHER TERESA* WOULDN'T GIVE THIS BALL BACK.
IF DANNY DINGS WANTED THAT HOME RUN BALL SO BAD, HE SHOULDN'T HAVE HIT IT OUT OF THE PARK.
THAT DOESN'T MAKE ANY SENSE.
WE HAVE IT NOW, POSSESSION IS NINE-TENTHS OF THE LAW, AND *THAT* MAKES PERFECT SENSE.
THEY AREN'T COMING OFF AS VERY *SYMPATHETIC,* ARE THEY?
SYMPATHETIC? EVEN *I* WANT TO GRAB A TORCH AND A PITCHFORK. LET'S JUST HOPE DAD DOESN'T SAY ANYTHING ELSE THAT MAKES THIS WORSE.
IF DANNY DINGS REALLY WANTS THIS BABY, HE CAN COME TO OUR AUCTION AND *BID* ON IT!
HRRRRMMM...
DOES DAD'S LIFE INSURANCE COVER IMPALING BY ANGRY MOBS?
LIFE INSURANCE?

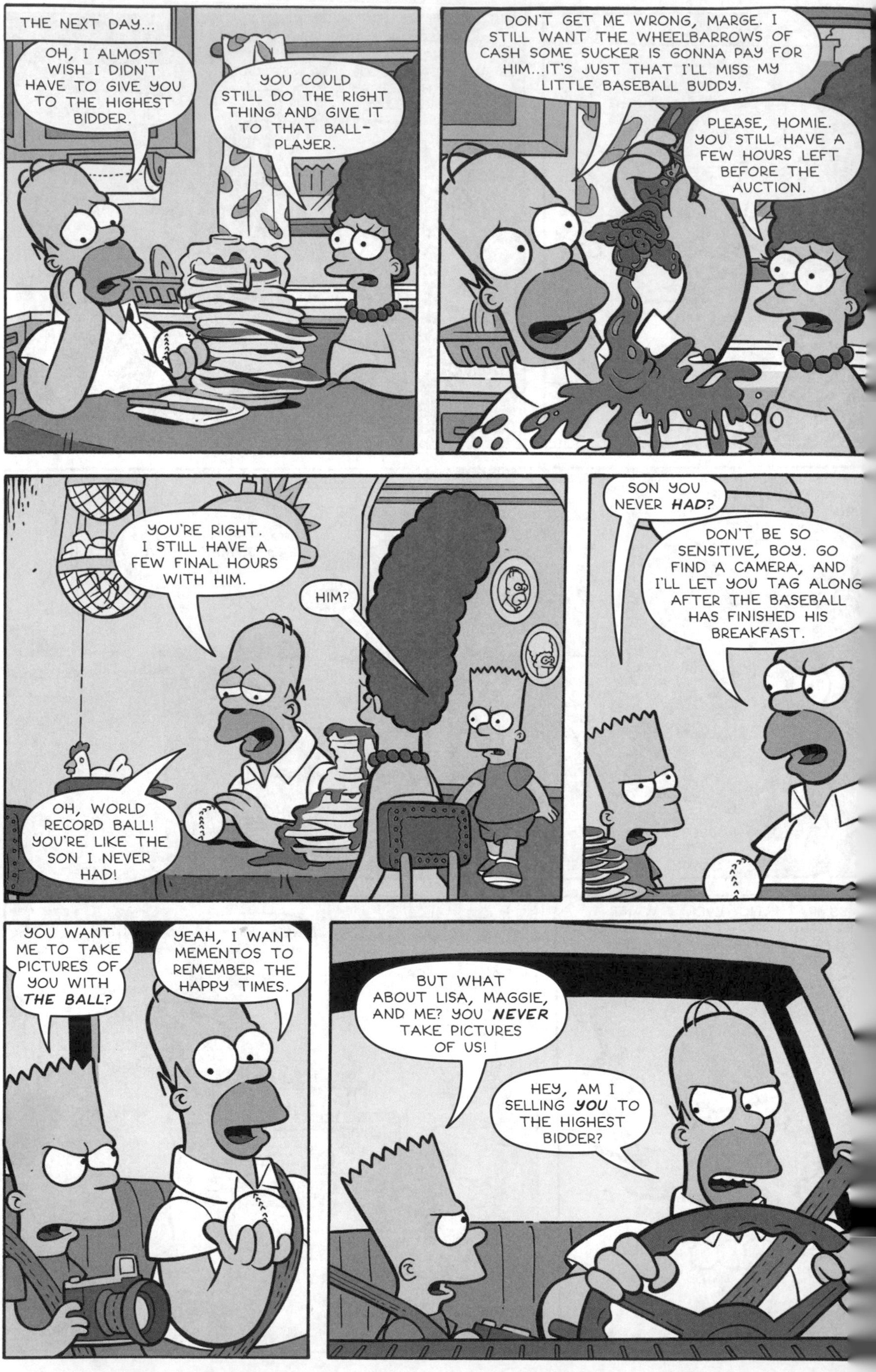
THE NEXT DAY...
OH, I ALMOST WISH I DIDN'T HAVE TO GIVE YOU TO THE HIGHEST BIDDER.
YOU COULD STILL DO THE RIGHT THING AND GIVE IT TO THAT BALL-PLAYER.
DON'T GET ME WRONG, MARGE. I STILL WANT THE WHEELBARROWS OF CASH SOME SUCKER IS GONNA PAY FOR HIM...IT'S JUST THAT I'LL MISS MY LITTLE BASEBALL BUDDY.
PLEASE, HOMIE. YOU STILL HAVE A FEW HOURS LEFT BEFORE THE AUCTION.
YOU'RE RIGHT. I STILL HAVE A FEW FINAL HOURS WITH HIM.
HIM?
OH, WORLD RECORD BALL! YOU'RE LIKE THE SON I NEVER HAD!
SON YOU NEVER ***HAD***?
DON'T BE SO SENSITIVE, BOY. GO FIND A CAMERA, AND I'LL LET YOU TAG ALONG AFTER THE BASEBALL HAS FINISHED HIS BREAKFAST.
YOU WANT ME TO TAKE PICTURES OF YOU WITH ***THE BALL***?
YEAH, I WANT MEMENTOS TO REMEMBER THE HAPPY TIMES.
BUT WHAT ABOUT LISA, MAGGIE, AND ME? YOU ***NEVER*** TAKE PICTURES OF US!
HEY, AM I SELLING ***YOU*** TO THE HIGHEST BIDDER?

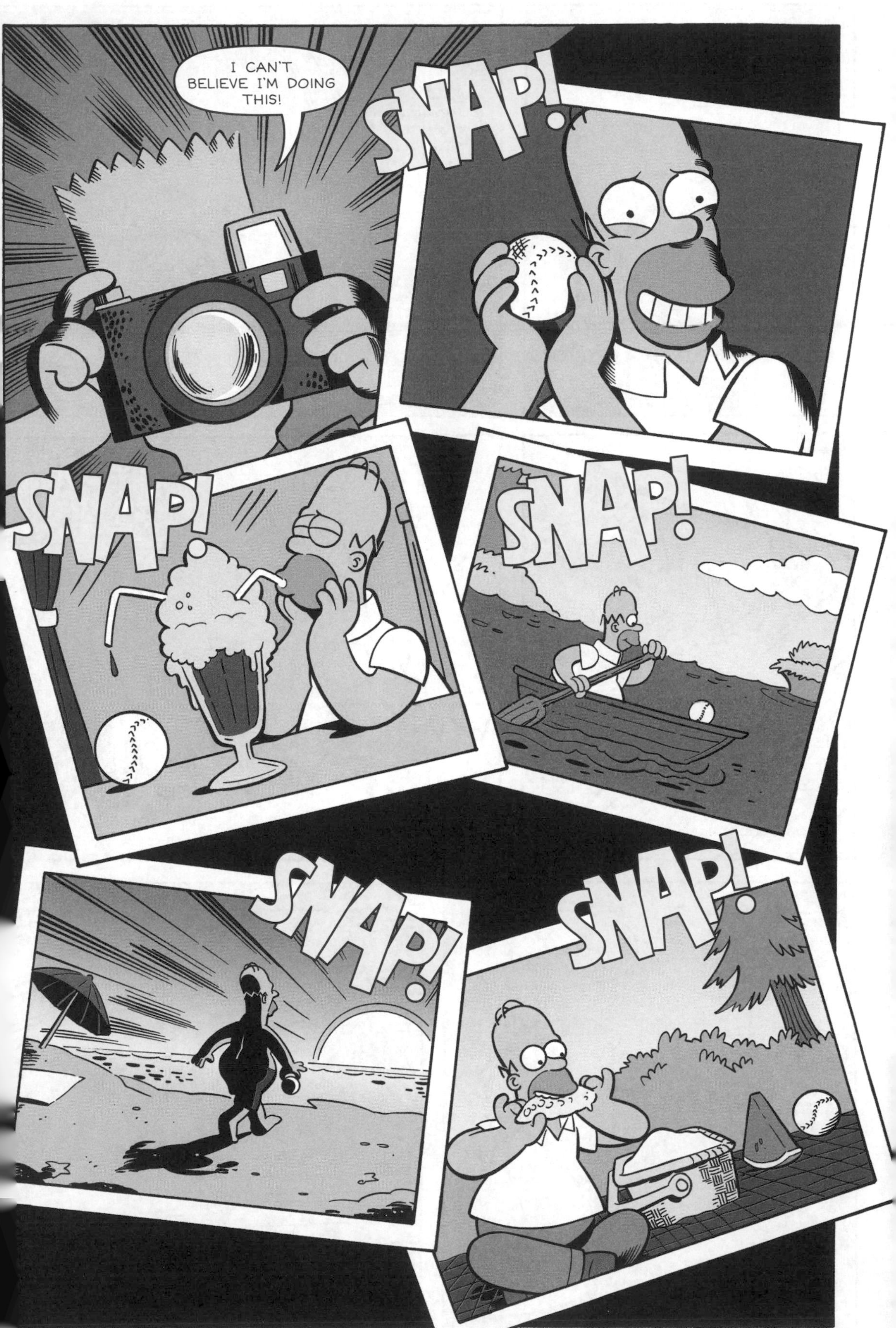
I CAN'T BELIEVE I'M DOING THIS!
SNAP!
SNAP!
SNAP!
SNAP!
SNAP!

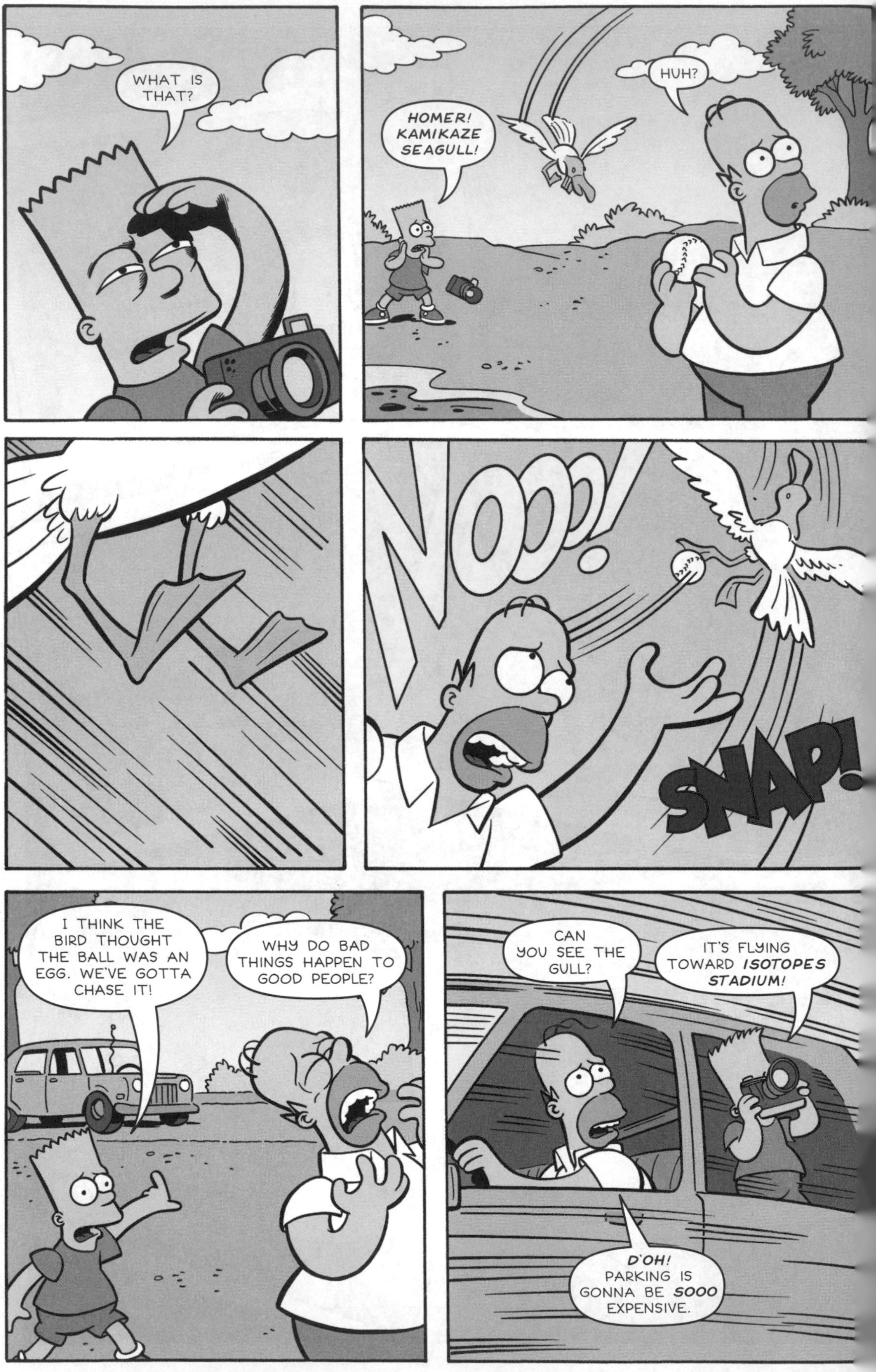
WHAT IS THAT?
HOMER! KAMIKAZE SEAGULL!
HUH?
NOOO!
SNAP!
I THINK THE BIRD THOUGHT THE BALL WAS AN EGG. WE'VE GOTTA CHASE IT!
WHY DO BAD THINGS HAPPEN TO GOOD PEOPLE?
CAN YOU SEE THE GULL?
IT'S FLYING TOWARD ISOTOPES STADIUM!
D'OH! PARKING IS GONNA BE SOOO EXPENSIVE.

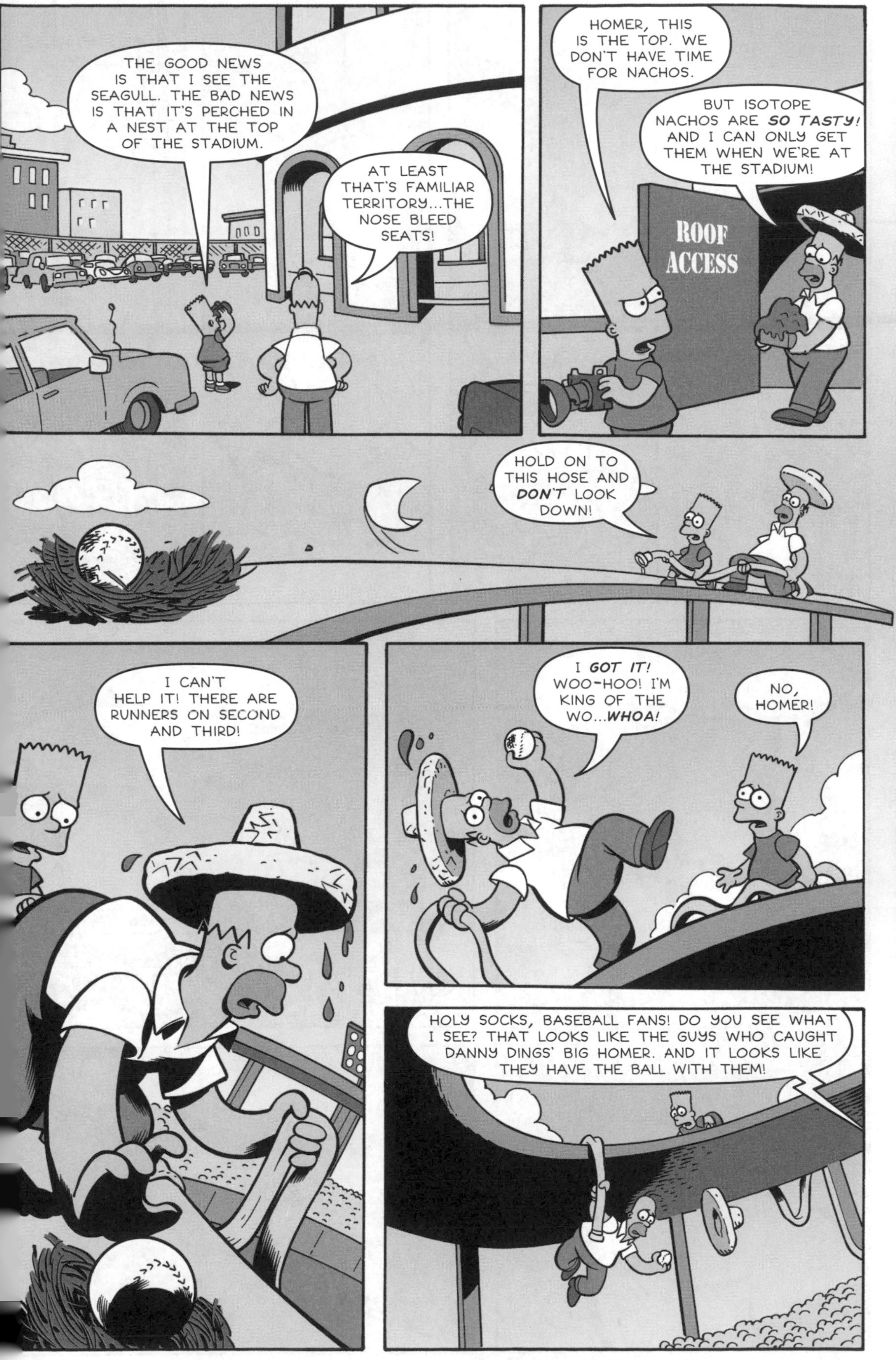
THE GOOD NEWS IS THAT I SEE THE SEAGULL. THE BAD NEWS IS THAT IT'S PERCHED IN A NEST AT THE TOP OF THE STADIUM.
AT LEAST THAT'S FAMILIAR TERRITORY...THE NOSE BLEED SEATS!
HOMER, THIS IS THE TOP. WE DON'T HAVE TIME FOR NACHOS.
BUT ISOTOPE NACHOS ARE **SO TASTY!** AND I CAN ONLY GET THEM WHEN WE'RE AT THE STADIUM!
ROOF ACCESS
HOLD ON TO THIS HOSE AND **DON'T** LOOK DOWN!
I CAN'T HELP IT! THERE ARE RUNNERS ON SECOND AND THIRD!
I **GOT IT!** WOO-HOO! I'M KING OF THE WO...**WHOA!**
NO, HOMER!
HOLY SOCKS, BASEBALL FANS! DO YOU SEE WHAT I SEE? THAT LOOKS LIKE THE GUYS WHO CAUGHT DANNY DINGS' BIG HOMER. AND IT LOOKS LIKE THEY HAVE THE BALL WITH THEM!

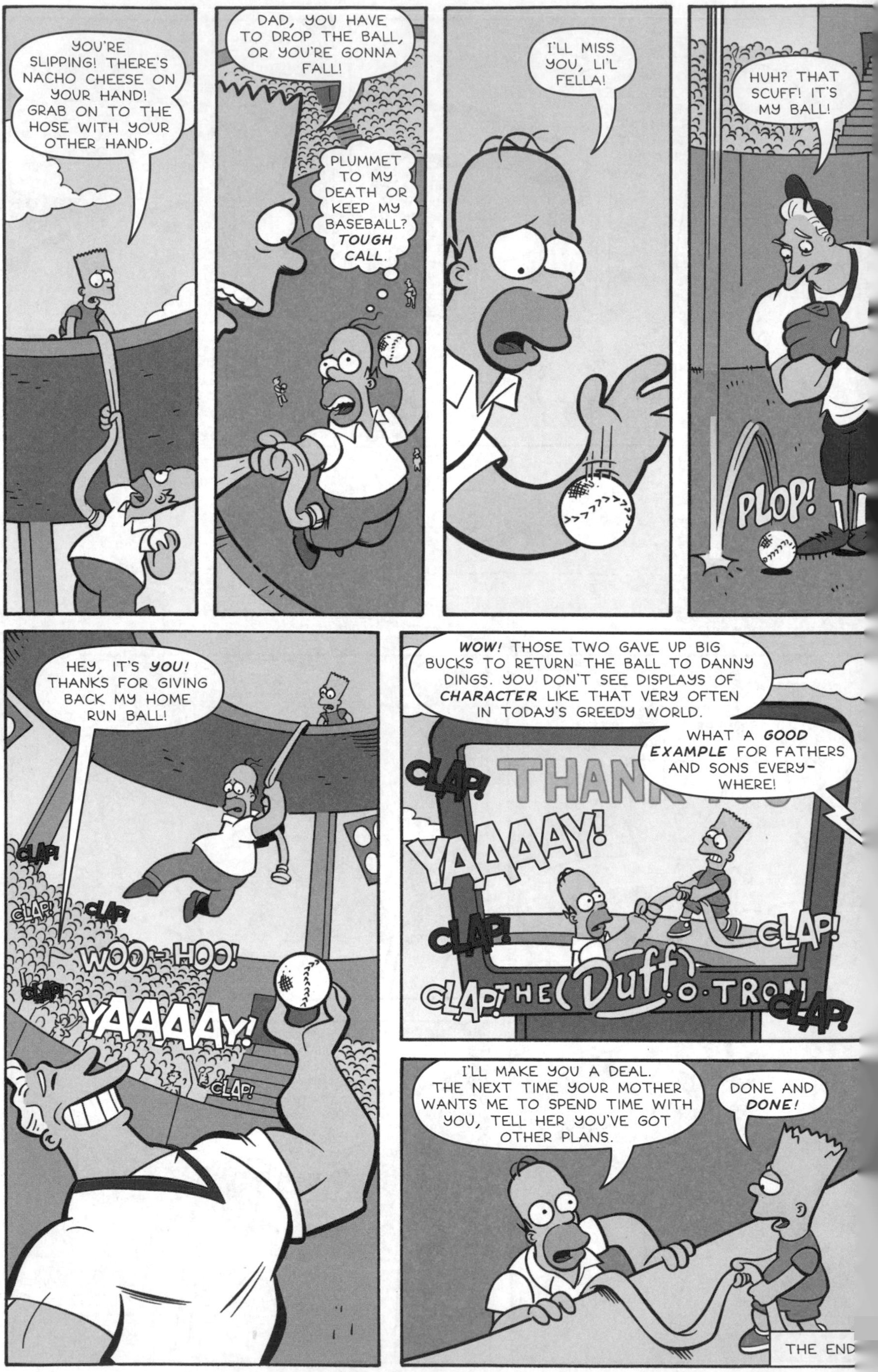
YOU'RE SLIPPING! THERE'S NACHO CHEESE ON YOUR HAND! GRAB ON TO THE HOSE WITH YOUR OTHER HAND.
DAD, YOU HAVE TO DROP THE BALL, OR YOU'RE GONNA FALL!
PLUMMET TO MY DEATH OR KEEP MY BASEBALL? TOUGH CALL.
I'LL MISS YOU, LI'L FELLA!
HUH? THAT SCUFF! IT'S MY BALL!
PLOP!
HEY, IT'S YOU! THANKS FOR GIVING BACK MY HOME RUN BALL!
CLAP!
CLAP!
CLAP!
WOO-HOO!
CLAP!
YAAAAY!
CLAP!
WOW! THOSE TWO GAVE UP BIG BUCKS TO RETURN THE BALL TO DANNY DINGS. YOU DON'T SEE DISPLAYS OF CHARACTER LIKE THAT VERY OFTEN IN TODAY'S GREEDY WORLD.
WHAT A GOOD EXAMPLE FOR FATHERS AND SONS EVERY-WHERE!
CLAP!
YAAAAY!
CLAP!
CLAP!
CLAP!
THE Duff-O-TRON
CLAP!
I'LL MAKE YOU A DEAL. THE NEXT TIME YOUR MOTHER WANTS ME TO SPEND TIME WITH YOU, TELL HER YOU'VE GOT OTHER PLANS.
DONE AND DONE!
THE END

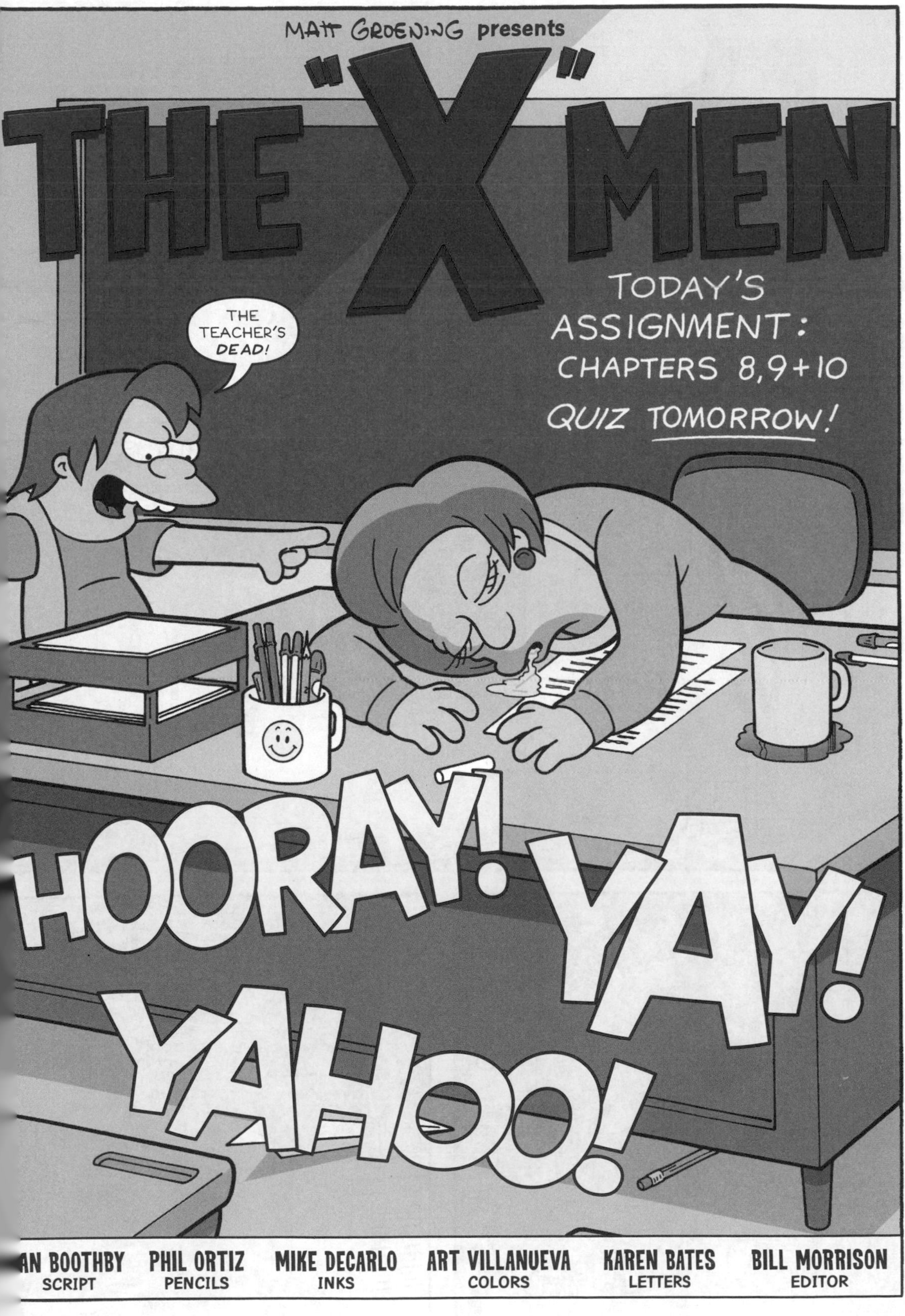
MATT GROENING presents
THE "X" MEN
TODAY'S ASSIGNMENT: CHAPTERS 8,9+10
QUIZ TOMORROW!
THE TEACHER'S DEAD!
HOORAY!
YAY!
YAHOO!

AN BOOTHBY SCRIPT | PHIL ORTIZ PENCILS | MIKE DECARLO INKS | ART VILLANUEVA COLORS | KAREN BATES LETTERS | BILL MORRISON EDITOR

SHE'S FINE! I JUST SNUCK INTO THE TEACHER'S LOUNGE EARLY TODAY...

COFFEE

"...AND REPLACED THEIR REGULAR COFFEE WITH *DECAFFEINATED!*"

TEACHER'S LOUNGE

De-CAF COFFEE

MEANWHILE...

ZZZZZ!

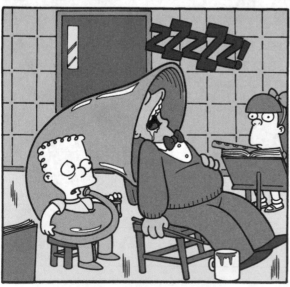

ZZZZZ

BUZZZZ

ZZZZZ!

DANGER! WOOD CHIPPER

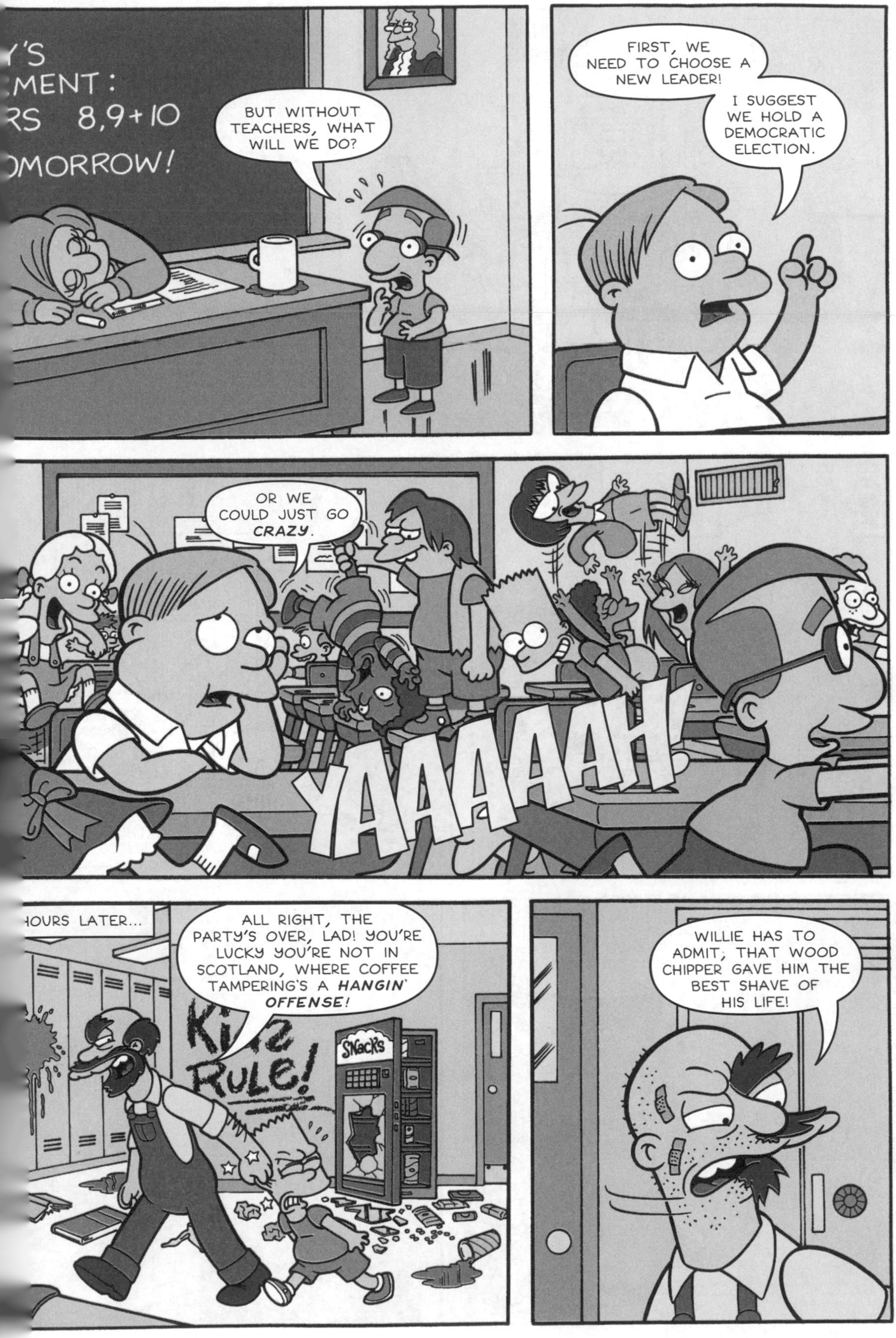
Y'S
MENT:
RS 8,9+10
OMORROW!
BUT WITHOUT TEACHERS, WHAT WILL WE DO?
FIRST, WE NEED TO CHOOSE A NEW LEADER!
I SUGGEST WE HOLD A DEMOCRATIC ELECTION.
OR WE COULD JUST GO *CRAZY*.
YAAAAAH!
HOURS LATER...
ALL RIGHT, THE PARTY'S OVER, LAD! YOU'RE LUCKY YOU'RE NOT IN SCOTLAND, WHERE COFFEE TAMPERING'S A *HANGIN' OFFENSE*!
RULE!
SNacKS
WILLIE HAS TO ADMIT, THAT WOOD CHIPPER GAVE HIM THE BEST SHAVE OF HIS LIFE!

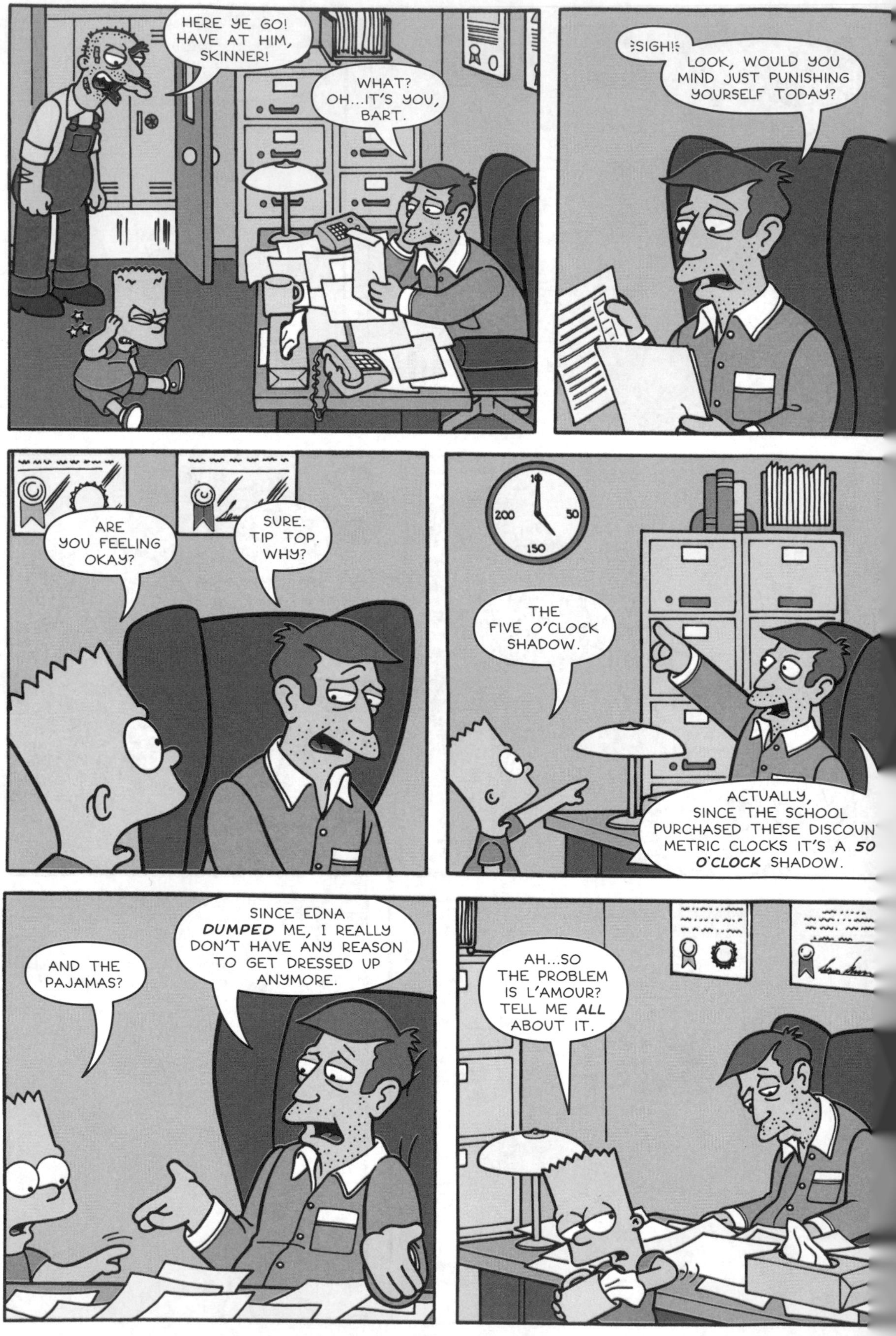
HERE YE GO! HAVE AT HIM, SKINNER!
WHAT? OH...IT'S YOU, BART.
SIGH!
LOOK, WOULD YOU MIND JUST PUNISHING YOURSELF TODAY?
ARE YOU FEELING OKAY?
SURE. TIP TOP. WHY?
THE FIVE O'CLOCK SHADOW.
ACTUALLY, SINCE THE SCHOOL PURCHASED THESE DISCOUNT METRIC CLOCKS IT'S A **50 O'CLOCK** SHADOW.
AND THE PAJAMAS?
SINCE EDNA **DUMPED** ME, I REALLY DON'T HAVE ANY REASON TO GET DRESSED UP ANYMORE.
AH...SO THE PROBLEM IS L'AMOUR? TELL ME **ALL** ABOUT IT.

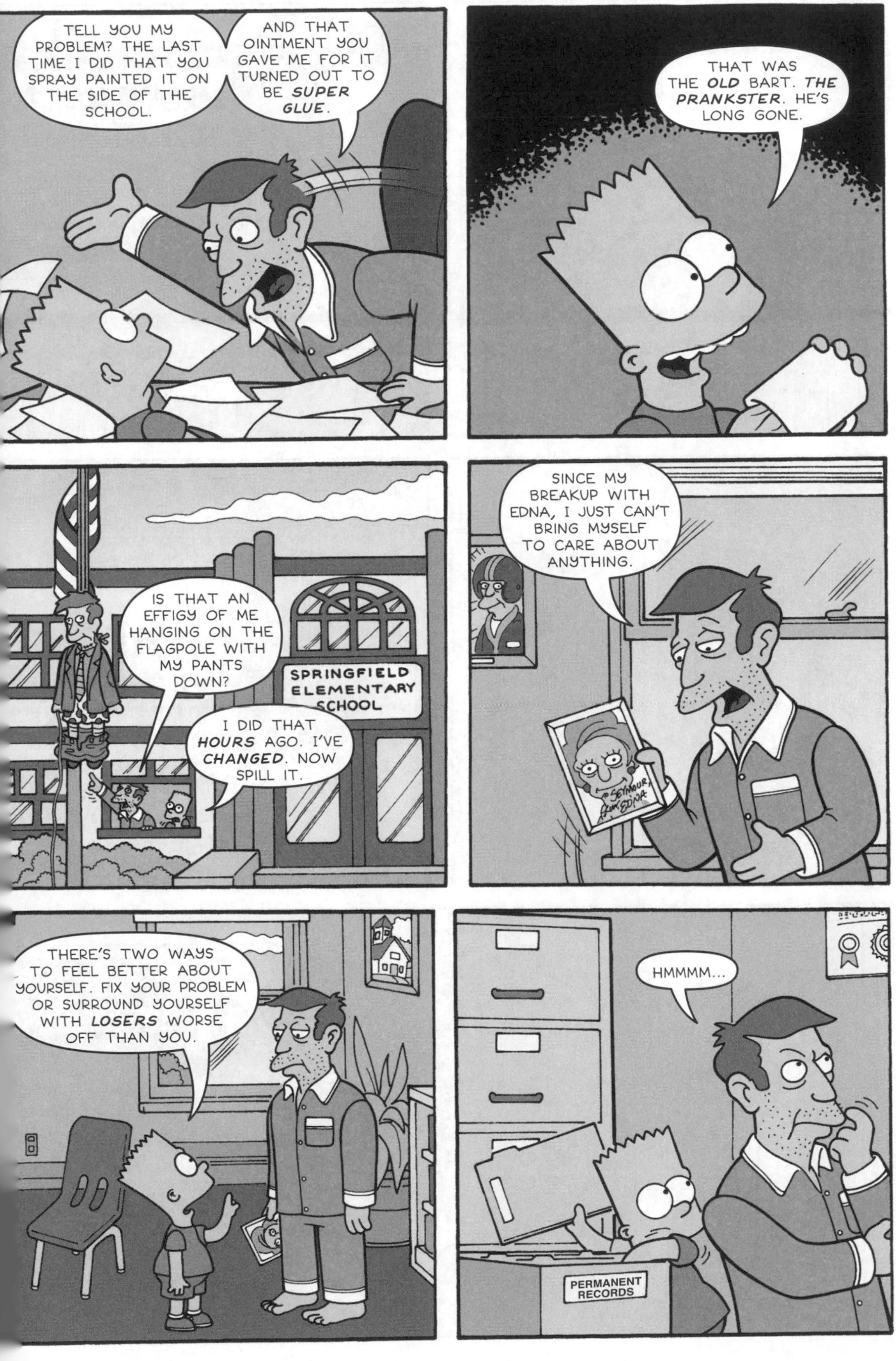
TELL YOU MY PROBLEM? THE LAST TIME I DID THAT YOU SPRAY PAINTED IT ON THE SIDE OF THE SCHOOL.
AND THAT OINTMENT YOU GAVE ME FOR IT TURNED OUT TO BE SUPER GLUE.
THAT WAS THE OLD BART. THE PRANKSTER. HE'S LONG GONE.
IS THAT AN EFFIGY OF ME HANGING ON THE FLAGPOLE WITH MY PANTS DOWN?
SPRINGFIELD ELEMENTARY SCHOOL
I DID THAT HOURS AGO. I'VE CHANGED. NOW SPILL IT.
SINCE MY BREAKUP WITH EDNA, I JUST CAN'T BRING MYSELF TO CARE ABOUT ANYTHING.
THERE'S TWO WAYS TO FEEL BETTER ABOUT YOURSELF. FIX YOUR PROBLEM OR SURROUND YOURSELF WITH LOSERS WORSE OFF THAN YOU.
HMMMM...
PERMANENT RECORDS

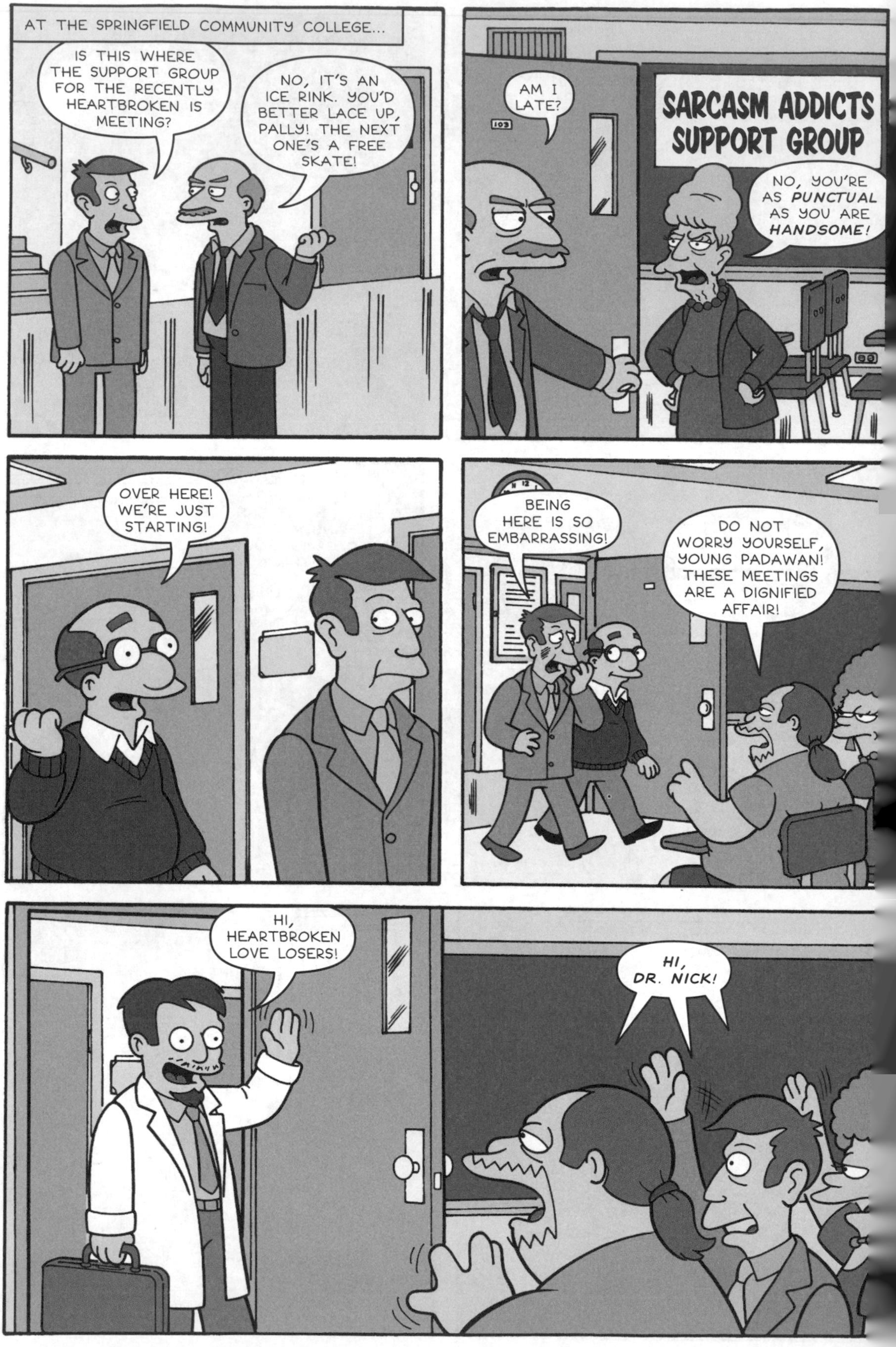
AT THE SPRINGFIELD COMMUNITY COLLEGE...
IS THIS WHERE THE SUPPORT GROUP FOR THE RECENTLY HEARTBROKEN IS MEETING?
NO, IT'S AN ICE RINK. YOU'D BETTER LACE UP, PALLY! THE NEXT ONE'S A FREE SKATE!
AM I LATE?
103
SARCASM ADDICTS SUPPORT GROUP
NO, YOU'RE AS PUNCTUAL AS YOU ARE HANDSOME!
OVER HERE! WE'RE JUST STARTING!
BEING HERE IS SO EMBARRASSING!
DO NOT WORRY YOURSELF, YOUNG PADAWAN! THESE MEETINGS ARE A DIGNIFIED AFFAIR!
HI, HEARTBROKEN LOVE LOSERS!
HI, DR. NICK!

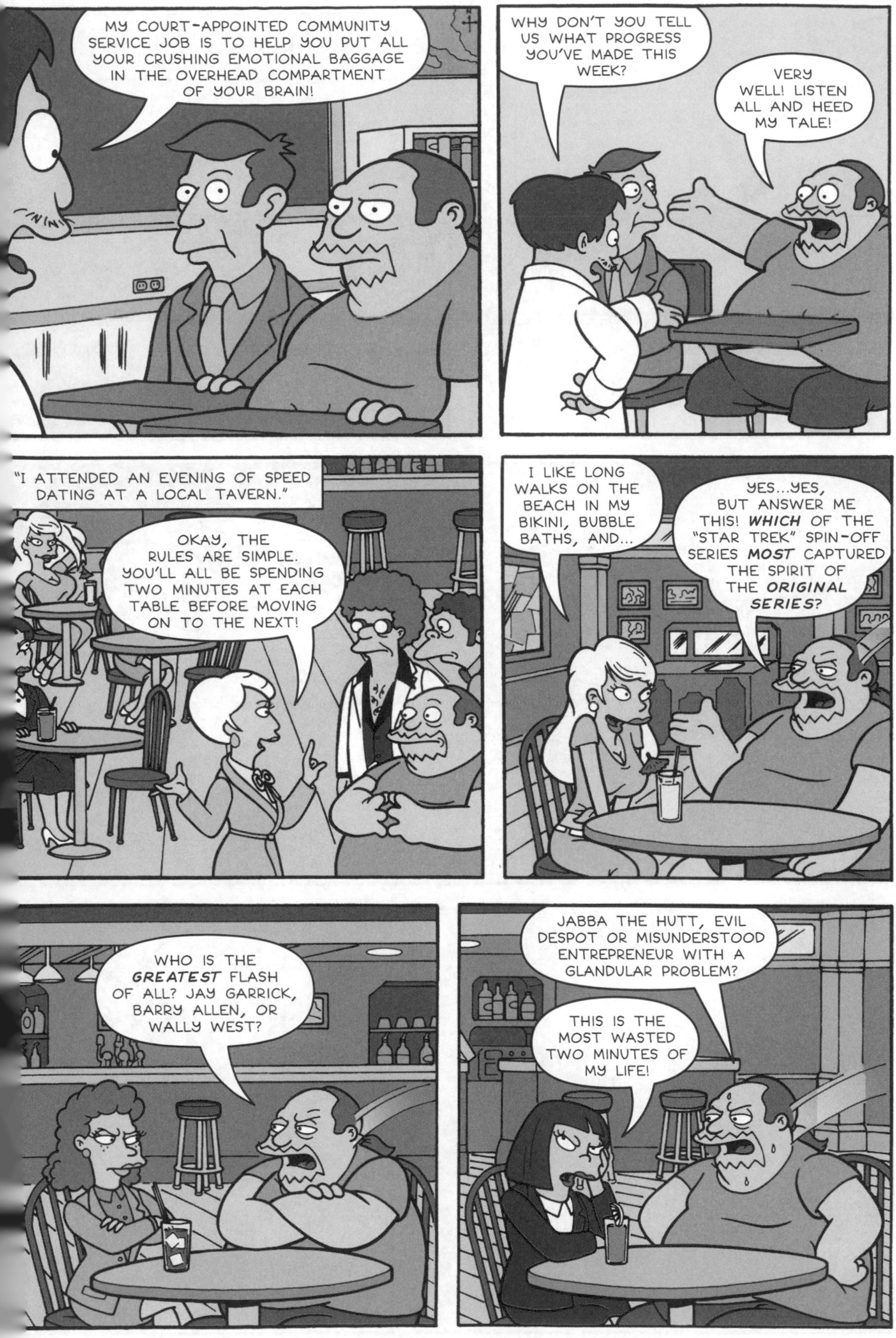
MY COURT-APPOINTED COMMUNITY SERVICE JOB IS TO HELP YOU PUT ALL YOUR CRUSHING EMOTIONAL BAGGAGE IN THE OVERHEAD COMPARTMENT OF YOUR BRAIN!
WHY DON'T YOU TELL US WHAT PROGRESS YOU'VE MADE THIS WEEK?
VERY WELL! LISTEN ALL AND HEED MY TALE!
"I ATTENDED AN EVENING OF SPEED DATING AT A LOCAL TAVERN."
OKAY, THE RULES ARE SIMPLE. YOU'LL ALL BE SPENDING TWO MINUTES AT EACH TABLE BEFORE MOVING ON TO THE NEXT!
I LIKE LONG WALKS ON THE BEACH IN MY BIKINI, BUBBLE BATHS, AND...
YES...YES, BUT ANSWER ME THIS! **WHICH** OF THE "STAR TREK" SPIN-OFF SERIES **MOST** CAPTURED THE SPIRIT OF THE ***ORIGINAL SERIES***?
WHO IS THE ***GREATEST*** FLASH OF ALL? JAY GARRICK, BARRY ALLEN, OR WALLY WEST?
JABBA THE HUTT, EVIL DESPOT OR MISUNDERSTOOD ENTREPRENEUR WITH A GLANDULAR PROBLEM?
THIS IS THE MOST WASTED TWO MINUTES OF MY LIFE!

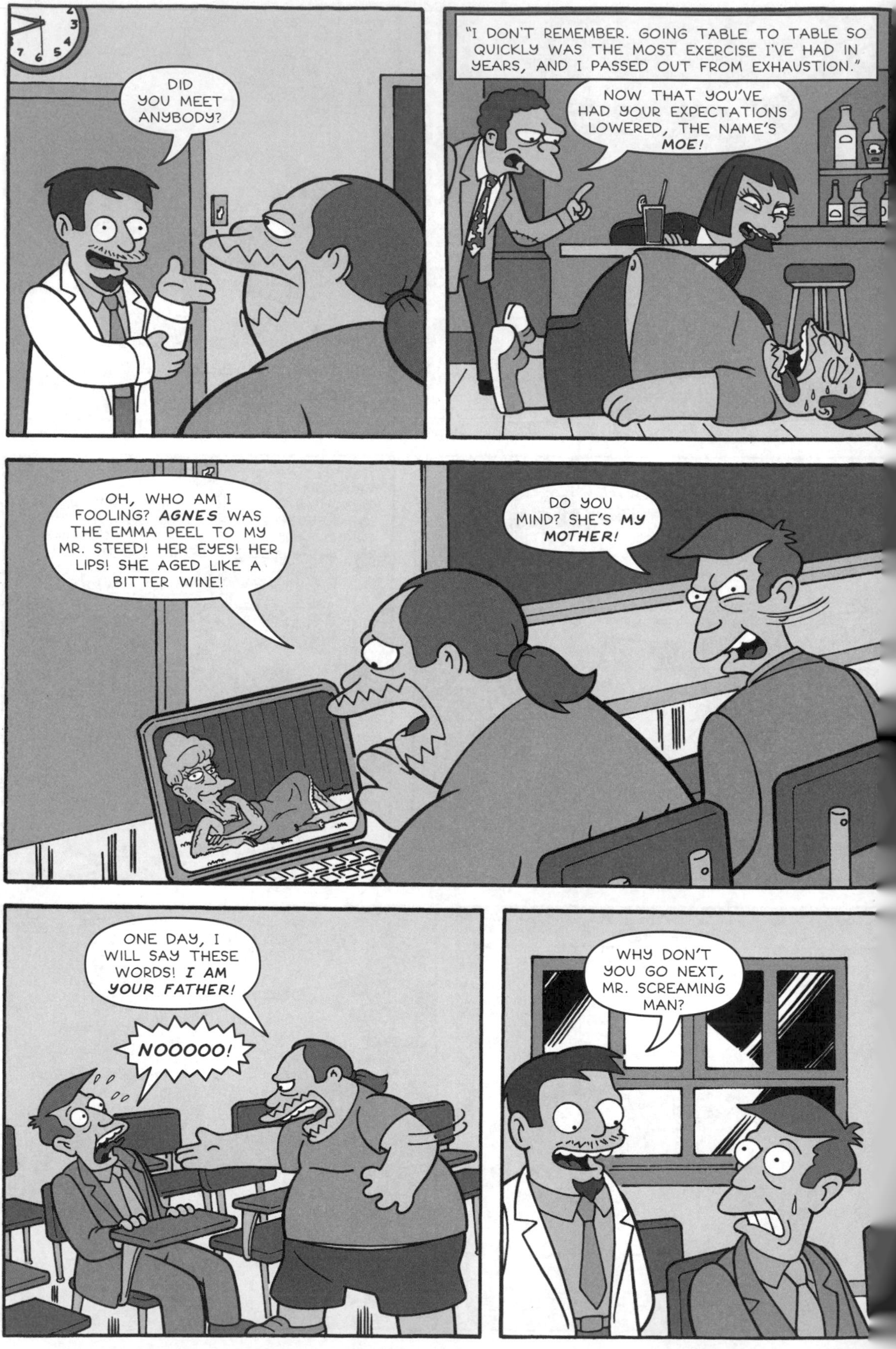
DID YOU MEET ANYBODY?
"I DON'T REMEMBER. GOING TABLE TO TABLE SO QUICKLY WAS THE MOST EXERCISE I'VE HAD IN YEARS, AND I PASSED OUT FROM EXHAUSTION."
NOW THAT YOU'VE HAD YOUR EXPECTATIONS LOWERED, THE NAME'S MOE!
OH, WHO AM I FOOLING? AGNES WAS THE EMMA PEEL TO MY MR. STEED! HER EYES! HER LIPS! SHE AGED LIKE A BITTER WINE!
DO YOU MIND? SHE'S MY MOTHER!
ONE DAY, I WILL SAY THESE WORDS! I AM YOUR FATHER!
NOOOOO!
WHY DON'T YOU GO NEXT, MR. SCREAMING MAN?

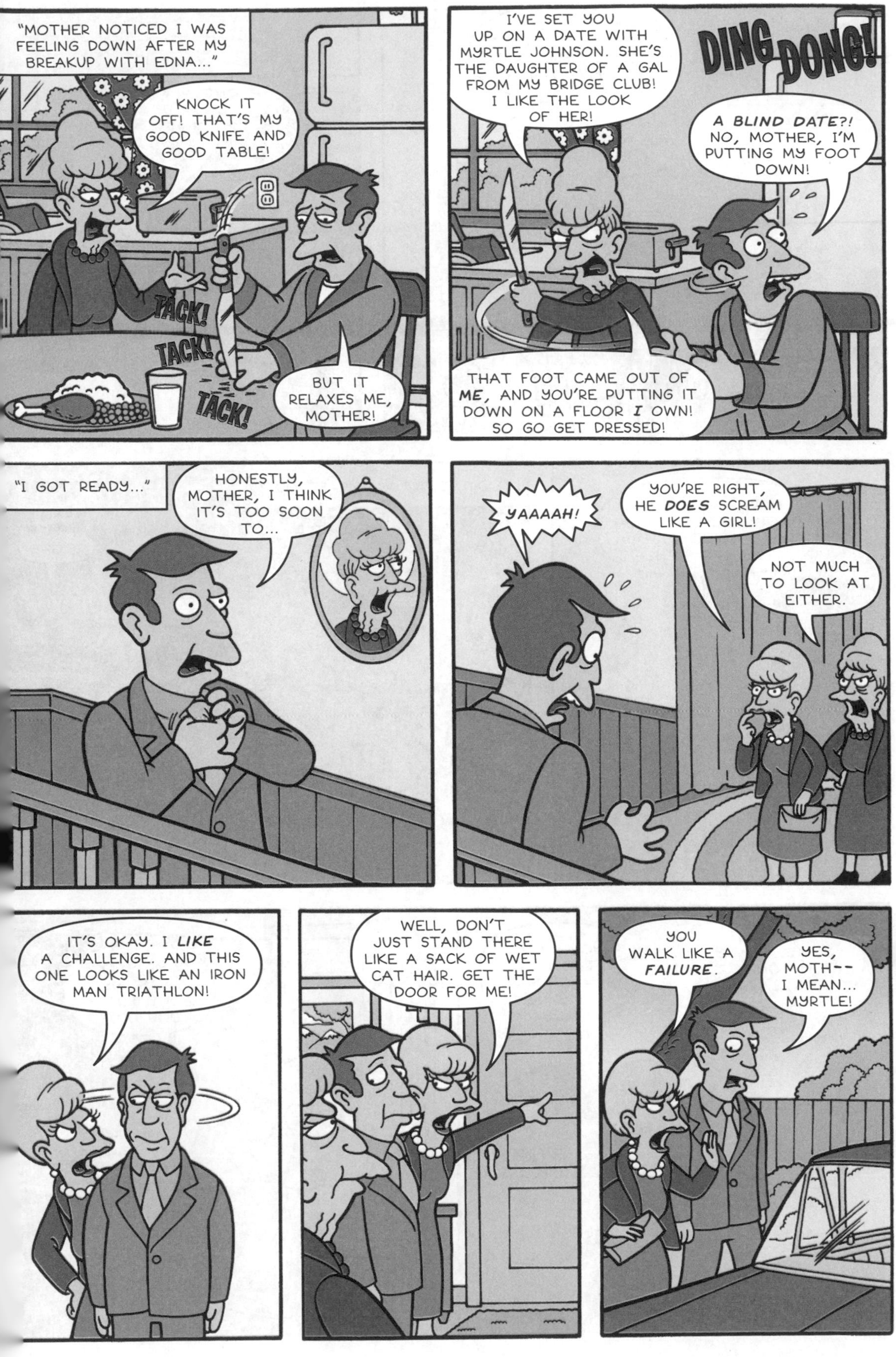
"MOTHER NOTICED I WAS FEELING DOWN AFTER MY BREAKUP WITH EDNA..."
KNOCK IT OFF! THAT'S MY GOOD KNIFE AND GOOD TABLE!
TACK!
TACK!
TACK!
BUT IT RELAXES ME, MOTHER!
I'VE SET YOU UP ON A DATE WITH MYRTLE JOHNSON. SHE'S THE DAUGHTER OF A GAL FROM MY BRIDGE CLUB! I LIKE THE LOOK OF HER!
DING DONG!
A BLIND DATE?! NO, MOTHER, I'M PUTTING MY FOOT DOWN!
THAT FOOT CAME OUT OF ME, AND YOU'RE PUTTING IT DOWN ON A FLOOR I OWN! SO GO GET DRESSED!
"I GOT READY..."
HONESTLY, MOTHER, I THINK IT'S TOO SOON TO...
YAAAAH!
YOU'RE RIGHT, HE DOES SCREAM LIKE A GIRL!
NOT MUCH TO LOOK AT EITHER.
IT'S OKAY. I LIKE A CHALLENGE. AND THIS ONE LOOKS LIKE AN IRON MAN TRIATHLON!
WELL, DON'T JUST STAND THERE LIKE A SACK OF WET CAT HAIR. GET THE DOOR FOR ME!
YOU WALK LIKE A FAILURE.
YES, MOTH-- I MEAN... MYRTLE!

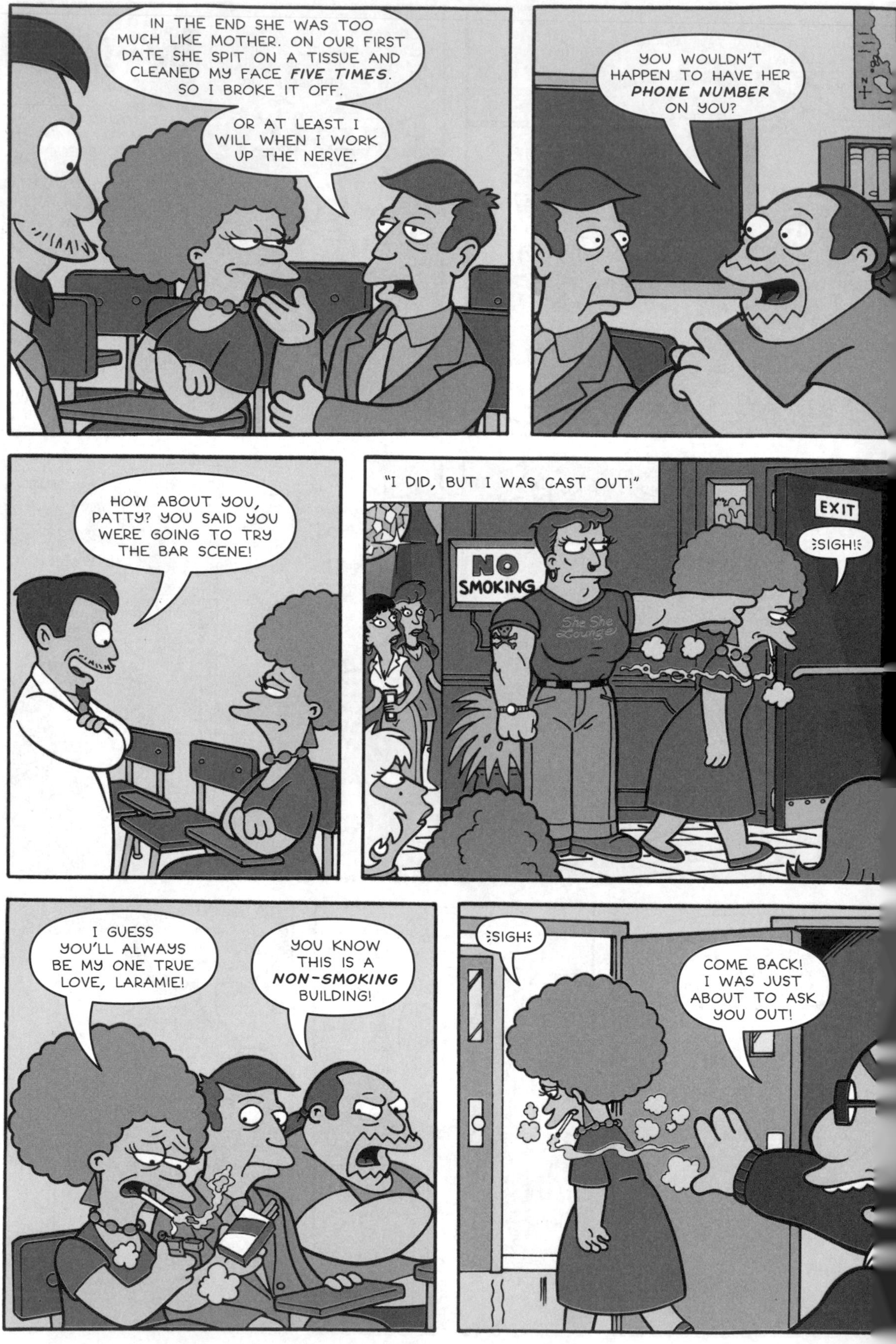

IN THE END SHE WAS TOO MUCH LIKE MOTHER. ON OUR FIRST DATE SHE SPIT ON A TISSUE AND CLEANED MY FACE **FIVE TIMES**. SO I BROKE IT OFF.
OR AT LEAST I WILL WHEN I WORK UP THE NERVE.
YOU WOULDN'T HAPPEN TO HAVE HER **PHONE NUMBER** ON YOU?
HOW ABOUT YOU, PATTY? YOU SAID YOU WERE GOING TO TRY THE BAR SCENE!
"I DID, BUT I WAS CAST OUT!"
NO SMOKING
EXIT
SIGH!
She She Lounge
I GUESS YOU'LL ALWAYS BE MY ONE TRUE LOVE, LARAMIE!
YOU KNOW THIS IS A **NON-SMOKING** BUILDING!
SIGH
COME BACK! I WAS JUST ABOUT TO ASK YOU OUT!

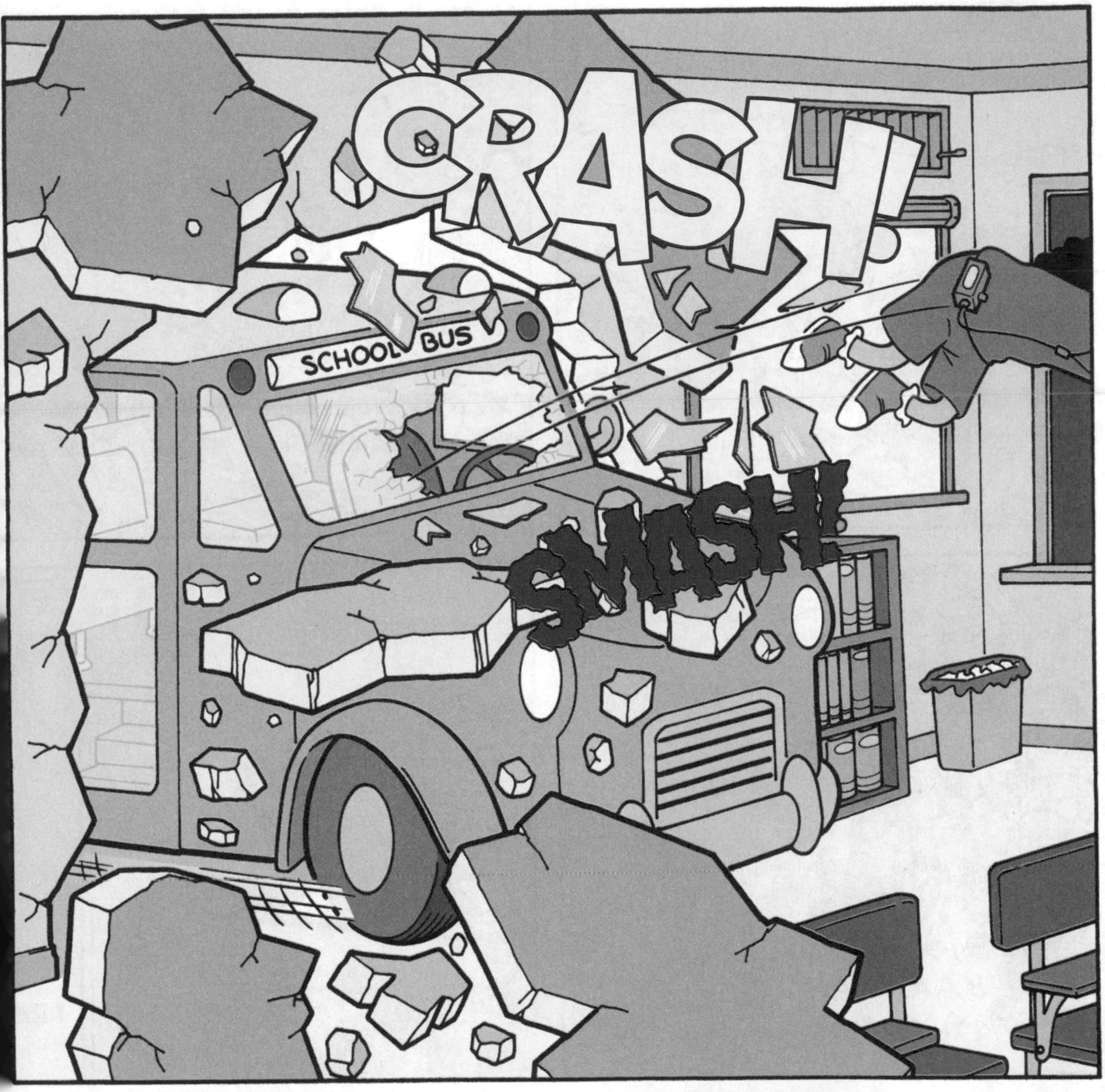
CRASH!
SCHOOL BUS
SMASH!

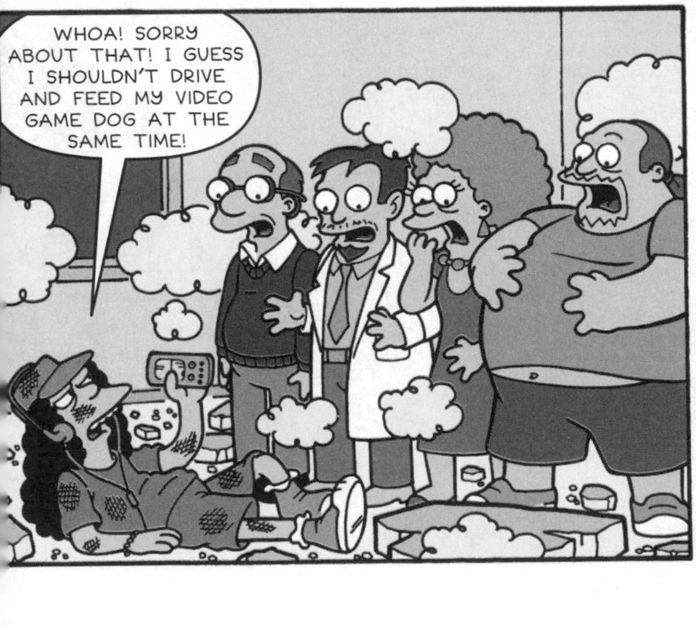
WHOA! SORRY ABOUT THAT! I GUESS I SHOULDN'T DRIVE AND FEED MY VIDEO GAME DOG AT THE SAME TIME!

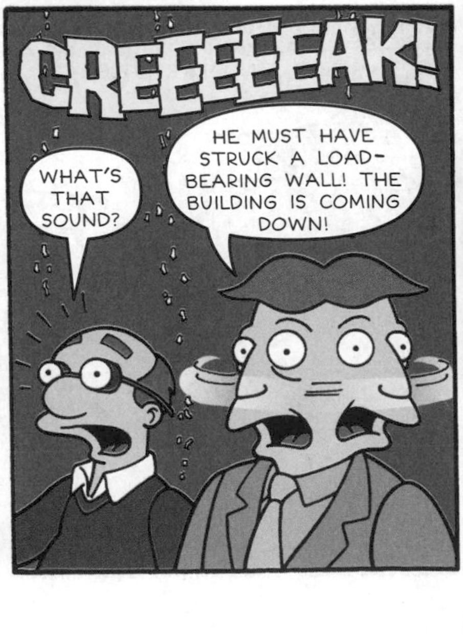
CREEEEEAK!
WHAT'S THAT SOUND?
HE MUST HAVE STRUCK A LOAD-BEARING WALL! THE BUILDING IS COMING DOWN!

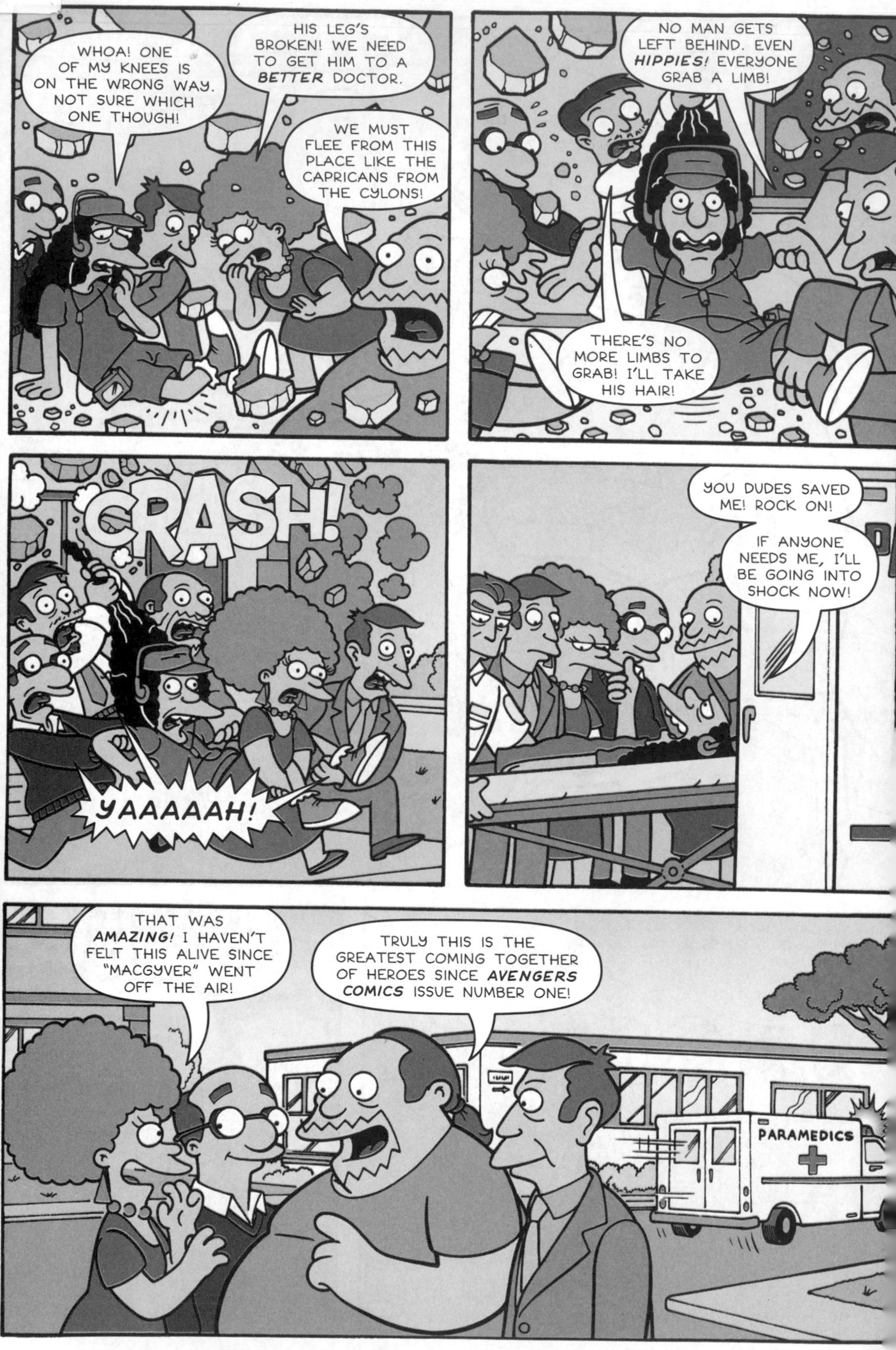
WHOA! ONE OF MY KNEES IS ON THE WRONG WAY. NOT SURE WHICH ONE THOUGH!
HIS LEG'S BROKEN! WE NEED TO GET HIM TO A BETTER DOCTOR.
WE MUST FLEE FROM THIS PLACE LIKE THE CAPRICANS FROM THE CYLONS!
NO MAN GETS LEFT BEHIND. EVEN HIPPIES! EVERYONE GRAB A LIMB!
THERE'S NO MORE LIMBS TO GRAB! I'LL TAKE HIS HAIR!
CRASH!
YAAAAAH!
YOU DUDES SAVED ME! ROCK ON!
IF ANYONE NEEDS ME, I'LL BE GOING INTO SHOCK NOW!
THAT WAS AMAZING! I HAVEN'T FELT THIS ALIVE SINCE "MACGYVER" WENT OFF THE AIR!
TRULY THIS IS THE GREATEST COMING TOGETHER OF HEROES SINCE AVENGERS COMICS ISSUE NUMBER ONE!
PARAMEDICS

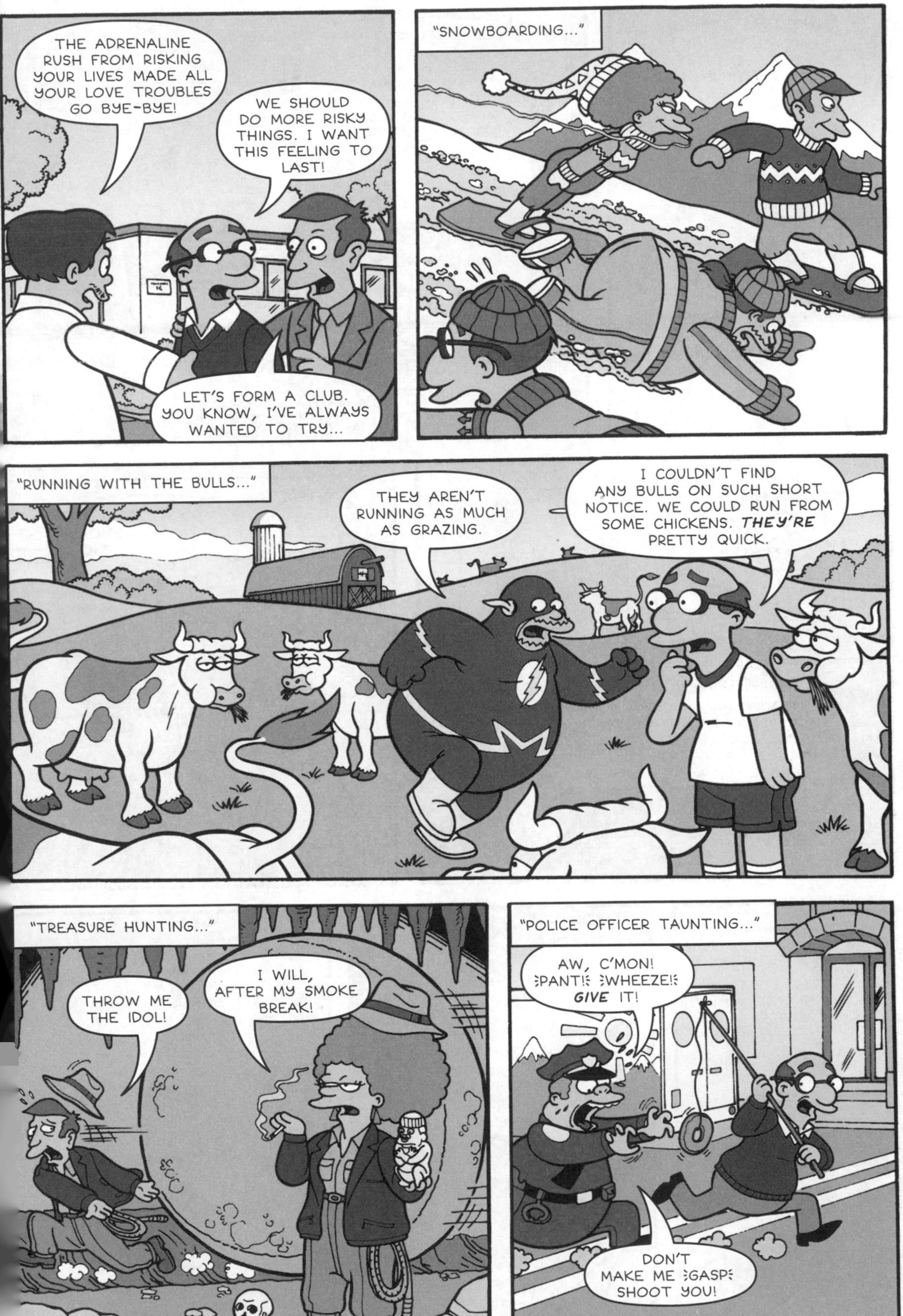
THE ADRENALINE RUSH FROM RISKING YOUR LIVES MADE ALL YOUR LOVE TROUBLES GO BYE-BYE!
WE SHOULD DO MORE RISKY THINGS. I WANT THIS FEELING TO LAST!
LET'S FORM A CLUB. YOU KNOW, I'VE ALWAYS WANTED TO TRY...
"SNOWBOARDING..."
"RUNNING WITH THE BULLS..."
THEY AREN'T RUNNING AS MUCH AS GRAZING.
I COULDN'T FIND ANY BULLS ON SUCH SHORT NOTICE. WE COULD RUN FROM SOME CHICKENS. *THEY'RE* PRETTY QUICK.
"TREASURE HUNTING..."
THROW ME THE IDOL!
I WILL, AFTER MY SMOKE BREAK!
"POLICE OFFICER TAUNTING..."
AW, C'MON! PANT! WHEEZE! *GIVE* IT!
DON'T MAKE ME GASP SHOOT YOU!

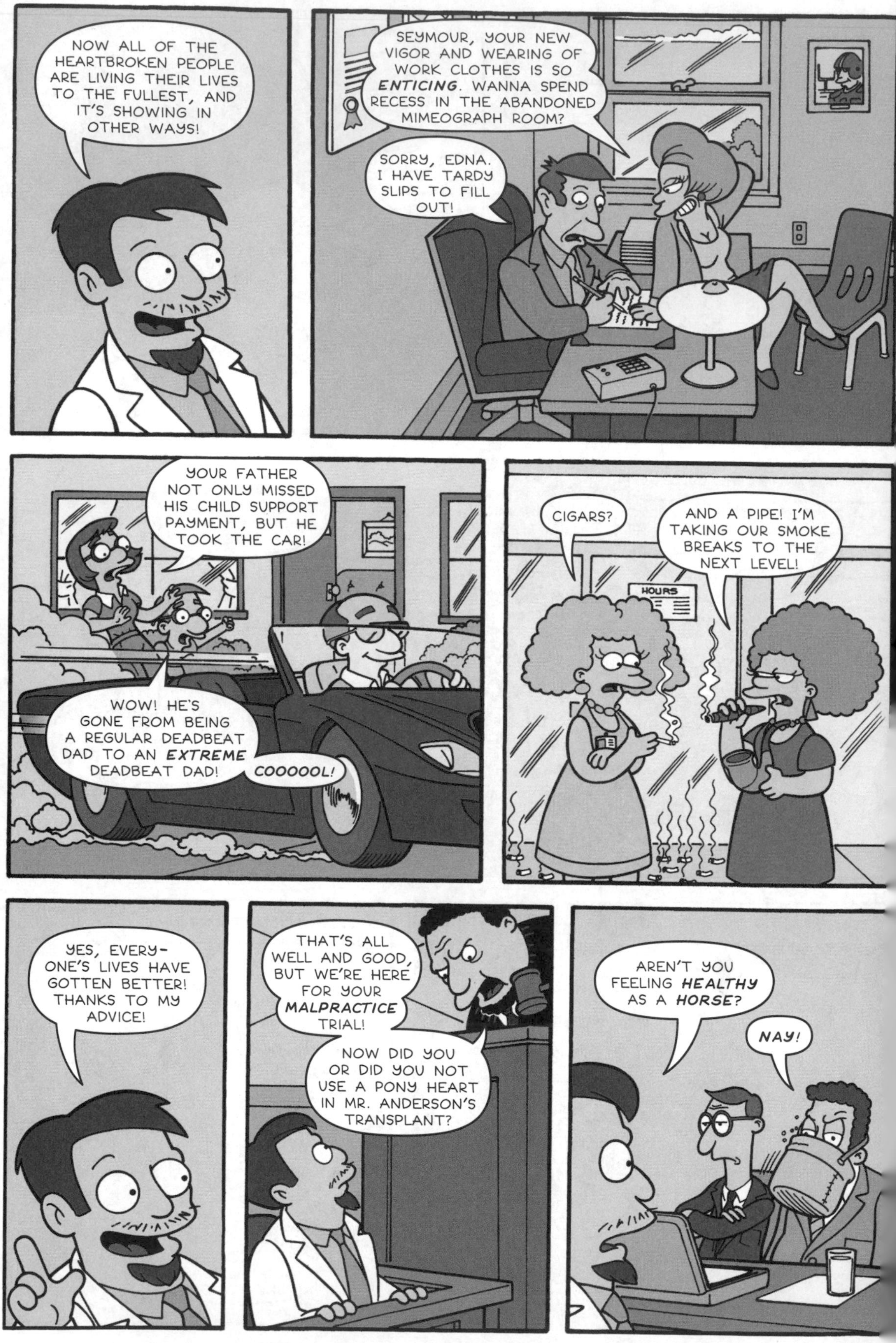
NOW ALL OF THE HEARTBROKEN PEOPLE ARE LIVING THEIR LIVES TO THE FULLEST, AND IT'S SHOWING IN OTHER WAYS!
SEYMOUR, YOUR NEW VIGOR AND WEARING OF WORK CLOTHES IS SO **ENTICING**. WANNA SPEND RECESS IN THE ABANDONED MIMEOGRAPH ROOM?
SORRY, EDNA. I HAVE TARDY SLIPS TO FILL OUT!
YOUR FATHER NOT ONLY MISSED HIS CHILD SUPPORT PAYMENT, BUT HE TOOK THE CAR!
WOW! HE'S GONE FROM BEING A REGULAR DEADBEAT DAD TO AN **EXTREME** DEADBEAT DAD!
COOOOOL!
CIGARS?
AND A PIPE! I'M TAKING OUR SMOKE BREAKS TO THE NEXT LEVEL!
HOURS
YES, EVERY-ONE'S LIVES HAVE GOTTEN BETTER! THANKS TO MY ADVICE!
THAT'S ALL WELL AND GOOD, BUT WE'RE HERE FOR YOUR **MALPRACTICE** TRIAL!
NOW DID YOU OR DID YOU NOT USE A PONY HEART IN MR. ANDERSON'S TRANSPLANT?
AREN'T YOU FEELING **HEALTHY** AS A **HORSE**?
NAY!

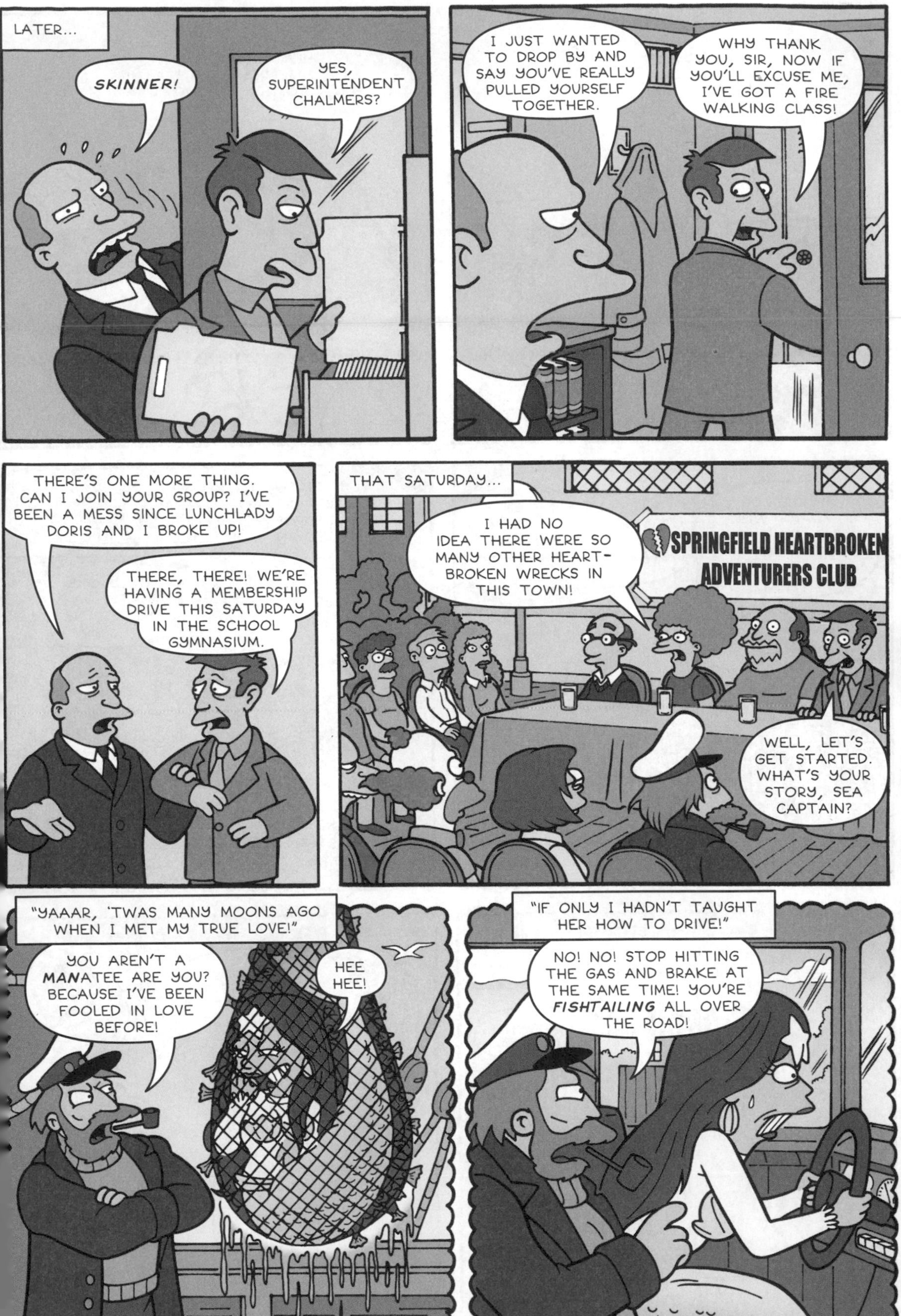
LATER...
SKINNER!
YES, SUPERINTENDENT CHALMERS?
I JUST WANTED TO DROP BY AND SAY YOU'VE REALLY PULLED YOURSELF TOGETHER.
WHY THANK YOU, SIR, NOW IF YOU'LL EXCUSE ME, I'VE GOT A FIRE WALKING CLASS!
THERE'S ONE MORE THING. CAN I JOIN YOUR GROUP? I'VE BEEN A MESS SINCE LUNCHLADY DORIS AND I BROKE UP!
THERE, THERE! WE'RE HAVING A MEMBERSHIP DRIVE THIS SATURDAY IN THE SCHOOL GYMNASIUM.
THAT SATURDAY...
I HAD NO IDEA THERE WERE SO MANY OTHER HEART-BROKEN WRECKS IN THIS TOWN!
SPRINGFIELD HEARTBROKEN ADVENTURERS CLUB
WELL, LET'S GET STARTED. WHAT'S YOUR STORY, SEA CAPTAIN?
"YAAAR, 'TWAS MANY MOONS AGO WHEN I MET MY TRUE LOVE!"
YOU AREN'T A MANATEE ARE YOU? BECAUSE I'VE BEEN FOOLED IN LOVE BEFORE!
HEE HEE!
"IF ONLY I HADN'T TAUGHT HER HOW TO DRIVE!"
NO! NO! STOP HITTING THE GAS AND BRAKE AT THE SAME TIME! YOU'RE FISHTAILING ALL OVER THE ROAD!

SHE DIED IN A CAR ACCIDENT?

NO, SHE DROVE OFF AND HAD AN AFFAIR WITH JACQUES COUSTEAU!

I DATED RAINIER WOLFCASTLE FOR A YEAR, THEN FOUND OUT IT WAS JUST RESEARCH FOR HIS COMEDY, "*I DATED A PLAIN GIRL*."

I FELL FOR A DAME WHO WAS A MIME. THEN I FOUND OUT SHE COULD ACTUALLY TALK!

YES, I HAD THE SAME EXPERIENCE DATING MARY PICKFORD. SILENT FILM STARS SHOULD *REMAIN* SILENT, I SAY!

BUT LISTEN TO ME GO ON. SMITHERS, DO *YOU* HAVE ANY TALES OF HEARTACHE TO SHARE? AN UNREQUITED LOVE, PERHAPS?

ONLY ONE THAT I DARE NOT SPEAK OF, SIR.

AW, WHY CAN'T I JOIN. I LIKE JOINING THINGS!

YOU'RE HAPPILY MARRIED WITH A FAMILY!

SIGH DON'T REMIND ME.

SPRINGFIELD
ADVENTURERS C

SHORTLY...

LOUSY LOVING FAMILY KEEPS ME FROM JOINING ALL THE COOL CLUBS!

SLAM!

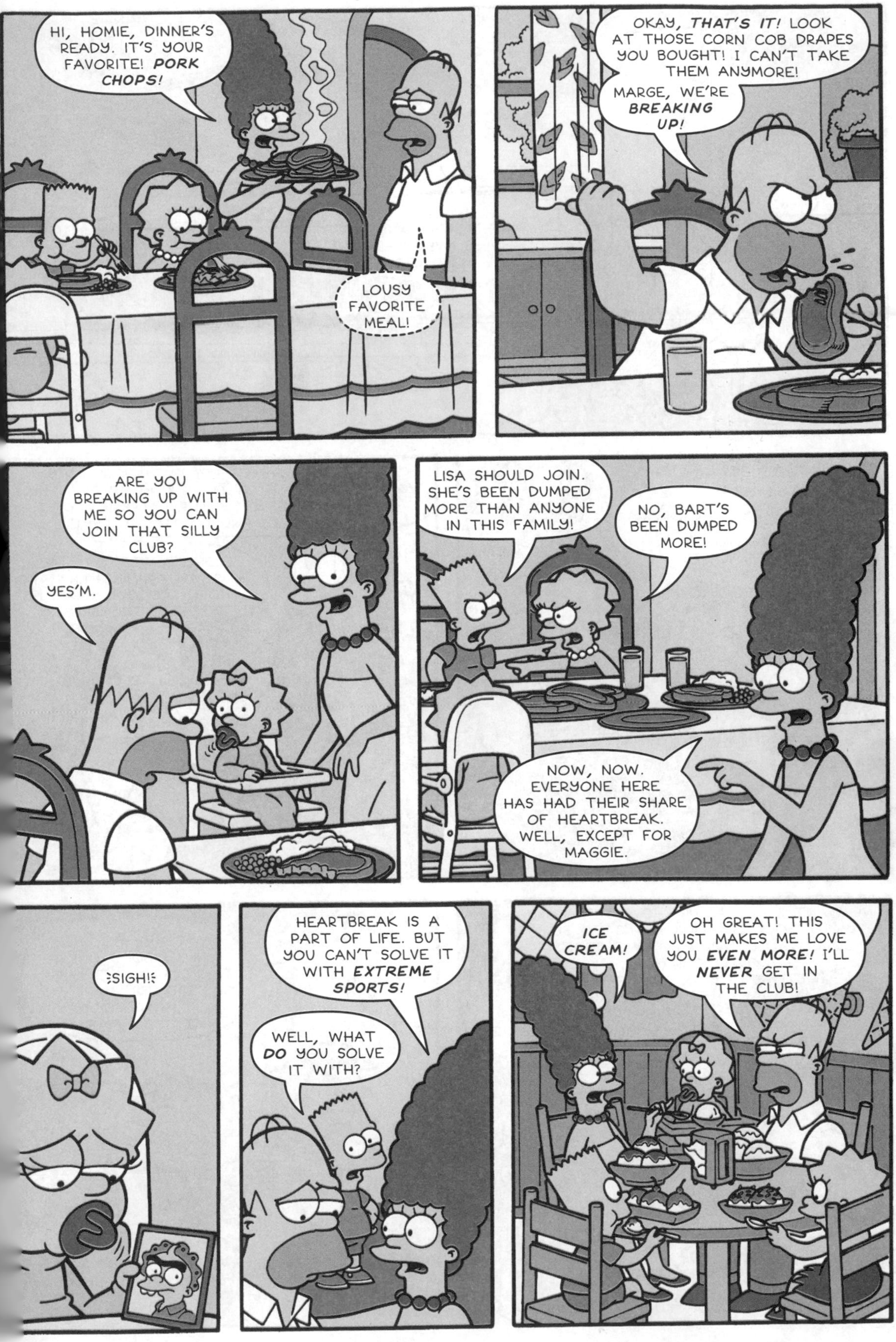
HI, HOMIE, DINNER'S READY. IT'S YOUR FAVORITE! PORK CHOPS!
LOUSY FAVORITE MEAL!
OKAY, THAT'S IT! LOOK AT THOSE CORN COB DRAPES YOU BOUGHT! I CAN'T TAKE THEM ANYMORE!
MARGE, WE'RE BREAKING UP!
ARE YOU BREAKING UP WITH ME SO YOU CAN JOIN THAT SILLY CLUB?
YES'M.
LISA SHOULD JOIN. SHE'S BEEN DUMPED MORE THAN ANYONE IN THIS FAMILY!
NO, BART'S BEEN DUMPED MORE!
NOW, NOW. EVERYONE HERE HAS HAD THEIR SHARE OF HEARTBREAK. WELL, EXCEPT FOR MAGGIE.
SIGH!
HEARTBREAK IS A PART OF LIFE. BUT YOU CAN'T SOLVE IT WITH EXTREME SPORTS!
WELL, WHAT DO YOU SOLVE IT WITH?
ICE CREAM!
OH GREAT! THIS JUST MAKES ME LOVE YOU EVEN MORE! I'LL NEVER GET IN THE CLUB!

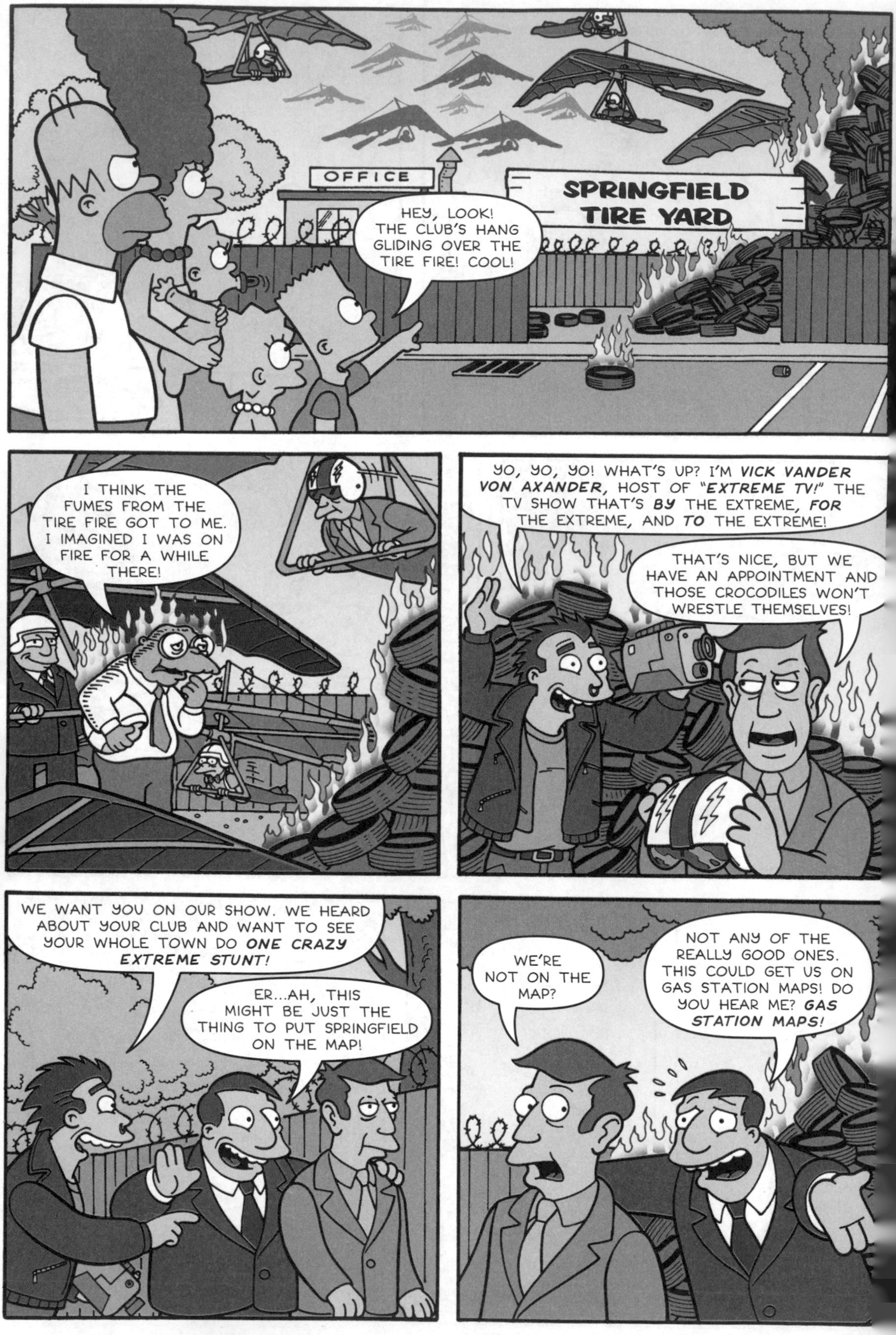
OFFICE
SPRINGFIELD TIRE YARD
HEY, LOOK! THE CLUB'S HANG GLIDING OVER THE TIRE FIRE! COOL!
I THINK THE FUMES FROM THE TIRE FIRE GOT TO ME. I IMAGINED I WAS ON FIRE FOR A WHILE THERE!
YO, YO, YO! WHAT'S UP? I'M VICK VANDER VON AXANDER, HOST OF "EXTREME TV!" THE TV SHOW THAT'S BY THE EXTREME, FOR THE EXTREME, AND TO THE EXTREME!
THAT'S NICE, BUT WE HAVE AN APPOINTMENT AND THOSE CROCODILES WON'T WRESTLE THEMSELVES!
WE WANT YOU ON OUR SHOW. WE HEARD ABOUT YOUR CLUB AND WANT TO SEE YOUR WHOLE TOWN DO ONE CRAZY EXTREME STUNT!
ER...AH, THIS MIGHT BE JUST THE THING TO PUT SPRINGFIELD ON THE MAP!
WE'RE NOT ON THE MAP?
NOT ANY OF THE REALLY GOOD ONES. THIS COULD GET US ON GAS STATION MAPS! DO YOU HEAR ME? GAS STATION MAPS!

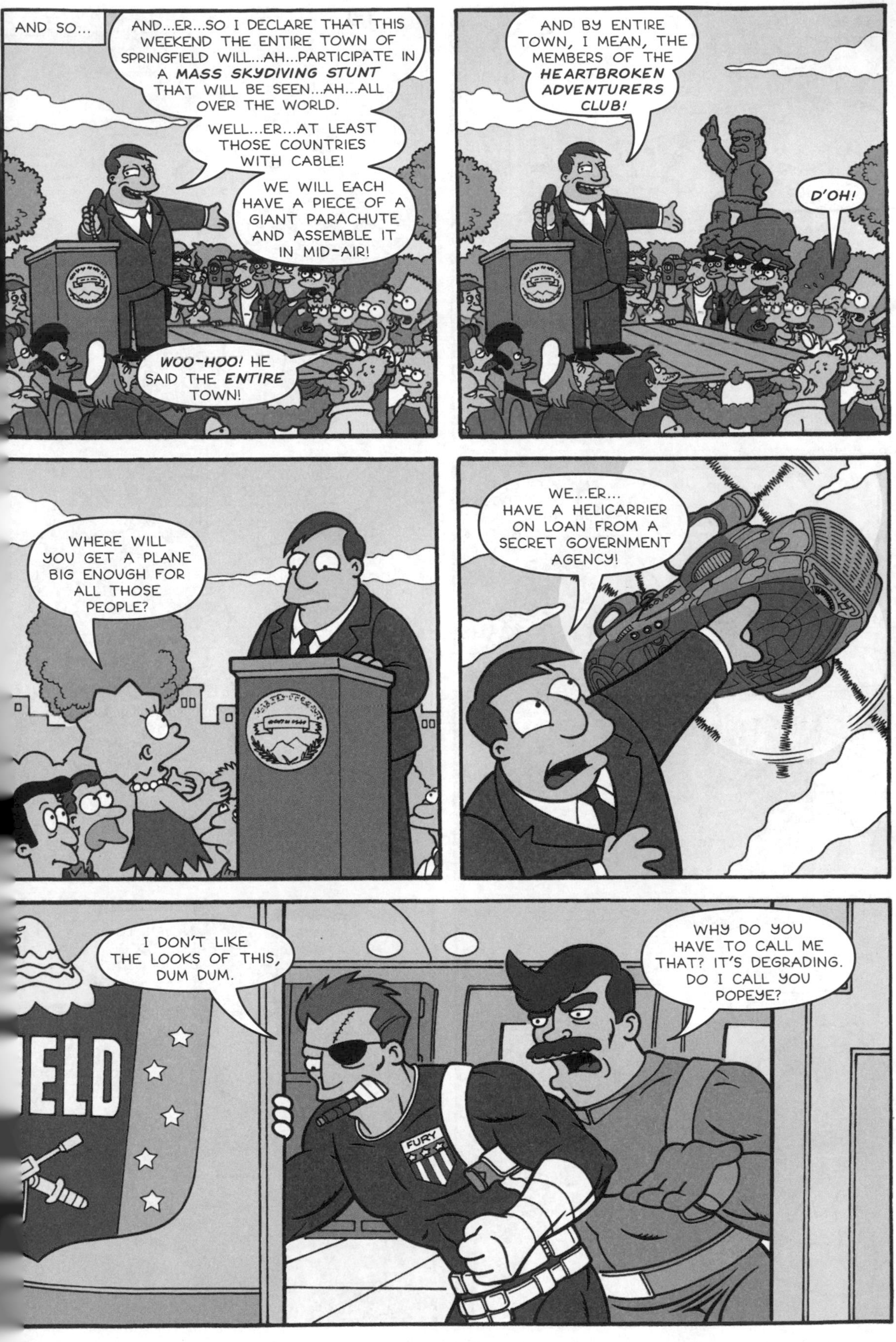
AND SO...
AND...ER...SO I DECLARE THAT THIS WEEKEND THE ENTIRE TOWN OF SPRINGFIELD WILL...AH...PARTICIPATE IN A MASS SKYDIVING STUNT THAT WILL BE SEEN...AH...ALL OVER THE WORLD.
WELL...ER...AT LEAST THOSE COUNTRIES WITH CABLE!
WE WILL EACH HAVE A PIECE OF A GIANT PARACHUTE AND ASSEMBLE IT IN MID-AIR!
WOO-HOO! HE SAID THE ENTIRE TOWN!
AND BY ENTIRE TOWN, I MEAN, THE MEMBERS OF THE HEARTBROKEN ADVENTURERS CLUB!
D'OH!
WHERE WILL YOU GET A PLANE BIG ENOUGH FOR ALL THOSE PEOPLE?
WE...ER... HAVE A HELICARRIER ON LOAN FROM A SECRET GOVERNMENT AGENCY!
I DON'T LIKE THE LOOKS OF THIS, DUM DUM.
WHY DO YOU HAVE TO CALL ME THAT? IT'S DEGRADING. DO I CALL YOU POPEYE?
FURY
IELD

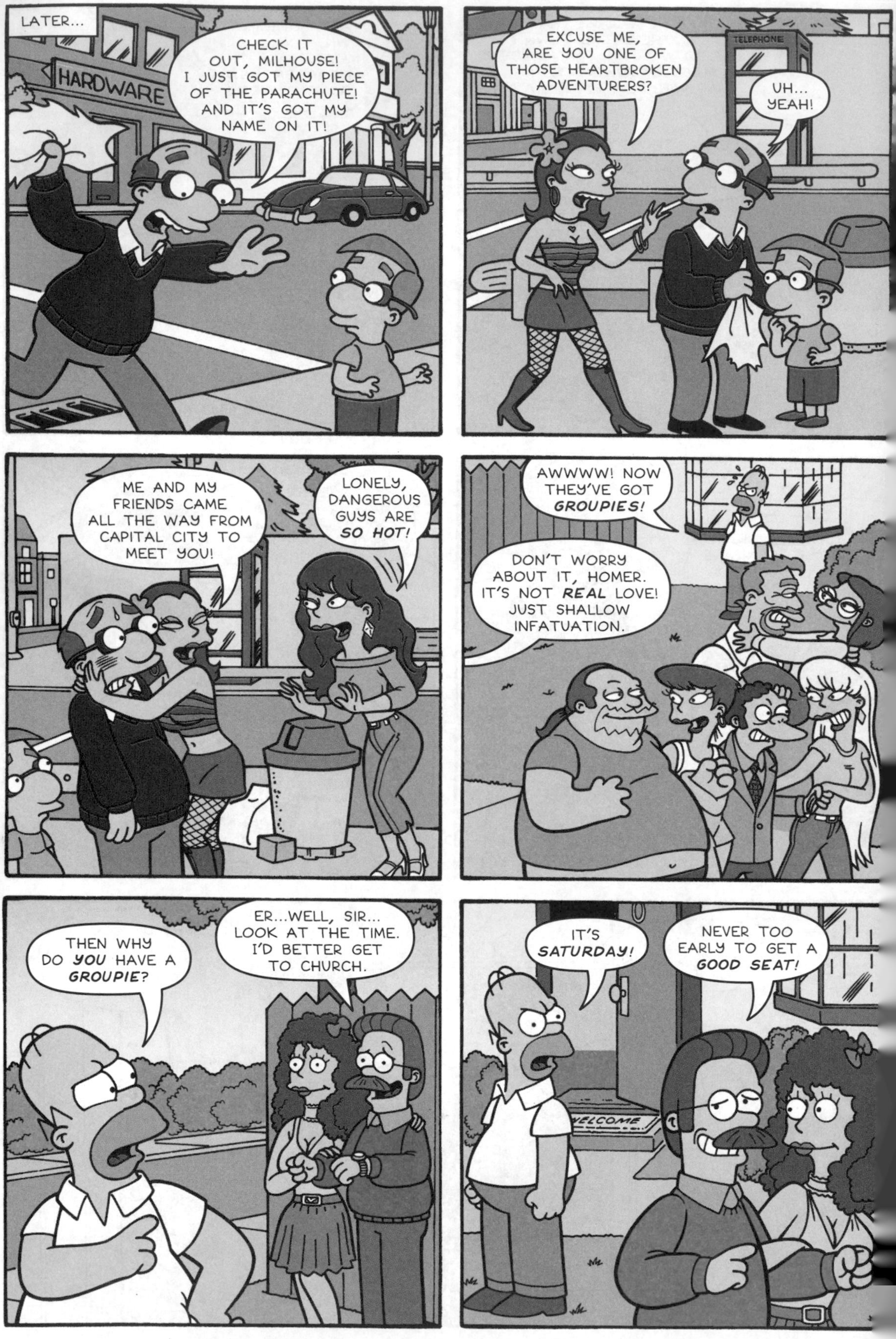
LATER...
HARDWARE
CHECK IT OUT, MILHOUSE! I JUST GOT MY PIECE OF THE PARACHUTE! AND IT'S GOT MY NAME ON IT!
TELEPHONE
EXCUSE ME, ARE YOU ONE OF THOSE HEARTBROKEN ADVENTURERS?
UH... YEAH!
ME AND MY FRIENDS CAME ALL THE WAY FROM CAPITAL CITY TO MEET YOU!
LONELY, DANGEROUS GUYS ARE *SO HOT!*
AWWWW! NOW THEY'VE GOT *GROUPIES!*
DON'T WORRY ABOUT IT, HOMER. IT'S NOT *REAL* LOVE! JUST SHALLOW INFATUATION.
THEN WHY DO *YOU* HAVE A *GROUPIE?*
ER...WELL, SIR... LOOK AT THE TIME. I'D BETTER GET TO CHURCH.
IT'S *SATURDAY!*
NEVER TOO EARLY TO GET A *GOOD SEAT!*
WELCOME

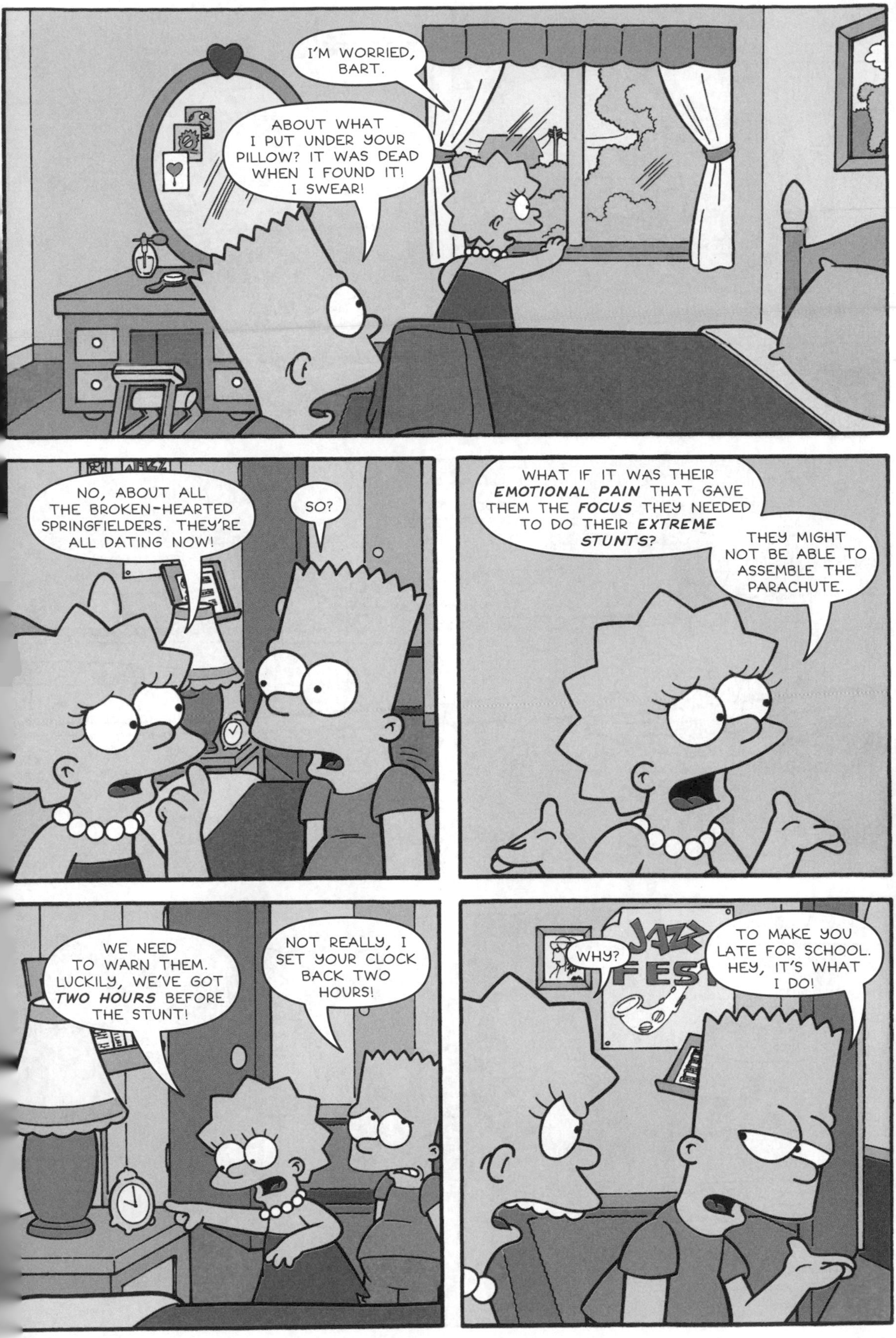
I'M WORRIED, BART.
ABOUT WHAT I PUT UNDER YOUR PILLOW? IT WAS DEAD WHEN I FOUND IT! I SWEAR!
NO, ABOUT ALL THE BROKEN-HEARTED SPRINGFIELDERS. THEY'RE ALL DATING NOW!
SO?
WHAT IF IT WAS THEIR EMOTIONAL PAIN THAT GAVE THEM THE FOCUS THEY NEEDED TO DO THEIR EXTREME STUNTS?
THEY MIGHT NOT BE ABLE TO ASSEMBLE THE PARACHUTE.
WE NEED TO WARN THEM. LUCKILY, WE'VE GOT TWO HOURS BEFORE THE STUNT!
NOT REALLY, I SET YOUR CLOCK BACK TWO HOURS!
JAZZ FEST
WHY?
TO MAKE YOU LATE FOR SCHOOL. HEY, IT'S WHAT I DO!

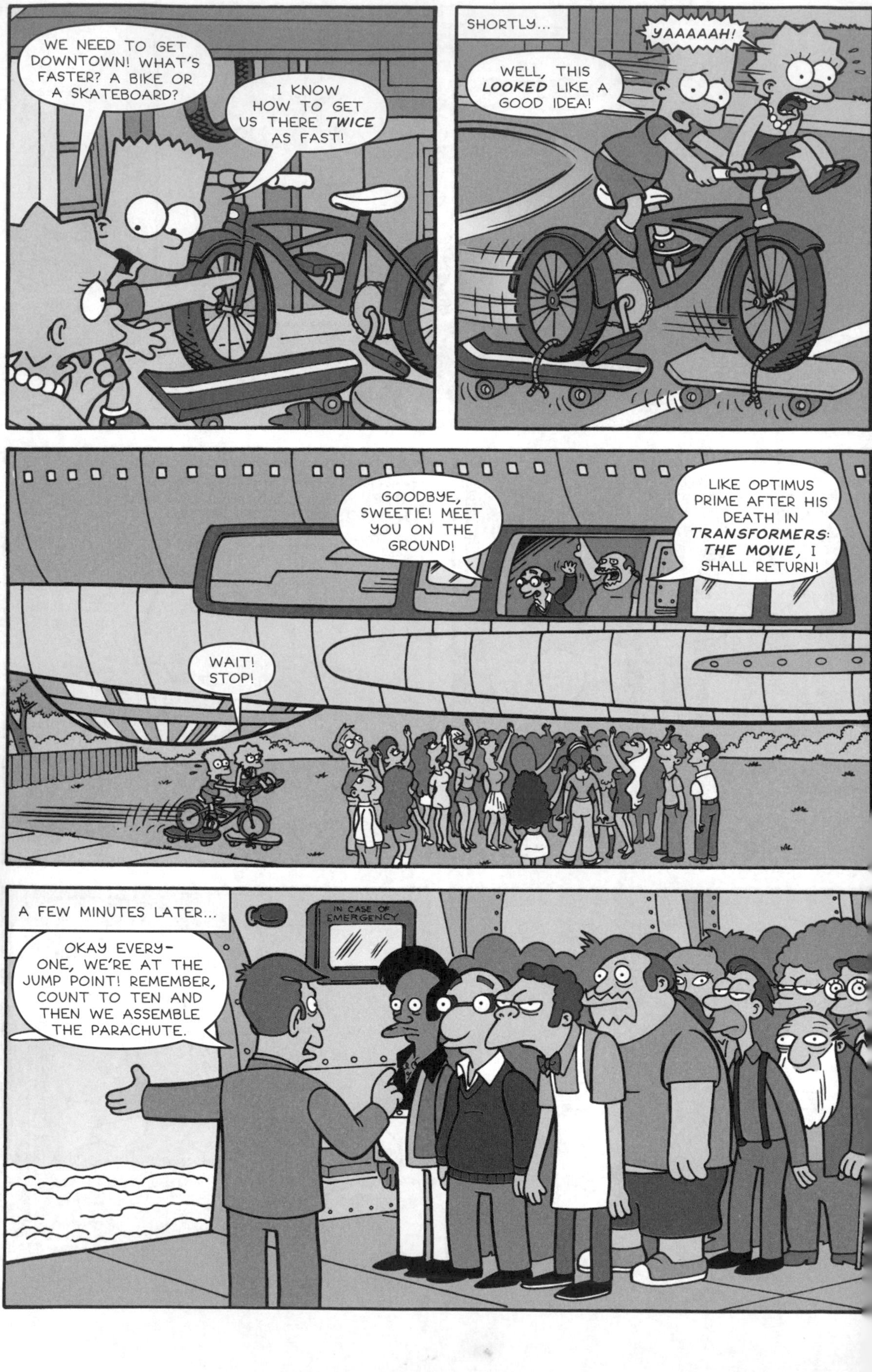
WE NEED TO GET DOWNTOWN! WHAT'S FASTER? A BIKE OR A SKATEBOARD?
I KNOW HOW TO GET US THERE TWICE AS FAST!
SHORTLY...
YAAAAAH!
WELL, THIS LOOKED LIKE A GOOD IDEA!
GOODBYE, SWEETIE! MEET YOU ON THE GROUND!
LIKE OPTIMUS PRIME AFTER HIS DEATH IN TRANSFORMERS: THE MOVIE, I SHALL RETURN!
WAIT! STOP!
A FEW MINUTES LATER...
IN CASE OF EMERGENCY
OKAY EVERYONE, WE'RE AT THE JUMP POINT! REMEMBER, COUNT TO TEN AND THEN WE ASSEMBLE THE PARACHUTE.

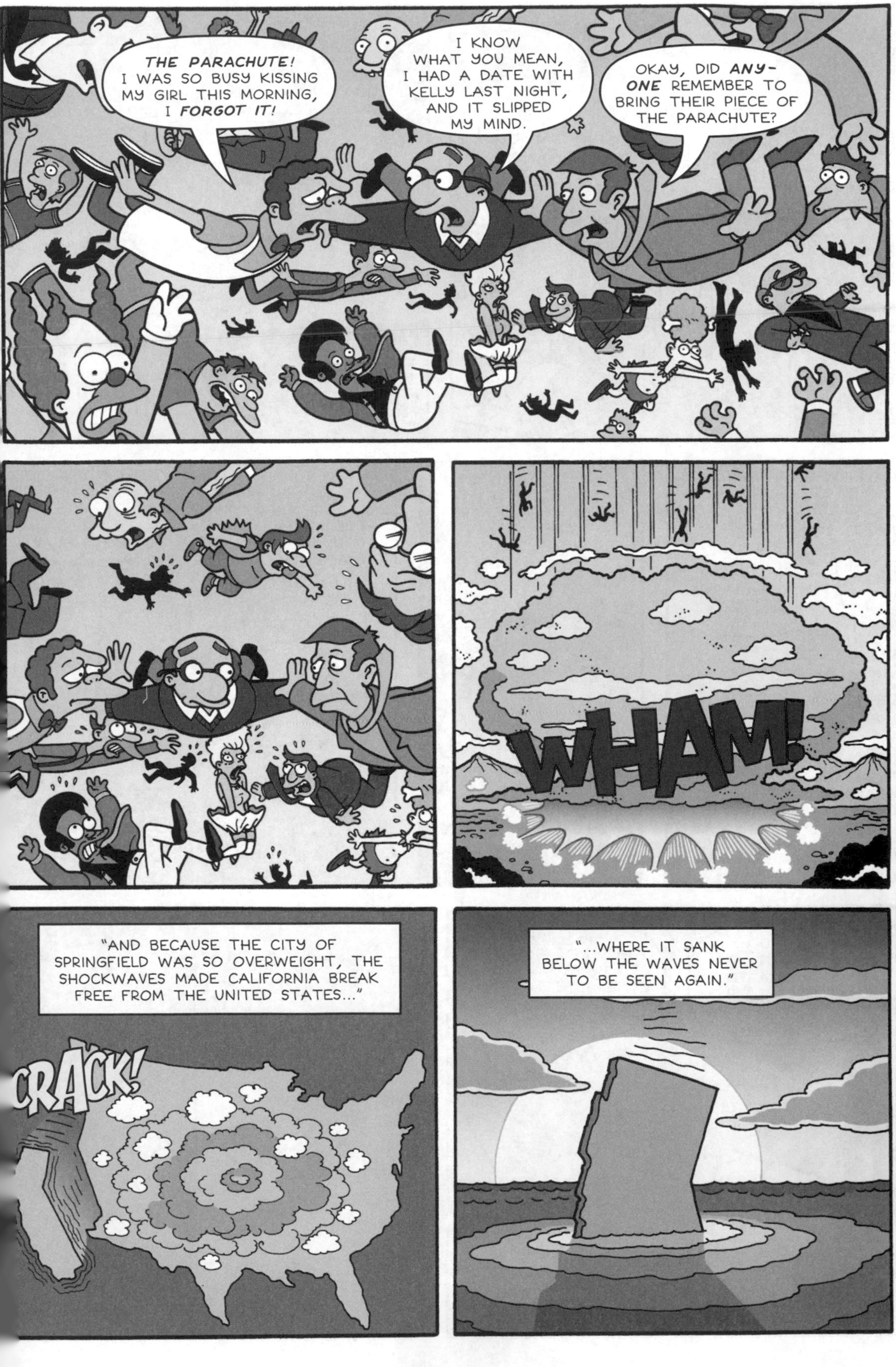
THE PARACHUTE! I WAS SO BUSY KISSING MY GIRL THIS MORNING, I FORGOT IT!
I KNOW WHAT YOU MEAN, I HAD A DATE WITH KELLY LAST NIGHT, AND IT SLIPPED MY MIND.
OKAY, DID ANY-ONE REMEMBER TO BRING THEIR PIECE OF THE PARACHUTE?
WHAM!
"AND BECAUSE THE CITY OF SPRINGFIELD WAS SO OVERWEIGHT, THE SHOCKWAVES MADE CALIFORNIA BREAK FREE FROM THE UNITED STATES..."
CRACK!
"...WHERE IT SANK BELOW THE WAVES NEVER TO BE SEEN AGAIN."

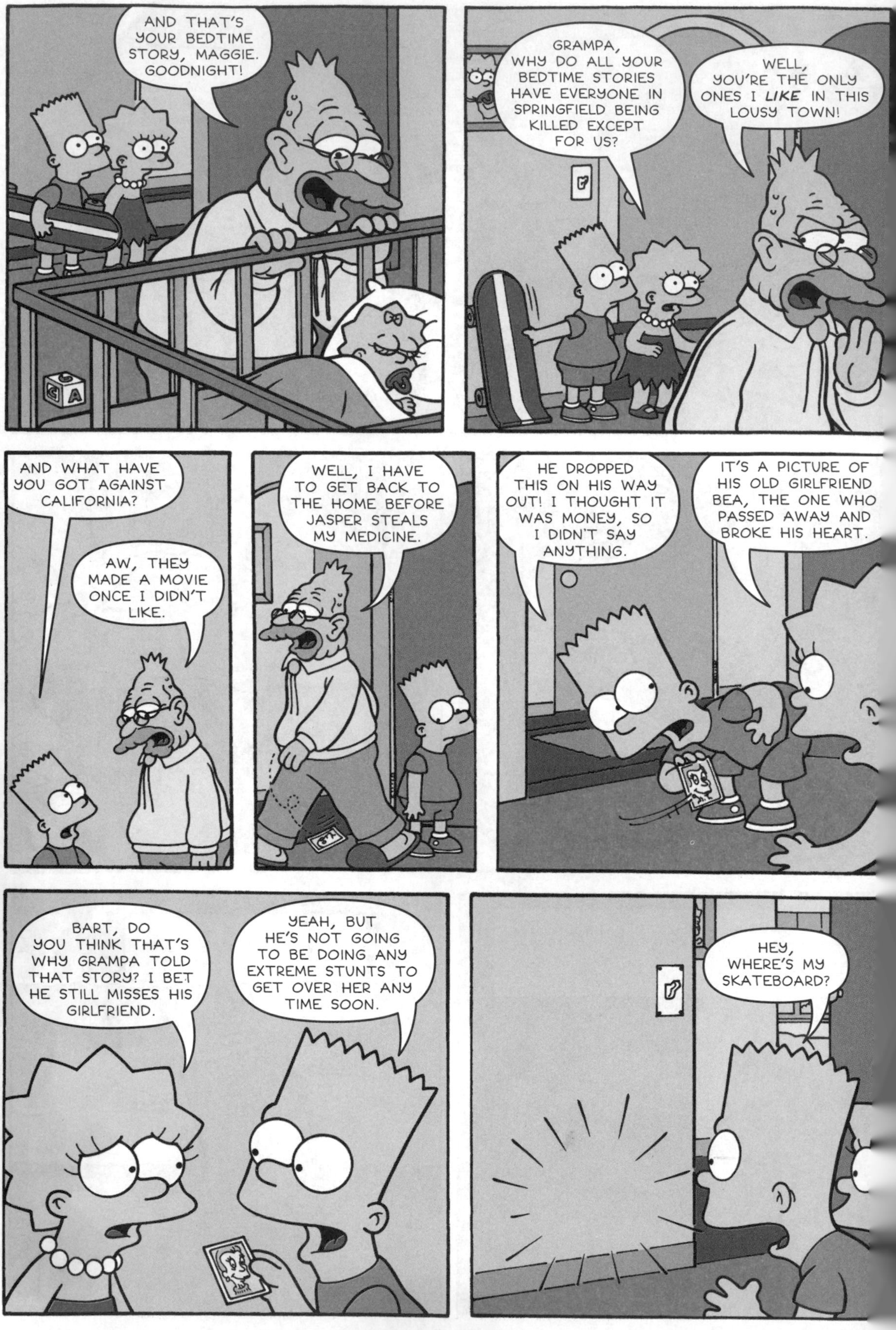
AND THAT'S YOUR BEDTIME STORY, MAGGIE. GOODNIGHT!
GRAMPA, WHY DO ALL YOUR BEDTIME STORIES HAVE EVERYONE IN SPRINGFIELD BEING KILLED EXCEPT FOR US?
WELL, YOU'RE THE ONLY ONES I *LIKE* IN THIS LOUSY TOWN!
AND WHAT HAVE YOU GOT AGAINST CALIFORNIA?
AW, THEY MADE A MOVIE ONCE I DIDN'T LIKE.
WELL, I HAVE TO GET BACK TO THE HOME BEFORE JASPER STEALS MY MEDICINE.
HE DROPPED THIS ON HIS WAY OUT! I THOUGHT IT WAS MONEY, SO I DIDN'T SAY ANYTHING.
IT'S A PICTURE OF HIS OLD GIRLFRIEND BEA, THE ONE WHO PASSED AWAY AND BROKE HIS HEART.
BART, DO YOU THINK THAT'S WHY GRAMPA TOLD THAT STORY? I BET HE STILL MISSES HIS GIRLFRIEND.
YEAH, BUT HE'S NOT GOING TO BE DOING ANY EXTREME STUNTS TO GET OVER HER ANY TIME SOON.
HEY, WHERE'S MY SKATEBOARD?

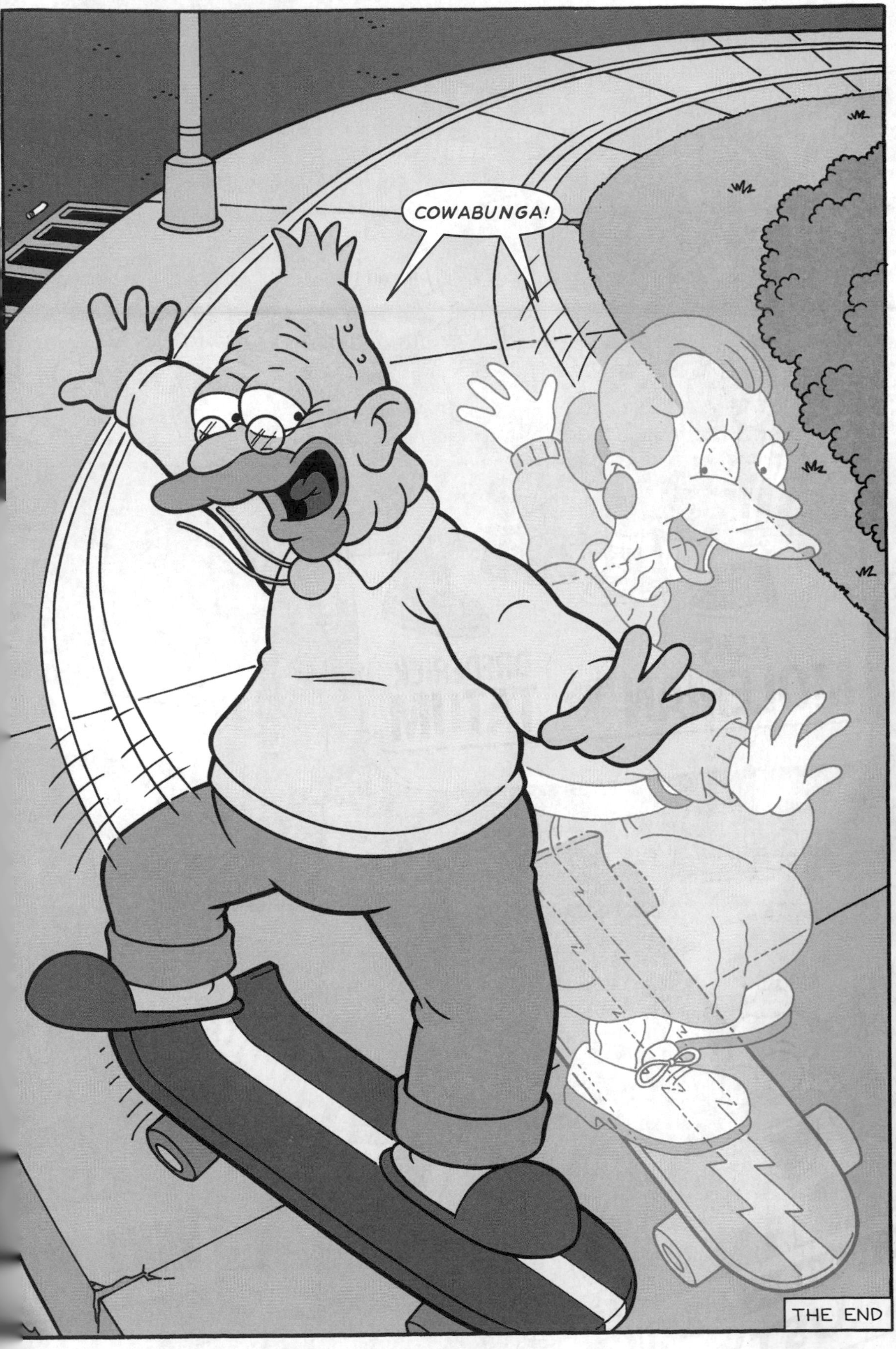
COWABUNGA!
THE END

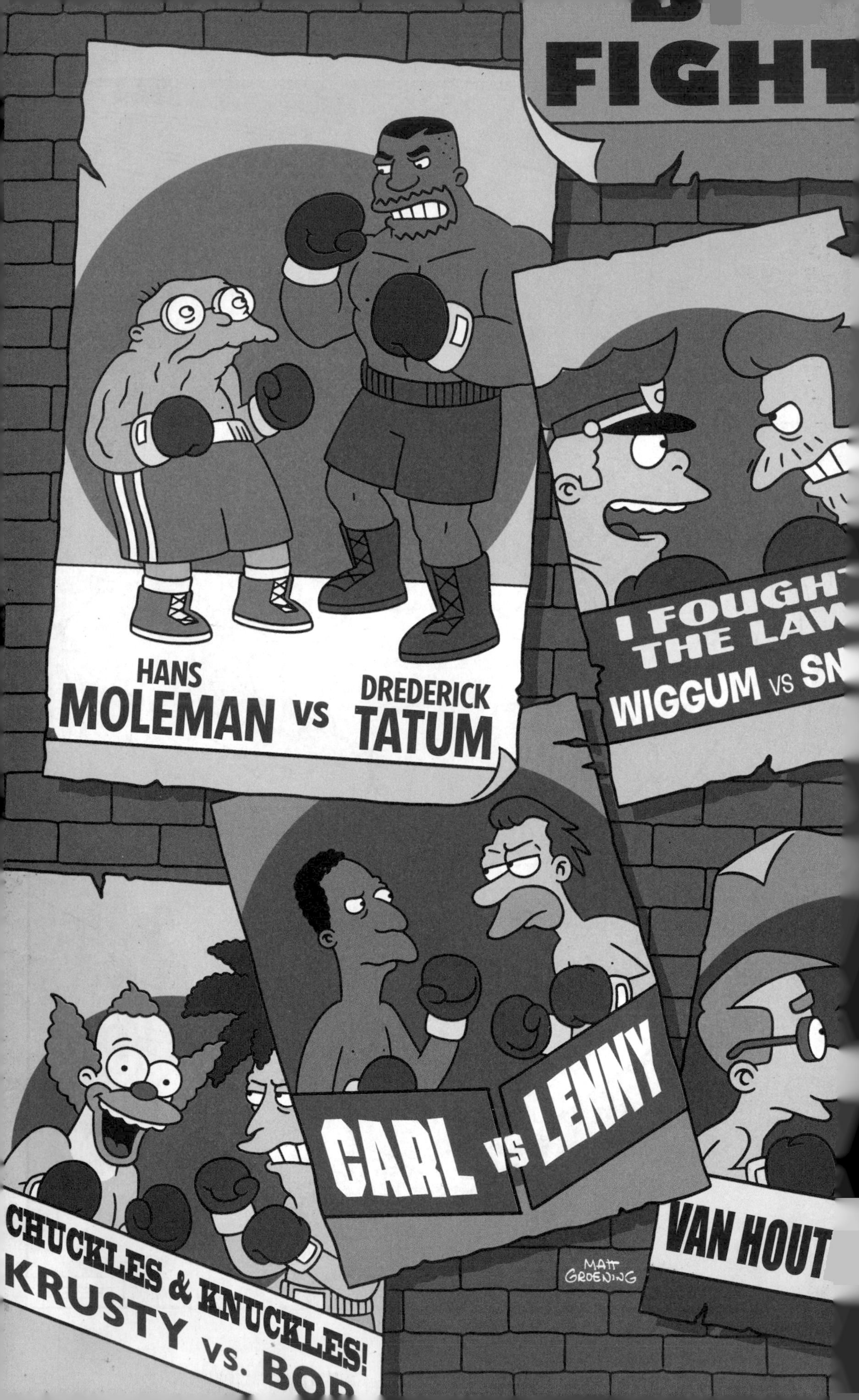
FIGHT
HANS MOLEMAN VS DREDERICK TATUM
I FOUGHT THE LAW
WIGGUM VS SN
CARL VS LENNY
CHUCKLES & KNUCKLES!
KRUSTY VS. BOB
VAN HOUT
MATT GROENING